CAROLE'S STORY...
A SCOTTISH GEM

CAROLE'S STORY...
A SCOTTISH GEM

BASED ON AN INCREDIBLE TRUE STORY
AND HELPING SUPPORT THE ALTERNATIVE
TREATMENT TO CANCER.

A NOVEL BY
MICHELE M. RODGER

ISBN: 978-0-9832576-0-8

Library of congress Control Number: 2010915336

Printed in the United States of America

Certain stock imagery © Thinkstock.

Because of the dynamic nature of the Internet, any Web addresses or links contained in this book may have changed since publication and may no longer be valid.

Edited by Frances Ghee Ross, PhD

Visit our Web site at www.alternativecancertreatmentproject.com for further information on how to support an alternative treatment to cancer and resources.

In Loving Memory of Carole

This book is dedicated to Carole's two children, who are a constant reminder of her beauty and wit. They were the loves of her life;

To her loving husband, who was a pillar of strength during trying times and never wavered from giving Carole his continuous support and unconditional love;

Her sisters and brother for being a steady source of support that only a sibling could give;

And to her mother, who loved her daughter dearly and kept a silent vigil in hopes for a miracle.

INTRODUCTION

I clearly remember the day I decided to write this book. It was September 10, 2008, a little over three months after my sister-in-law, Carole, passed away from stage 4 breast cancer at the age of 42. I made a promise to myself to honor Carole's life, and once that commitment was made, there was no stopping me. For the next twelve months, Monday through Thursday, after finishing my day's work, having some family time, and putting my boys to bed, I'd write my book from 9:00 pm until the early hours. Most weekends were taken up revising and researching aspects of Carole's life. It was indeed an awesome task and one I now look forward to sharing with the world. Please join me on this unique journey of hope, which you are about to become part of.

Carole's story is one of strength, triumphs, tribulations, spirit, romance, love of life, and love for her family. I invite you to live vicariously through her, as she was inspirational in many ways and had a zest for life bigger than life itself. In more ways than one, it was her spirit that helped me write this book.

Although her life was much too short, sometimes quality is more important than quantity. Celebrate her life, which was full of laughter, excitement, and joy, but also share in her tribulations, which is the other reason why I wrote this book.

Oddly enough, what started out solely as a tribute to Carole's life has blossomed into something much larger in scale. In essence, the book serves as a vehicle to support alternative treatments to cancer in the hope that other families won't have to experience the same emotional challenges our family has had to bear. I don't know anyone whose life has not been touched by cancer, whether it's been a family member or friend or one's own self. This experience has had a profound effect on me; however, what really matters is what I do with how it's changed me.

I *will* support alternative treatments to cancer through portions of the proceeds of this book and (one day) a blockbuster movie. I *will* see to it that other families won't go through what my family and more than 560,000 other families have had to endure in the past year alone: They all lost a loved one to cancer in 2009. I *will* lift the world higher through my efforts, because frankly we (you and I) must take action and stop thinking we can't possibly be part of supporting the alternative. "Hoping" for an alternative without taking action is no longer an option. It is our action that will eventually help foster a change. That is what I *will* do...what *will* you do?

I can hear you saying, "I don't have thousands of dollars to spend on this." The exciting thing is you can still be part of supporting an alternative, and it doesn't take hundreds or thousands of dollars from each of us; however, it does require everyone to take action...it does need people like you and me to make a difference. How awesome would it be to be able to say one day, "I helped advance an alternative treatment for cancer, which saved my sister, brother, mother, father, child, in-law, friend," or your own life!

There has got to be a better way, and I believe one of the alternatives is the Kanzius Non-Invasive Radio Wave Cancer Treatment. The Kanzius Cancer Research Foundation is a nonprofit organization supporting ongoing research and clinical trials for the Kanzius Non-invasive Radio Wave Cancer Treatment, an alternative method that has no side-effects. It does not require surgery, and 100 percent of cancer cells are destroyed without damage to neighboring "good" cells or tissues! In 2010, upon receiving approval from the FDA to build a larger, human-sized device, pre-clinical testing will begin. The Kanzius Cancer Research Foundation's goal is to begin Phase I Human Clinical Trials by 2012.

When Carole was running out of options, this non-invasive radio wave cancer treatment gave her hope, as I am sure it has given thousands of others. Other then purchasing this book, there are several ways you can make a difference. Write to your local government (Governor, Senators, and members of Congress) in support of alternative methods to treat cancer. A letter is already drafted for you at Carole's Story web site. Visit www.alternativecancertreatmentproject.com download it, sign it, and mail it - that's your second step in supporting the mission to conquer cancer.

If it's a financial contribution you'd like to make, give what you wish, but also realize that if each family gave just a dollar for each member of their family, it would make a difference and quickly add up to millions of dollars.

It's time to ask yourself a few questions. There are alternatives out there, so are you ready to take action and support them? Are you ready to seize the moment, move forward and make a difference? I am, and in so doing, I can't think of a better way to honor my sister-in-law or your _____ (mother, father, sister, brother, son, daughter, child, cousin, friend, brother-in-law, grandparent, aunt, uncle, niece, nephew...) - you fill in the blank.

Michele

SHARING UNEXPECTED NEWS

It was Friday morning, December 31, 1999, the eve of the Millennium. Carole McMann stepped out of her house and was greeted with cold rain and wind hitting her face. She grinned as she looked up at the sky, and took a deep breath of fresh air. Carole kept inhaling until there was no room in her lungs, and then exhaled through her mouth and relaxed her shoulders. She got into her blue Ford Focus and drove down the long driveway looking at her lovely new house through her side view mirror.

Carole lived in her dream house with her family and, before they decided to move into the town of Linlithgow, Scotland, she had made sure it had everything they needed. A good school district was important. It also needed to be close enough to her mum and sister's house. An added bonus was the town's history. It had it all, plus the Linlithgow Palace, an old ruin with its earliest reference dating back to 1301. Mary Queen of Scots was born here. Carole loved her Scottish roots and was very proud of them.

She and her husband, Richard, had outgrown their bungalow in Neilston, Glasgow, and moved into this house in August. Although it was a bit out of their budget, Carole was confident that, with two incomes, they would be just fine.

She was headed for Edinburgh, 15 miles to the west. Carole needed to get out of the house and get some peace before her family and friends arrived to celebrate the New Year. Her mum, Margaret, and sister, Linda, were already at her house helping her get ready for the party and taking care of her two children - Kristy, 5, and Joseph, 2. Carole had started planning this New Year's Eve party in November and had everything organized for when her guests arrived. She knew who was sleeping where, and what the menu would be for dinner that evening and breakfast the following morning. Loud party horns, sparkly princess crowns, and rainbow-colored streamers were already purchased to help bring in the New Year, and *plenty* of alcohol was on hand. She just needed to run into the city quickly to pick up an order of sausage rolls and steak pies from her favorite butcher shop, which gave her some time to think. Carole had news to share with her family and friends, but had not yet decided when would be the right time to tell them.

The city was buzzing; everyone she passed in the street seemed to be laughing, smiling, and full of joy. Carole smiled back at them, but what she was feeling inside was numbness and despair.

"I will find that feeling of happiness again. I know I will," she said out loud with a tone of determination, but for now she just needed to get through the next two days.

***

Carole had met Richard in Glasgow, in 1982. She had an interview at Beejay's Snooker Club where he was the manager. He looked at Carole as she entered the club with her big '80s hairstyle and her oversized shoulder-padded blouse. Carole had long red hair, large smiling brown eyes, and a tall, slender body.

"Can I help you with something, Hen?" asked Richard.

"Yes, I have an interview with Richard for a receptionist position. Is he in?"

"Yes, I'm Richard. You can call me Dick. Come over here, and let's sit down and have a chat."

The Snooker Club smelled like an ashtray that nobody had emptied for months. The daytime was when it slept, and it rocked during the night.

"Do you have any experience as a receptionist?" he asked.

"No, but I do catch on quickly…just tell me what I need to do," she said with a big grin that was saying, please, please hire me.

"How old are you?"

"I'm 17. Can I have the job, please?"

Dick smiled. "Don't you want to know what you'll be doing?"

"Oh, yes, please," she said as she felt her face go red, thinking that she'd just blown it.

"Well, I need someone to answer the phones, file, and fax," he said.

"I can do that," Carole said, barely allowing him to finish his sentence.

"Okay, then…when can you start?" he asked with a giggle.

"How's tomorrow? What time should I be here?"

"I'll see you at 11:00 am."

"Brilliant! I'll see you at 11:00 am, sharp!" she said as she started to walk towards the front door. "Oh…and thank you!"

Carole felt like skipping, but managed to keep her cool until she got outside.

"Wow, that wasn't hard at all," she thought. Carole was over the moon that she had just gotten her first proper job, and even more excited that she would be working for Dick. His long, jet-black, layered, Duran-Duran hairstyle suited his thin stature, and it wasn't long before Carole and he were dating. She was dating an older man...five years her senior.

They dated for eight years, and every time he would bring up the idea of getting married, Carole would voice her concerns and fears. She by no means ever wanted to be in the same situation as her mother: divorced, with children. Carole lived through it and never wanted to return to that place.

CHILDHOOD MEMORIES

As a child, Carole had lived in a two-bedroom house at 12 Springhill Road, in Port Glasgow, Scotland. Her family had lived in Birkenhead, England, for the first four years of her life, until her parents decided to relocate to Scotland and purchase a starter house with the intention of getting a bigger house one day. Everything was good in Carole's little world until that very dark day when her dad left her mother. By this time, however, two additional siblings were part of the family and the living conditions were, needless to say, tight. Her mother slept in the bedroom with the youngest child, Christine, who was one year old. She and the rest of her siblings - Elaine, 3; Linda, 8; and Deka, her 11-year-old big brother, all shared the second bedroom. Carole herself was 6.

Carole's mother was a proud woman who ran her home with a heavy hand. If nothing else, she wanted everyone on the outside to see she had control over her five children, which she indeed did. There was a dull, gray cloud over Carole's little world, and her family life and the neighborhood she lived in made it bleak and gloomy. Winter coats served two purposes…coats during the day and blankets during the long, cold, winter nights. The kitchen was

6'x 5'with a stove and a sink where clothes were washed by hand. When it was Carole's turn to experience the heavy hand, Deka would say to her, "Carole, just cry and she will stop," but she would not cry. Carole had a strong spirit, even as a child. She knew the only thing she was able to control were her own emotions, and that's what she did. Carole would not be broken. The heavy-handedness ended as soon as Deka turned sixteen, as he was able to protect himself and his sisters against any further eruptions by threatening the same treatment in return.

Carole and older sister Linda – Birkenhead, England

Carole would carry those childhood memories with her, and it was a constant reminder of what she didn't want. She was determined to make a different life for herself.

STARTING A FAMILY

When Carole was 26, she was ready to get married. Dick and she had been together for nearly 10 years. "Surely, we will have a good strong marriage," she thought. They were wed on Saturday, October 19, 1991.

Carole had grown into a stunning young woman who had confidence and style as well as a great sense of humor. Three years later, on August 21, their first child was born. They named her Kristy. She had lovely brown hair, big green eyes, and ruby-red lips. Carole was often asked if she put lipstick on them, to which she would reply, "Oh no, it's her natural color...aren't they lovely?" They were proud parents and loved spending time together as a family, going to the park and taking long walks. Then, in July of 1996, Carole shared her exciting news with Dick that they were having their second child, and on the following April 18, Joseph was born. He had a round face with big blue eyes and very light blonde hair. At a young age Joseph already showed his humorous side by making funny faces which made his mother laugh. He had a contagious little giggle. Carole wrote in her journal the things her children did and said, so she could remember to share them with her friends and family. Carole could not have been happier, with two lovely children, a devoted and loving husband, and plans to move into another house. Carole had an undeniable desire to have the good things in life. One by one she was reaching her goals and the next large milestone would be moving into 58 Kettil Stoun Mains.

Carole in her 20's

***

Carole returned from Edinburgh and was hurrying about so she'd be ready for her guests when they arrived. Linda helped in the kitchen while her mother watched the children. Dick was not home, and nobody was talking about his whereabouts.

"Shall I set the table?" Margaret, her mum, asked.

"Yes, please," said Carole. "I've made up a place setting for everyone and we'll need soup dishes and spoons as well. Let's use the tartan ribbons for napkin holders. They're in the dining room

"Did you make your signature soup?" Linda asked.

"Yes, I did; I just hope everyone likes carrot coriander soup."

"I'm sure they will," said Linda.

As the eldest female sibling, Linda had a motherly way about her. She was always supportive of her sisters – Carole, in particular. Her loyal and sincere mannerisms always shone through, and when she promised something, the promise was kept. Linda had straight, brown shoulder length hair, and her blue eyes were framed most of the time by her glasses. As with to Carole, family was very important to her, so when they needed her, she was there for them.

Carole was expecting her big brother, Deka, his wife, Michele, and Deka's son, Andrew. Mick and Sue Stamp, who were close friends of the family, were invited as well. There were ten people in total, the perfect number for a formal dinner.

The front doorbell rang. "I'll get it," Carole said. "Hi, Mick!" she said as she welcomed him with a big hug and kiss. "Sue, you look lovely! How are you?"

"Yes, I'm good. And yourself?"

"Yeah, yeah, I'm fine. Come on in; let me take your coats."

"Michele, Deka, and Andrew are right behind us. We followed each other up," Mick said.

Deka and Mick had been in the British Military together, and Mick was Deka's best man when he got married. Both Mick and Sue were really more like family than friends. Mick was a gentle soul, but had the exterior of a tough guy. He had a short, square-top hairstyle, full mustache, and looked like Charles Bronson. Sue was a petite, blue-eyed blonde who wore her hair in a short bob style.

She was soft-spoken, always had a warm smile on her face, and was quite a stylish dresser.

"Is anyone home?" Deka said in a disguised voice, as he entered the house with a big smile.

"Hey, big Bro," Carole said and gave him a hug. Although they didn't see each other very often, when they did, they enjoyed each other's company and always knew they were there for each other.

Deka was a redhead like Carole, but he wore his hair so short it was barely noticeable; however, it did make his lovely blue eyes stand out. He had a dry sense of humor and was the practical jokester of the family. Deka's passion for being the best at everything he did was what kept him off the streets of Port Glasgow as a kid and in the boxing ring, which eventually lead him to box for his country and ultimately became the Army Welterweight Champion. Physical fitness would remain part of his daily routine, which gave him a very well-defined body. When Michele and he were dating, she'd tease him and ask him where his neck was, as his shoulders were so big it made him look like he didn't have a neck. Michele was an American who had moved over to England in 1998 after they got married. She was petite, with long, curly brown hair, hazel eyes, and although she didn't get most of her husband's jokes, she enjoyed every bit of his British culture. She was innately a very kind-hearted person, who sincerely enjoyed helping others.

Linda and Margaret came out from the kitchen and everyone exchanged their greetings. "My goodness, Andrew, you are getting big," said Margaret.

"Aye, Granny, I'm 14 next month," Andrew said with his thick Irish brogue.

He lived with his mother in Ireland and was visiting Michele and Deka during the holiday season. Andrew was a tall, well-behaved boy, and he, too, was a redhead.

"How was the ride up?" asked Linda.

"Not bad, love," said Mick.

"Can I get you a drink?" asked Carole.

"Yes, I'd love a cuppa,"

"Absolutely," said Carole, "I'll put the kettle on."

"Nice house, Carole," Deka said. "Come on, give us a tour!"

"Sure, shall I show you upstairs first? There are four bedrooms and two bathrooms. The master bedroom is my favorite room. I love the big closets, which I'll be filling with loads of shoes one day, and the on-suite bathroom," she said with a smile.

As they walked up the stairs, the first door to the left was Carole and Dick's room.

"Wow, I can see why it's your favorite room, it's huge and it has great high ceilings. A far cry from Port Glasgow, huh, Caz?" Deka said.

"You said it -- days of the past. Let's keep them there."

The kids' rooms and the guest room were down the hall, and straight ahead at the end of the hall was the main bathroom. All were nice-sized rooms; there would be plenty of space for everyone to sleep comfortably that evening.

"Downstairs is an office, the lounge, an eat-in kitchen, a toilet, and, on the other side of the kitchen is the dining room."

"Wow, this is some set-up," Deka said.

"Yes, I love it. We haven't done a lot of decorating yet, really, but little by little we will get there," said Carole.

"Well, the best of luck, and I hope you make many good memories here," Michele said, "It's lovely."

"Thanks! Now what can I get you to drink?"

"I'll have a cuppa as well," said Deka.

"Where is Dick?" asked Mick.

"Oh, he has to work all night because of Y2K," Carole said.

"What! You're joking!" Deka said in a surprised tone.

"No. I'm sure you know what's happening…the date on computers has to turn from 1999 to 2000 and everyone in business is afraid that the computers will not recognize 2000, and they will go back to 1900 again. That could shut down electric grids, and turn electricity off, which would affect the alarm systems at the mall, causing all sorts of problems," Carole said.

Dick was the regional site manager for one of the local malls in Edinburgh. Part of his responsibility was to make sure everything ran smoothly there.

"That's a shame, isn't it? He's missing his own house party," Michele said.

"Well, hopefully he will be home early tomorrow morning. Besides, you and Deka could have our bedroom and I'll sleep with Joseph," Carole said.

"Oh, that's very nice of you. Are you sure?" Michele asked.

"Yes, I insist."

***

"Wow, your table looks fabulous. I love the centerpiece," Michele said.

The table was fully dressed for a formal dinner. It had two gold and two silver candles, and assorted colored flowers lying on a bed of pine branches with silver and gold ringlets, which looked like confetti, placed throughout the arrangement, which gave the room an aroma of fresh-cut pine trees. The white linen tablecloth was freshly pressed, the tartan ribbons held the napkins firmly in place, and her finest flatware and silverware were displayed proudly.

"Thanks, I made it myself! Now, can you please ask everyone to come and sit down for dinner?" Carole lit the candles, and dinner was served. The five-course meal started with soup served with warm rolls, and ended with a selection of fine cheeses, including Mick's favorite, Stilton. Everyone was feeling quite full and very merry.

"Would anyone care for some port?" asked Carole.

"I would," said Deka. "I would as well," said Mick. "None for me," said Michele, "The last time I had port, I was wearing it."

"That's because you Americans can't drink," said Deka.

"Very funny, Honey," said Michele. "It's because you spilled it on me. Who's the one who can't drink?" she said with a smile.

"What did you say?" said Deka.

"I said, who is the one who can't drink?" Michele said again.

"Do you have a stutter?" asked Deka with a big smile on his face.

Michele looked at him, shook her head, and rolled her eyes as the others giggled at Deka's humor.

"Yeah, yeah, one day I won't fall for that."

Mick and Deka looked at each other and said, "The Queen," as they drank their port. Toasting the Queen was always another reason to have additional drinks when they were serving in the military, as no one was allowed to leave the bar when the Queen was being toasted. This tradition remained intact even after they left the military.

While the banter was going on, Carole had a moment to think about how she was going to share her painful news. She was still trying to figure it all out herself and shook her head until the thought left her mind.

"It's time to get outside and bring in the New Year with all the neighbors. I'll get the bottle," announced Carole.

"Don't forget the hats and horns!" said Linda.

One of the holiday customs they enjoyed was to visit each neighbor's house, share a drink with them, and then move onto the next house. Carole's mum stayed at the house to watch the sleeping children upstairs and to welcome anyone visiting their house. The music was blaring and people were dancing in the streets. Horns were being blown and everyone was yelling "Happy New Year!" Everyone kissed and hugged. A new century had arrived. "What will the 21st century bring?" Carole wondered.

They all headed back to Carole's house, and the party resumed in the living room, which quickly became the dance floor, and the song "I Will Survive," sung by Gloria Gaynor, was playing - one of those girly songs that females all around the world love to sing to their hearts' content. Even if they hadn't recently been scorned by a man, they'd sing it in support of a friend, as it was deemed an unofficial female-empowerment anthem.

However, something was different with the way Carole and Linda were singing the song to each other. Both had great passion and emotion behind every word. It was as if nobody else was in the room and the lyrics meant something to them. Michele had a weird gut feeling and thought, "What's that all about?" but as quickly as it came into her mind it left.

***

"Good night everyone," Michele said, "I can't keep my eyes open anymore."

"What time is it?" asked Sue.

"It's almost 3:30," said Michele.

"Oh, I'm off as well," added Sue.

Michele could hear them carrying on downstairs, but it suddenly got quiet. When Deka went to bed in the wee hours of the morning, he whispered into Michele's ear, "Are you sleeping?" "Not anymore," she said. "Carole is getting a divorce," he told her. "Please tell me you are kidding," said Michele. "I wish I was…Dick is having an affair and has moved out of the house."

NEW YEAR'S DAY

The next morning everyone was a wee bit under the weather from too much drinking and not enough sleep. Nobody spoke of the news that was shared the night before. It was a rainy, cold, dark day, which fit everyone's mood.

"What does everyone want for breakfast?" Carole asked. "I was going to make a traditional breakfast, if that's all right with everyone."

"That's fine," said Linda. "Let me help you."

"What a perfect way to start the day, after the kind of drinking session we had last night. Fried eggs, slice sausage, black pudding, beans, tomatoes and potato scones -- um, um," Deka said.

"Yes, that sounds great, but I'll pass on the black pudding, if you don't mind," said Michele.

"Still haven't acquired a taste for black pudding, Michele?" asked Mick.

"No, call me crazy, but pig's blood just doesn't do it for me. Especially at 10:00 in the morning, after a night of drinking. As a matter of fact, just the thought of it can put me off my breakfast."

"Good, more for me," said Deka with a smile.

After breakfast, Margaret and the kids started to watch *It's a Wonderful Life* on TV. It seemed to be an odd film to be watching, given the news that was revealed the night before, but perhaps there was a message there that none of them could see. Could something good somehow come out of this bad situation?

"We're going to start heading out," Deka said.

"How long will it take you to get to Leeds?" Linda asked.

"About 4 ½ hours. We're going to take the A74 down. It's the scenic route and we'll see the piper on the border of England and Scotland, which is something Michele will like," said Deka.

He gave his sisters a big hug and kiss. He whispered in Carole's ear, "Just keep your pecker up. You are a Rodger and you'll get through this. Give me a ring if you need to chat." Michele gave Carole a hug and held onto her for a bit as to say, "Hang in there, you **will** survive." It then dawned on Michele why she felt that way the night before, when she saw her sisters-in-law singing the song to each other. Carole was in survival mode.

Carole's eyes welled up with tears, as the words of her brother and sister-in-law rang in her head. "I know I will get through this, but at the moment I'm hurting so much I feel numb, and I'm so angry that he did this to me…to us."

"How could this be happening?" Michele exclaimed on the ride home. "So many things must be rushing through Carole's mind. I mean, they just moved into that huge house, they have two young kids, and they have been together for a total of 18 years. It just doesn't make sense, because they seemed so in love at our wedding, only two years ago. How does that happen?"

A VISIT TO THE BIG APPLE

Michele and Deka got married in July 1998 in Long Island, New York, which gave Carole and Dick an opportunity to visit the United States for the first time.

"We're going to the Big Apple, we're going to the Big Apple," Carole sang over and over again as she danced around her house.

"Can we ask your parents to watch the kids? We've never left them for a whole week. What do you think?" she asked.

"I think they'll be fine for a week and I'll give my parents a ring today and ask them," said Dick.

It took Carole three days to pack because she wanted to make sure she had the right clothes for meeting her American in-laws.

"We are flying British Airways, aren't we?" Carole asked. "Yes, and we will have to be at the airport three hours ahead of time. Do you think you'll have your bags packed in time?" Dick asked playfully.

"I'll give it my best shot, and if it doesn't all fit in my luggage, I'll sneak some stuff in yours," she said with a grin.

Linda flew over with Carole and Dick, and they met Mick and Sue at JFK Airport in New York. There was a man with a sign with the name "Stamp" on it.

"That's me," Mick said, as his chest pushed out like a proud peacock's. He took them out to a big, black stretch limousine.

"Oh, my God, would you look at the size of this thing! It's got to seat about 10 people! Can I stick my head out the sun window and tell everyone we have arrived?" Carole asked. "I could definitely get used to this. We don't have too many of these cars around Neilston," she added with a giggle.

They were all staying in the city for a few days before going out to Long Island for the wedding. Carole was excited about being in Manhattan and seeing the lights and enormous buildings. "Would you look at the size of that building! That's the Empire State Building, isn't it?" said Carole. "Yes, it is," said Linda, "I've seen that building in the movie *When Sally Met Harry*. Who would have thought that we'd ever be in New York City looking at the Empire State Building in person and not just looking at it in a movie or in a book? This is brilliant," Linda said.

"There is so much to see, but more important, let's figure out where the great shops are!" Carole said with excitement. "I need to go to Bloomingdales and Macy's! You can't visit New York City and not go to those two shops!"

Dick just smiled, "Okay, just as long as we get in all the other sights as well." They checked into the Edison Hotel, right in the middle of Times Square, and then took a taxi up to Central Park. They had a delicious meal that evening at Tavern on the Green and then went on a horse-and-carriage ride through the Park.

The next morning Carole and Dick met Linda, Mick, and Sue in the lobby, and they walked to the corner of 8th Avenue and 53rd Street to get on the big red double-decker tour bus.

"Let's get a good view from upstairs," Carole suggested. They all climbed up to the upper deck and enjoyed the sun on their faces. The tour took them as far downtown as Battery Park and back up to Central Park. They got off the bus downtown and walked over to the World Trade Center, and took elevators to the top of the tower. "What did you think of the speed of those elevators? I'm surprised I didn't get a nosebleed," Carole said. "We are 110 stories high! What an awesome view!" said Dick. "Let's enjoy the view for a wee bit longer and then walk on over to South Street Seaport and have some lunch. I have a map, so it shouldn't be hard to figure out how to get there," added Carole.

They had lunch on the pier overlooking the Brooklyn Bridge. "We'd better start making our way back uptown if we want to stop in Midtown before we go back to the hotel to get ready for the theater," said Sue.

They hopped back on the bus until they reached Macy's. "Let's go shopping!" Carole sang. "I'd like to get a pair of shoes in New York." Macy's was massive to Carole. "I'll need a whole week in here just to figure out where everything is!" she said. "Oh, aren't they lovely tan sandals? I like the way they fit, and the two thick straps make them quite comfortable."

"Do we have time to go up the Empire State Building?" asked Mick.

"What time is it? I feel like I need a quick nap before we go out tonight," said Sue.

"It's 3:30. What do you think? Yah, let's do it. How often will we be in New York City?" said Mick. They walked over to the large pencil-shaped building and rode up to the observation deck.

"One view is better then the other. What a great view of the city -- both uptown and downtown," said Carole.

They slowly made their way back to the hotel, and that evening they went to see "Les Miserables."

The following day they traveled out to Sea Cliff, Long Island, and had a great time at the wedding of Carole's brother, Deka. The reception was held at San Sousa, and the view of Long Island Sound was beautiful. Carole wore a beige suite with a Black Watch tartan sash that draped across one shoulder and tied at her waist. Her hat was shaped like a bell with a squared-off top gently wrapped with beige tulle. Carole loved fashion. Whenever she had an opportunity to dress up, she did it with style. She stood out like the regal lady she was. As Carole and Dick danced to the song "Through the Years," sung by Kenny Rogers, Carole whispered to him, "I love you" and he whispered back, "I love you too."

Carole's sister Linda, brother Deka, and Carole on Deka's wedding day.

***

"So how do you go from 'I love you' to 'I want a divorce' in two years!" asked Michele. "I mean, they are on our wedding video clear as day, professing their love for each other, and then he leaves her? What is wrong with this picture? Unbelievable! How the heck did she remain so calm at the house? I would have needed a box of tissues and a Xanax. I'll need to write her a letter when we get home. Just to offer her my support."

Perhaps because the whole thing came as such a shock, nobody talked about it the next day. Michele thought maybe it was a British thing. Something along the lines of "keeping a stiff upper lip" and all that sort of dysfunctional behavior. Regardless, it was alien to her and it kept gnawing at her until she put pen to paper.

> *Dear Carole,*
>
> *It was really nice to see you on New Year's Eve, and you are definitely the "hostess with the mostest!" (An American saying which means you are very good at hosting parties...I'll need to take lessons!)*
>
> *On a more serious note, although I'm a mere "in-law" :) , I do want you to know that I think of you often and I'm sure you'll find the strength to get through this. As the song goes, you will survive, and I have no doubt you will emerge stronger. I know you have a lot of friends and family, but if you ever want to have a chat, just pick up the phone. Hang in there, Carole, and we'll talk soon.*
>
> *Love,*
> *Michele*
> *xox*

Carole did have a good support system around her. She had told her sister Linda and her mum a week earlier that Dick wanted a divorce, and they were supporting her as best as they knew how.

Linda said, "Just cancel the party. They will all understand and you don't have to entertain everyone up here when you are feeling like this."

"It's too late to cancel. Besides, I need to tell them all anyway and I'd rather tell them in person. It will be fine."

"How is she able to think about hosting a party with her friends and family whilst her whole world is falling apart around her? It's just unthinkable," Linda said to her mum.

For the most part, Carole was able to keep up appearances, even for her sister and mum, but her heart felt like it was made out of glass thrown to the ground and shattered into sharp little bits that were stabbing her from the inside out. Every night for months she would cry herself to sleep, a side of Carole that nobody saw.

"Why is this happening to me?" she asked herself over and over again. The feeling that her life was spiraling out of control was a foreign one to her, as she always felt she knew the direction her life was going in. But this ordeal was causing her extreme stress and there was no end in sight.

LEARNING THE TRUTH

"Did you sense it was happening, Carole?" Linda asked.

"No, the only sign I got was the two months running up to Christmas. He was working a lot of hours and sometimes he didn't even come home. I'd call him at work to ask what time he was coming for tea. He'd say, 'Oh, I've got a lot going on at work with this Y2K preparation and the Millennium bug looming just around the corner, so don't expect me home tonight,' or he'd say he was going to be very late. I thought, well, that makes sense, but every time it happened, I'd wonder and say to myself, "No, everything is all right.' I didn't say anything to anyone because I felt foolish, and quite frankly, I didn't want to think it could be true. I feel like such an idiot."

"Carole, you've done what any other wife who loves her husband would do, and that is to give him the benefit of the doubt. He unfortunately didn't deserve it. When did you actually find out that he was leaving?"

"Two days before Christmas. Can you believe that?" Carole said.

They sat there in silence – it felt like hours - trying to comprehend what was happening. Carole's head shook back and forth in disbelief, and all they heard was the ticking of the clock in the living room and the rain hitting the side windows of the house.

"Oh my God, Carole, I am so sorry you have to go through this," Linda finally said.

"The crazy twist to this whole thing is, I always said to Dick I didn't want to get married. I didn't want to do it, because my biggest fear was to get married, have children, and get divorced, like Mum did. I just never wanted to relive what Mum went through. The hardship, the struggle, and here I am about to live her hardship and struggle. Isn't that insane? What I was thinking about and constantly dreading has become my reality. That saying should be 'Be *careful what you **don't** wish for',* because that's what will come true. "

"You certainly didn't wish for this! Mum's situation was much different from yours," Linda said. "You will be fine and you'll handle this differently than Mum because you know what not to do. And I will help you; you are not alone," she said, crying.

"Yes, yes, you are right on both accounts, but isn't it ironic that what I thought about constantly came about?" Carole said, joining her sister in crying.

As the weeks went by, Carole got more information from Dick on who he was having an affair with. Her name was Catherine, a dyed blonde wee thing who was a sales clerk at the card shop in the mall that he managed. Oddly enough it was Dick who never trusted Carole and was always jealous of her and her friends. He didn't like it when she wanted to socialize with her family or friends. Yet it was he who was out there getting involved in another relationship. If it was up to him, it would just be him, her, and the children. He wanted to keep them isolated, but Carole never allowed him to fully isolate her.

During the initial months of separation, Dick was in constant contact with Carole, and he would cry that he wanted to come home.

"Please, Carole, I swear, I left her and I want to come home," Dick said.

"Are you having a laugh? How can I trust you? You can't just walk back into this house like nothing has happened. The kids want to know where Daddy is, and it is breaking my heart making up lies to them about your whereabouts. What should I say? 'Oh, Daddy is at his girlfriend Catherine's house having a play date!' You call yourself a man? You are not a man, you're a *prick!* No, actually, you are not a prick, because a prick is a useful thing. You fold under pressure and responsibility, and go looking outside before you even give us a chance, and have the nerve to tell me two days before Christmas. You are a pathetic human being. I'm not sure if you truly are a human being, but one thing is for sure, you are a worthless piece of crap."

As the words came out of her mouth, she could feel the pent-up feelings of hurt, anger, and betrayal flowing out of her like a faucet running. 'Phew, that was a long time coming,' she thought to herself.

"I know, I know, I deserve all of it, but you have to believe me when I say I am sorry. I would even be willing to go to marriage counseling, if you want," Dick said.

"Let me think about it, and we'll talk next week when you come to see the children."

Carole knew the only way she'd be able to try to make this work was if she learned how to trust him again, and maybe marriage counseling was the way forward. Despite everything he had done, she still loved him.

The following week Dick and Carole were having a chat at the kitchen table when the front doorbell rang.

"I'll be right back," Carole said.

At the door was a petite woman with bleached-blonde hair who Carole didn't recognize.

"Hello." Carole said with a smile.

"I'm Catherine. Is Dick here?" she said.

THE OTHER WOMEN

It felt like time was moving in slow motion as Carole looked at this woman who had come between her husband and her. So many thoughts went through her mind including "This is what he left me for?" and "Should I slam the door in her face in an effort to lock her out of my life literally as well as physically?" Carole's wit came to her rescue.

"Oh, I wish I could say it is a pleasure to meet you, but I would be lying. Do forgive me," she said.

"Is Dick here?" Catherine repeated as if she was annoyed.

"Why do you want to know?"

"I want to make sure he is telling you what he is supposed to be telling you," Catherine said.

"What do you mean by that? Are you still seeing him?"

Carole was feeling outraged and was furious by the absolute gall of this *cow* wanting to talk to her husband in their house. Surely this can't be happening at the front door of her home with her children upstairs! As Carole stood in the doorway, her stance was like one of a Swiss Guard guarding the jewels of the Queen. Her message was clear: "You will not be going any further."

"Yes, I'm still seeing him. Why do you think I'm here?" Catherine asked.

"What?" said Carole in a loud, disturbed tone. "Have you ever stopped seeing him?"

"No! Is he here?" Catherine said again as if she was losing patience.

"Well, that is interesting," Carole said, ignoring the fact that Catherine had now asked three times if Dick was in the house. "He said that he left you and wanted to come home. I suppose once a liar, always a liar," Carole said, as she slammed the door in her face.

Dick started walking towards the front door.

"What's going on?" he asked.

"Why are you constantly lying to me? That was Catherine," she said through her tears. "You have not left her at all. You just lie, on top of a lie, on top of another lie. Get out of here, **NOW**," Carole yelled.

"That's okay," Dick said as he was leaving the house, "I didn't get a chance to tell you what I was here to talk to you about, but I've changed my mind. I don't want to try to make this work."

As Carole closed the door behind him, she put her back to the door and slid down into a fetal position. She started to weep as she pressed her hands against her aching heart. The realization of her marriage being truly over hit her like a ton of bricks.

The months that followed had Carole replaying in her mind what happened to her marriage and how Dick was able to leave her and their two young children, without looking back for more than a second. Was he not struggling with the thought of not seeing his children everyday? Over and over again she asked herself, "What happened? Why did it happen?"

Dick did say several times that he thought the house was too expensive for them, but Carole would have sold the house if she had thought the stress of it was going to end her marriage. After months of sheer heartache and pain, Carole was convinced that he was going through a midlife crisis. Dick had just turned 40 and didn't want the responsibility of a wife, children, and a large mortgage. Carole started to notice that when he visited the children, his sense of style was changing. He was wearing trendy clothes, had a sporty car, and had moved on with his life.

One evening, as she was getting ready for bed, Carole thought to herself, "It's time for me to move on as well, or this breakup is going to be the death of me." As she went to sleep, she seemed more relaxed, as she now knew exactly what she needed to do.

NEW BEGINNINGS

Carole put her dream house up for sale, but she knew that one day she would have it all again. In the short time that she had lived there, Carole would see her neighbor when she was out gardening. They would exchange cordial greetings and go along their merry ways. While Carole, Linda, and Margaret were busy packing up the house, there was a knock at the door. There stood a petite lady with short brown hair holding a tray of sandwiches.

"Oh, thank you, come on in," Carole said to her next-door neighbor.

"How is the packing coming along? Do you need help? Steve can come over and carry some of the heavy things if you need him," Eve said.

"No, that's all right; the movers will take care of the rest. We are just about done. These sandwiches came at a perfect time. This is our last night here, and I am ready to leave this house behind me now," Carole said.

"Well, the good news is, you are not going too far," said Eve.

Carole had decided that the children and she would stay in the same neighborhood. They moved to 21 Ashley Hall Gardens, a quaint semi-detached house with a lovely garden and large trees in front. The children each had their own bedroom upstairs, and Carole's room was across the hall. She loved the house and was pleased that it marked a new beginning for her and her children.

Carole quickly got everyone back onto a schedule: Monday through Thursday the children would be at the child-minder's house. Linda would come up to the house on Thursday evenings after work and stay until Sundays to help out. Carole was working full time for PricewaterhouseCoopers in Edinburgh, in the marketing department. She had previously worked for Price Waterhouse in their London office and had the company to thank for her transfer back up to Scotland. It was there in London where she had met three ladies – Jacqui, Fay, and Daryl - who would eventually become her closest friends.

LIVING IN ENGLAND

Prior to getting married, Carole and Dick had lived together in a flat in Croydon, England. She was very excited about moving down to Croydon, because she liked the thought of living outside a big city like London. It was only a thirty-minute train ride into the city, and she had planned on getting a job in the heart of London.

"I can't wait to decorate the flat," she said to Dick. "And I'll get to see my brother more often as well. I spoke to him yesterday, and his flat is literally around the corner from ours. Isn't that brilliant! Let's invite him over for tea."

"That's fine, but let's wait until next weekend," Dick said.

Carole had set up some interviews while still in Scotland and had a chat with the personnel recruiter at Price Waterhouse. The recruiter liked what she heard and set up an interview to meet Carole in person. On Monday, September 10, 1984, Carole started her career working full time in the marketing department at Price Waterhouse.

"Wish me luck! I hope I do well," she said to Dick as she was leaving the flat for her first day of work.

"You'll do great," he said. "Let's meet up in the city for dinner tonight to celebrate your first day."

"Okay, I'll call you during my lunch break to let you know how it's going, and we can arrange a time and place to meet," she said.

As Carole waited on the platform for her train to arrive, she felt very pleased with herself. She was where she wanted to be in life and was starting a new chapter. She loved her new work clothes and new shoes. The train pulled up and was packed with fellow commuters going into the city. She quickly learned where she needed to stand on the platform in order to get a seat when the train pulled in.

She arrived at the office, and Julia, from Personnel, greeted her.

"Good morning, Carole; I'll walk you down to the marketing department," she said.

"Great, thank you," Carole said politely.

"This is Carole Rodger," announced Julia to the marketing employees. "She'll be joining you from today onward – so I do hope you will look after her well."

A fourth person was being added to their office, and the three other women weren't quite sure how it would work out. Carole stood there looking poised and well groomed. From head to toe everything matched. She was pretty as a picture and they all fell in love with her soft Scottish accent. It was there and then that she met Jacqui, Fay, and Daryl. Four very different individuals, yet from that day on, their lives were entwined. They learned everything about one another and, through the good and bad times, they were always there for each other. Every Friday evening they'd go to Happy Hour at the same pub and soon were referred to by the bartender as the "Four Usuals," since they'd always get the same drink.

As the years passed by, one by one, the "Four Usuals," as they eventually nicknamed themselves, took off on their lives' journeys. There were weddings and children, and good times. Carole and Dick decided to relocate back up to Scotland. The others were traveling all over the world, but they always found time to reunite and, when they did, it was always magical, full of reminiscing, lots of red wine, and laughter until they cried.

The Four Usuals

Carole enjoyed working at Price Waterhouse, so when Dick and she decided to relocate to Scotland in 1991, Carole requested a transfer and remained employed with them until 2003. This not only gave her the independence she needed, but the income as well, especially once she became a single parent.

REVISITING HER CHILDHOOD

Since she was alone now, Carole relied on her mother's support to help her watch the children. She had decided to go back to school for her marketing degree while she was working full time.

"Mum, can you come over and watch the children Tuesday and Thursday evenings? I've only got one more semester to go before I get my degree, which means I'll be done by the spring. I'll sign up for the classes I need at Stevenson College and go there straight after work, if that's okay."

"Whatever you need, Love, just let me know what time I have to be there, so I can get the bus schedule sorted."

It was during this time that Carole was able to see the love her mother was capable of giving her and her children. This was a different person from the one she had grown up with. She was able to relate to what her mother went through as a single parent, which prompted Carole to talk to her mother about those dark days in Port Glasgow, at 12 Springhill Road.

"Mum, I am so touched by the way you show your love to Kristy and Joseph. It's nice to see, but why didn't you love me like that?" she asked.

"What are you talking about? I loved you...all of you."

"But you never showed it; actually, you gave us no affection at all. We were just there and you had to be there because you were our mum."

"Och, God forgive you. You are telling lies." There was silence and then, "I did the best I could."

At that moment it dawned on Carole that the past was too painful for her mother to relive. Although her mother didn't recall or admit to being abusive, she didn't have to, because it was time for Carole to take the first steps in letting go, forgiving her mother, and starting to heal.

Carole and her Mum

She shared the chat she had had with her mother with her older siblings and encouraged her brother to do the same. It gave Carole a warm feeling to see how much her children loved her mother and, although it was something she was unable to feel as a child, somehow over time that same person who had given her such pain as a child had now come to her aid and the aid of her children during a time when she was needed most.

"You know I love you, Carole," her mother said.

"Yes, I know that, and I love you too," Carole replied.

As they were finishing up their conversation, there was a knock at the front door.

Building New Friendships

"Hellooo, anyone home?" Eve sang as Carole walked toward the door. "I was just on my way to the shops and thought I'd stop by to see if you needed anything. How are you? Are you pretty much settled in now?"

"Yes, we are just about there. All the boxes are unpacked, which is brilliant, because I was starting to think it was going to take us another month to get through all of them. We've been through a lot of changes, but things should start settling down now. At least I didn't have to change the child-minder or acclimate myself to a new area."

"I'm sure that had to make things easier. You know, if you need anything, just give me a ring," said Eve.

"Thanks for that; I'll take you up on your offer," Carole said.

And she did. They didn't have much time to get acquainted when they were neighbors, but they quickly befriended each other and spent hours chatting over cups of tea and glasses of red wine. Carole shared her recent woes from her separation from Dick, and Eve could see the stress it was causing Carole.

"You are doing a lot of things, but there seems to be one thing missing," Eve said one evening as they shared a bottle of red wine.

"What do you mean?" Carole asked.

"Well, between going to work full time, and school part time, you then spend all your time in your garden and with the children, but there is no adult fun. Spring is here, the start of new beginnings; do you fancy coming with me to do some indoor rock climbing? I belong to a club. I've been doing it for almost a year now. I really enjoy it. You can give it a go on an indoor wall to see if it's something you'd like and then move towards outdoor climbing. You might enjoy getting out. What do you think?" Eve asked.

"That sounds quite exciting, but I don't know the first thing about rock climbing. What would I have to bring with me?"

"I know you can rent equipment at the arena. I'd suggest doing that until you're sure it's something you'd like to do before you buy your own equipment. And I think the best way to get a feel of what the sport is about is to start on an indoor wall. These walls were originally designed as training aids for traditional rock climbers. Once you get hooked, like I did, think about joining the climbing club. It's a great way to meet other climbers and make a load of new friends. You'll also benefit from the knowledge of other climbers, just by watching them climb, talking to them, and learning from their experiences. It's actually more fun doing it with a friend. However, I would recommend that you take a basic information course first."

"Hmm, that really sounds good. What do they typically go over in a course?" Carole asked.

"In my course, they went over rock-climbing equipment, knots, rope handling, belaying, abseiling, safety, and the basics on various climbing techniques, those sort of things."

"That sounds good. I have to say, I could use a little pick-me-up. I haven't felt excited about anything in a long time," Carole said.

"Oh, this will pick you up, all right!" said Eve with a giggle. "I really love it. To me, climbing is both physically and mentally challenging. It's a sport that anyone can try out. Once I had my first taste of success, I was hooked and determined to go higher the next time. I have a feeling that will happen to you as well."

"I could certainly use an outlet to help me get away from it all, close out everything else, and just focus on the climb. Not to mention, it's got to be good exercise," said Carole.

"It's an excellent workout for your whole body and it constantly builds your mental strength."

"When are you going again?" Carole asked.

"This Saturday, actually. Should I pick you up around 10:00?"

"Okay, I'll see if my mum or Linda could watch the children for a few hours," said Carole.

"Why don't you ask Dick to watch them?" Eve asked.

"Unfortunately, it's not that easy. Every time he knows I have to be somewhere, and we've agreed on a time to pick the children up, he arrives hours late. For instance, we had arranged for him to come and get them at 11:00 because I had a 12:00 appointment. He came at 4:00 pm, and the kids were waiting for him, asking every five minutes, 'When is Daddy going to be here, when is Daddy going to be here?' Waiting for hours for Dick to show up is a lifetime for them. So now when he is due to pick them up, I don't tell the kids until he's at the door, so they don't get disappointed, and I don't tell Dick what I am doing so he can't mess up my plans. He is so pathetic. If it's his weekend to see them and I have plans, I just have Mum or Linda here to see the kids off, which really gets his goat because he doesn't have control over what I do anymore. And he still won't take the children overnight," said Carole.

"Why is that?" asked Eve.

"I truly don't think he is capable of taking care of them by himself, which I'm fine with, but I've asked him to stop messing the kids about. Sometimes he just doesn't show up for his scheduled visits...no call, nothing. He doesn't help out at all, and I think he just gets joy out of messing up my whole day. He is supposed to move on with his life, but apparently he doesn't want me to move on with mine. Thing is, he doesn't have much to say about what I want to do. Like I said, I can't rely on him and so I won't even ask him," Carole said.

"That's a sad excuse of a father, isn't it?" said Eve.

"This is the way I have to look at it and, believe me, it has taken some time to get here. What goes around, comes around, and I do believe things happen for a reason. Sometimes, when you are in the middle of it, it's hard to see the light at the end of the tunnel, but there is always a light if you look for it. I've got to believe that. It does get a bit frustrating dealing with him, but I never want to pitch the children against their father and, one day, they will learn the truth. In the meantime, I'm really looking for a new beginning and I have a good feeling about this."

ROCK CLIMBING

When Eve picked Carole up at 10:00 am sharp, she couldn't help but notice the big grin on Carole's face.

"What are you smiling about?" Eve asked.

"I'm quite excited and can't wait to try this out," she replied.

The climbing arena was huge. Eve helped Carole find the rental shop, and she got climbing shoes, ropes, and a harness. She had decided to take Eve's advice and enroll in a start-up course. A tall, young, man in his late 20's stood in front of a sign that said "10:30 am Start-up Course". He had a soft smile and his light brown hair nearly covered his eyes.

"Okay, guys, we're going to get started. I'm Ken and I'm going to be your climbing instructor for the next three hours. This course is very interactive. Not your typical type of class. How many of you have tried this before?"

There were a total of four people in Carole's session, two woman and two men; nobody raised their hands.

"Okay, great. We have a bunch of new climbers. I love introducing people to this sport. You're going to have a blast! If you don't, I haven't done my job properly," Ken said, in a thick

Scottish accent. "We've got walls from 12 metres to 35 metres high, and routes from simple to technically complex, so it is really up to you how much you want to challenge yourself. The good news is, we've got something for all levels and abilities, and we have a team of talented instructors, including myself," he said with a big smile and added, "who can give you tips to help move you to the next level."

Carole had butterflies in her stomach as she looked up at the wall. Smiling, she felt half excited and half nervous. "What the heck am I doing here? Calm down," she told herself, "You can do this. Just listen to the instruction and follow it."

"Right, I'll be going over essential information on rock climbing for the next 45 minutes and then I will stop talking, I promise, and get you started on the wall. I'll talk about technical climbing gear, use of knots, climbing harnesses, abseiling, climbing techniques, and safe anchoring. We'll take one topic at a time and then we will get on the wall. Any questions?" he asked. "Okay, let's get started."

He went over all aspects in great detail and Carole picked up everything extremely well, from putting on her harness correctly, to belaying and tying knots. It was like bees to honey for her.

"Okay," Ken said. "Everyone, pick up your harness. I'm going to demonstrate how to put it on. Hold the harness at arm's length in front of you to get it straight. Fit the strap around your waist as if you were tying a normal buckle. Feed the end piece through the buckle, and then go back over the bit on the buckle that says 'DANGER', and feed the belt back through the other end of the buckle. Let me clarify that part; some of you have a Petzl harness on. I personally use one and they all have the word 'DANGER' on the buckles to remind you to feed the belt back over the buckle.

Quite a helpful reminder, I'd say; in other words, if you can still see the word 'DANGER' when you are about to climb, you've forgot to do something, and you are indeed in 'DANGER'. It's a locking device which will ensure the buckle will not come undone. We follow the same procedure for the leg loops, making sure we always feed the leg loop strap back over the bit of the buckle that says 'DANGER.'"

Twenty minutes later everyone was comfortable with their harnesses. Next was learning how to use a knot and how to make them.

"Carole, come up here and let me demonstrate on you how to tie into your harness by using the Figure of Eight knot. If you need to learn one knot, then it should be the Figure of Eight knot because it could be used for a number of functions."

The most difficult part of climbing was mastering the belaying technique, which is a system used for protecting one's climbing partner in the event of a slip or fall.

Ken paired Carole off with one of the male students. They practiced belaying on the ground until they both felt comfortable, and then it was time to go on the wall. Carole felt a few butterflies in her stomach again, but this time because she was more excited than anything else and just wanted to get on the wall.

"Okay, who wants to be the first climbers?" asked Ken.

Carole and one other student raised their hands first.

"Right, then, you two will be partners and I'll supervise in the middle. The wall is 35 metres. Let's see how you get on."

Carole was ready to climb and she always gave it her all, no matter what she was trying. She had a competitive edge and liked challenging her mind and abilities. Her heart was racing and her adrenaline was pumping. Each move she made, she made sure she was also looking at the next place she would be putting her foot. She was halfway up and excited to feel the rush that she was going to be able to reach the top. "You can do it, Carole," a little voice inside her was saying. As she reached the top, she could hear cheers down below from Ken and the other climbers. "Well done, Carole," Ken yelled up. "Now abseil down like we practiced…easy does it."

"Oh, this is *absolutely* brilliant," Carole yelled as she was descending. "What a rush, and going up is just as much fun as coming down!" she added with a feeling of accomplishment.

The class was ending and Ken handed out progress cards to everyone, explaining how they did and what they needed to focus on the next time they climbed.

"You're a natural, Carole, and I'd think about investing in a good pair of climbing shoes if I were you, because you'll get good use out of them," her card said. Carole was over the moon with her report and went to find Eve to share her news.

"So, what do you think?" Eve asked.

"I have two words," Carole said with a serious look on her face. Eve was wondering if maybe she was off with her initial thoughts that she'd love it. "*ABSOLUTELY BRILLIANT!*" Carole said with glee. "Do you think we have time to go up the wall again?" she asked Eve.

"You had me going for a wee bit. But I don't see why not - let's do it."

They went up the wall three more times before they left for the day. Eve was right: Carole was hooked. She couldn't believe how much she had learned in three hours. On the drive home, she shared with Eve the different techniques Ken had taught them and there was no doubt: Carole had found a new passion.

The next day Carole's legs hurt and she could hardly walk. "No pain, no gain," she thought to herself, and the gain outweighed the pain by a long shot. She practiced her knots during the week and from that point on went climbing on a regular basis.

"Are you going to join the Climbing Club?" Eve asked.

"Yes, I think I am. I've got all the gear now. I love it and it's getting me out of the house, so why not meet people who could possibly help me with my climbing?" Carole said.

"The next time we go, let's get you signed up. You'll like them...they are a nice bunch of people. Some of the climbers actually go walking the hills as well," Eve said.

Carole's sister, Christine, was up visiting from Wales the following weekend and Carole had planned on going climbing. Carole loved when she visited, as she always had a good time with her little sister.

"Would you be interested in coming climbing with me tomorrow morning and then we'll go out for a meal with Linda around 7:30?" Carole asked her sister.

"That sounds good to me, but I've never climbed before."

"That's okay - come and see if you like it. If so, you can think about taking a class or just stay with me. I've got to call Mum and ask her if she'll watch the children on Saturday. It would be pretty much all day and night if we go out for a meal," said Carole.

"I don't think she'll mind at all. Do you want to go for an Indian meal?" asked Christine.

"That sounds good to me, as long as they serve wine!" Carole said.

After getting signed up for the club and climbing for a few hours, they went back to Carole's house. Linda had just arrived, and their mum was getting dinner ready for Kristy and Joseph.

"Should we have a little happy hour before we go out?" asked Christine.

"*Ab-so-lute-ly* - red or white?" asked Carole.

Carole's favorite word was *absolutely*, and what a great word it is when used in a positive way, which was the way she used it. If you'd ask her a question and the first word was "absolutely," it would put a smile on your face, knowing the second part of the answer could only get better. It's no wonder it was her favorite word, because it fit her personality just right. The best part was she never just said the word…she'd sing it.

"I'll just put the wine out and then I'm going to jump into the shower. Let's try to be out of here by 7:00, okay?" said Carole.

"Not a problem; give me a shout when you are out of the shower and I'll jump in," said Christine.

"Linda, can you call a taxi and ask them to be here for 7:00?" asked Carole.

The plan was set and they were in the taxi at 7:00 pm sharp on their way to start their evening of fun. As to be expected, the night was full of joke telling, reminiscing, and talking about starting new relationships. Carole was getting used to her new life, but she knew something was missing. Climbing was fun, but it had been well over six months since her marriage ended, and she thought it was time to start thinking about dating again. "What would that be like?" Carole thought to herself. Dick and she had met when she was only 17 years old, so dating was going to be a very different experience for her this time around.

The evening ended with a few glasses of red wine too many. As the taxi driver dropped them off at the front door of Carole's house, he had to interrupt their trio rendition of "Sisters" to let them know they were home and it was time to pay him. He smiled as he looked at how much fun they were having in one another's company. The next morning they hung out in bed and giggled about the night before.

"Well, one thing was decided last night for sure," Carole said at breakfast. "It's time to start dating."

But that would have to be put on hold for a wee bit longer.

An Unwelcomed Surprise

It was May 13, 2000, and Carole had just finished gardening and went in for a shower, when she felt her breast and thought she detected a lump. She got out of the shower and felt the need to tell someone, but at the same time didn't want to talk to anyone about it.

Carole sent a text to her sister Linda, "I think I found a lump in my breast." Linda wrote back, "I'll give you a call." Carole replied, "No, don't bother, I'm just putting the children to bed and I am headed to bed myself."

The next day she called Dr. Stewart and got an appointment to see him. He said it was very small and was amazed that she had found it at all. He reassured her it was nothing to worry about, so she breathed a sigh of relief and did just what the doctor ordered: she didn't worry too much. Carole spoke to Linda and told her what the doctor had said. She said she was going to keep an eye on it and, if it felt like it was getting bigger, she would go back to the doctor.

Three months later, it felt like the lump was getting bigger, which shocked her because she was convinced all was fine. She made another appointment to see Dr. Stewart and, upon examining her, he recommended that she get a biopsy. She asked him to explain what that meant, not fully wanting to hear the explanation, as she feared the worst.

"Well, we'll remove a small sample of breast tissue for pathology analysis," he said. "It's often the only way to be certain if a suspicious area in your breast is breast cancer. A breast biopsy helps identify any abnormalities in the cells that make up breast lumps, and a biopsy can help determine whether or not you need surgery or other treatment."

It was a little too much for her to take in, but she was able to ask, "Why are you recommending it now?"

"The lump in your breast has gotten bigger, and I'd like to get a good idea of what we are dealing with. I know just the fact that I've recommended it might make you quite anxious, but let's just take one step at a time."

"Okay. When will I get the results back?"

"It may take a few days. The report will have details about the size, color, and consistency of the tissue samples," said Dr. Stewart.

Carole had the biopsy done two days later and, two days after that, she was called back to get the results. She was still feeling quite confident that it was nothing, since it had been only three months earlier that the doctor had first seen her. Eve went with her to hear the results and, as they sat patiently in the waiting area, one doctor and two nurses approached them and asked Carole to come with them into the doctor's office. Carole thought to herself, "This can't be good news. It doesn't take a doctor and 2 nurses to give a person good news."

Dr. Stewart explained that cancer cells were present and discussed the type of breast cancer she had: estrogen-based breast cancer. She would need to see a specialist who would work through a treatment plan that best suited her needs.

Everything the doctor was saying became muffled as if he were talking under water after she heard him say the words, "Cancer cells are present."

She walked out to the waiting area in a fog and saw Eve sitting there. Carole said to Eve, "I've got cancer and I have to go see a specialist."

As soon as she got home, Carole called Linda and shared the news with her and her mum.

"I can't believe this…it's been some year. First my marriage falls apart and then I'm told I have cancer!"

"What? What did the doctor say?" Linda asked.

"He said that cancer cells are present, and I have to go see a specialist," Carole said.

Carole made an appointment to see the doctor right away and, after going over the results of the biopsy, the specialist recommended additional surgery. He told Carole that they would remove the tumor but if, once they were in there, it had spread, they would remove her breast. The doctor said, "Think of the breast as an egg and the yoke as the tumor. If the tumor spreads to the white of the egg, we want your permission to take the breast off at that point, so we don't have to do two surgeries. In other words, we would take the tumor and the breast all once, but we would need a signed consent form from you giving us permission to do so."

All Carole could think about was not an "egg," but how did the prognosis go from "Don't worry about it; it's so small" to "I need your permission to remove your right breast" in three short months? "What kind of option is that…one surgery or two?" she thought.

"I guess not having surgery isn't an option?" she asked the doctor.

"I would not recommend it, as the tumor grew quite fast in three months."

"When should I go into the hospital?" asked Carole.

"I'd like to get you in within a fortnight," said the doctor.

A week later Carole was in the hospital. Her surgery was scheduled for the following day. Her thoughts were consumed with asking God to get her through the procedure. She had signed the form allowing them to remove her breast, but was praying that she would wake up with her breast intact. Linda and her mum were taking care of the children, and Eve and a few of her friends from work -- Julie, Jackie and Lindsay -- were by Carole's side.

THE RECOVERY

Carole woke up in the recovery room and was bandaged up across her breasts. She had small breasts so she couldn't tell if all was fine or not. The doctor was told by the nurses that Carole was coming around and he was there to talk to her.

"Hi, how are you feeling?" he asked.

"I feel like going dancing," she said with a grin, managing to keep her sense of humor. "How did it go?" Carole asked.

"We had to do a mastectomy, but we caught it all," the doctor said.

The room went silent. Carole thought she was in a bad nightmare, just waiting to wake up. She closed her eyes tight and could feel a tear run down the side of her face. "Please, God, tell me this is not happening," she said to herself.

The doctor continued, "It spread and we didn't want to take any chances, so we removed the breast, but we got it all and once you are feeling up to it, we'll talk about hormone treatments."

Carole had been in the hospital for three days, and Linda and the children went to see her on the weekend. Eve was going during the week after work along with Jackie, Julie and Lindsay, who were other friends of Carole's from work, but Carole was feeling alone and just wanted to go home. She got up out of bed and started to walk the halls of the hospital. She was still highly medicated, but knew she wanted to get out of the hospital. "I've had enough of this place," she told herself and proceeded to get lost in the corridors until a nurse found her.

"Where do you think you are going, Sunshine?" said the nurse.

"I want to go home. I've had enough of this place and need to be with my children," Carole said.

"Okay, let's go back to your room and I'll call the doctor on call."

"If I don't get discharged tomorrow, I'll be signing myself out," Carole said.

The following day the doctor was back and they spoke about her treatment going forward. She would be getting hormone injections in her abdomen once a month instead of chemo and radiation treatment. Carole was pleased with that because she wouldn't be losing her hair, but she had to go for physical therapy and talk to the doctor about breast reconstruction. That evening, when Eve came to visit, Carole told her she was signing herself out of the hospital. Eve drove her home to where she wanted to be, which was around her children, her mum, and her sister Linda.

Throughout her whole recovery Linda, her mum, and Eve were by her side. Eve drove her to all her appointments, and her sister and mother made sure the children were looked after. Carole asked Dick to take the children for a few days at a time while she was recovering at home to which he replied "No", but she was able to arrange for the children's grandparents to care for them a few times. Dick commented to her while she was recovering that he wouldn't ever be able to help her because he was unable to care for a sick person. He never ceased to amaze her or her family on how pathetic a human being he was able to be. Even when Carole was recovering from a major operation, the only thing he felt the need to do was to explain how he wouldn't be able to cope with it and wouldn't be there for her emotionally. Carole didn't have the energy to get into it with him, but just nodded her head and thought to herself, "Don't worry, I know you are a selfish, weak, person and I can't have those sort of people around me when I'm recovering. I'll get through this without you." And she did.

The operation affected her right arm, and the treatment she was getting gave her severe abdominal pain, but she was told if the estrogen was killed with the hormone treatment, she would be fine. This treatment also brought on menopause quickly, but she kept on thinking that as long as the cancer was gone for good, she was fine with it all.

Carole was out of work for the month of August and was recovering quite nicely. When Deka and Michele were called with the news, it was if it was no big deal. "Yes, I have breast cancer, but they removed my breast and I'm fine," she said to her brother.

"What!?" Michele said, horrified. "When did all that happen?" she asked Deka.

"I don't know. The last time I spoke to her, the doctor said not to worry, all would be fine. Maybe she truly thought all was fine and wasn't making a big deal about it. Besides, talking about cancer isn't a topic people feel comfortable about, is it?"

"I understand that. Not too long ago I wasn't able to even say the word, I used to call it the Big C," said Michele. "But you have to talk about it. That's how you help support the person and help them through it.

They shouldn't feel like they are alone. Did she have to go for radiation or chemo?"

"No, the doctors didn't think it was necessary."

"Wow, not that I am a doctor, but that sounds unusual. I'm sure she was relieved that she didn't have to lose all her hair," Michele said.

"I suppose...I didn't ask her. She asked how you were feeling and I told her you only had a few more weeks to go. Maybe that's why she didn't tell us sooner," Deka said.

Michele was pregnant with their first child. The family was waiting for the new addition, who arrived on November 10, 2000. Bradley Howard Rodger was born; the year was to end on a high note.

Deka and Carole made plans for the family to spend Christmas together in Scotland. Linda, their mum, Kristy, Joseph, Carole, Deka, Michele, and Bradley were together for the holidays. They stayed in a lovely hotel, the Inchyra Grange, in Grangemouth.

The kids opened their Christmas gifts on the floor of the hotel room and, although Carole's right arm was sore from the surgery, it didn't stop her from cuddling her new nephew.

***

For a long time Carole didn't want anyone to see her scars, but she'd showed her children to help them understand what their mother had gone through, in hopes that explaining everything to them would eliminate any fears they might have. Carole had a couple of reconstructive surgeries to get through and then she'd be done with it all. As she was trying to see something positive come out of the horrifying ordeal, she thought to herself, "I'm going to get a 'boob job' for all my pain and suffering."

"I think I'm going to go from a 34A to a 34C! Hey, why not!" she told Linda. "But the insurance company is giving me a hard time at the moment because of the timing of changing my insurance plan. I had changed my plan about two months before I was diagnosed, to cover the house just in case anything happened to me. They are telling me that they will only pay for the right breast and not the left breast," Carole said.

"That is shocking! How could they expect you to be lopsided?" Linda said.

"I know, that's what I told them, but I think if I get my doctor to write a letter and explain when I was diagnosed, it will be fine," Carole said.

"Although not planned, that was good timing," said Linda.

"I know. The insurance money paid for the house and bills while I've been out of work," Carole said.

Within a month, Carole got her boob job and was quite pleased with the results. She felt whole again and was looking forward to buying shirts to fit her new body. The only thing that needed to be completed was the nipple and areola reconstruction, which would be a separate surgery in three to four months' time.

"Right," Carole said, "I need to get myself out of this house. I've got a lot to live for and this health scare has given me a wee wake-up call that I have to live life to its fullest."

And that is what she did.

THE DATING SCENE

During the next couple of months, Carole returned to work part time, met new friends through the climbing club, and socializing became part of her weekend enjoyment again. She and Julie, her friend from work, were out one evening when they met a mutual friend of Julie's.

Charlie was a tall, distinguished-looking man with black hair, graying temples and striking hazel eyes. He had a handsome, well-to-do look about him and was 12 years older than Carole. She was attracted to him and couldn't help but stare at his chiseled features. "Absolutely stunning," she thought. Charlie was a successful stockbroker who was divorced with two grown teenage girls.

"Hi Charlie this is Carole. Carole, Charlie," Julie said.

"Nice to meet you," said Charlie, "Can I get you both a drink?"

"Sure, I'll have a glass of pinot noir," said Carole. "I'll have the same," said Julie.

"Oh, red wine drinkers, I'll have the waitress bring over a bottle," Charlie said.

The waitress poured the wine and waited for someone to taste it. Charlie motioned to Carole to do the honors. Carole took the glass of wine and looked at it. She gently swirled the wine around the glass and slowly put her nose to the inside of the glass to smell it. Then she took a sip of the wine. She rolled the wine around on her tongue for a few seconds and then swallowed. Carole knew she didn't know what she was doing, but hoped nobody else thought so as well.

"That has a nice, rich, spicy flavor to it with gorgeous aromatics and a mild taste. Just lovely, thank you," Carole said to the waitress.

"Wow…we have a wine connoisseur amongst us!" said Charlie with a surprised tone.

"No, not really. I just always wanted to say that. I haven't a clue of what it all meant, but it sounded good," Carole said, laughing as she picked up her glass with a devilish little smile.

Charlie enjoyed Carole's humor. They had a lovely evening, chatting away, as Julie flipped back and forth from the other group of friends that were at the bar. At the end of the evening, Charlie asked Carole if he could call her.

"*Absolutely,* I would like that," she said.

They started to see each other regularly on the weekends. She knew dating would be much different than when she dated as a teenager, and of course she had her children to be concerned about. She didn't want them worrying about her dating and what that might mean for them. Carole was always as open as she should be with her children and explained to them that Charlie was a new friend of hers who would eventually come over and meet them. After a few months of dating, she decided to introduce Charlie to her family. Kristy, Joseph, her mum, Linda, and her sister Christine had planned on going out for a meal for Christine's birthday, and they met Charlie in Glasgow. He had asked Carole if she'd like to go on a cruise with him to Spain, France, and Italy. Being pampered was one of Carole's favorite pastimes. It didn't take her very long to decide she was going, so meeting her family in Glasgow was good timing.

A MEDITERRANEAN FANTASY

This was a holiday Carole was truly looking forward to. She had had quite the year and believed the tides were changing in her favor. The thought of being away for seven glorious days gave her an instant smile. She could almost feel the sun warming her face as she pictured herself lying on a lounge chair on the deck of the ship.

Carole anticipated excitement, joy and pleasure, which made her feel like a little girl looking forward to her first vacation. She wasn't sure if it was the trip itself, yearning to have the companionship and attention of a man, or just being happy that she was able to feel alive again. She told herself over and over again during the past year "Be strong, Carole, you'll get through this. You *will* get through this," and now that she was finally seeing the light at the end of the tunnel she felt an overwhelming sense of relief.

On the way to the airport Carole was humming the Cliff Richards song, "We're All Going on a Summer Holiday," which made Charlie start humming as well. They both broke out in song and started to laugh at their giddiness.

Their flight to Barcelona, Spain was at 9:00 am, and because the ship didn't depart until 6:00 pm, they had several hours to explore Barcelona. Carole planned out what they would see while in the city.

They strolled up Las Ramblas arm in arm at a snail's pace. They were enjoying all the charm and attractions the old city had to offer along the promenade lined with shops and cafes. Charlie stopped to listen to street performers singing and then snuck away to the flower stall and bought Carole one long-stemmed red rose. As he gave it to her, she smiled and thanked him by giving him a kiss on the cheek. She knew it was going to be a good holiday and really liked his company. They both enjoyed sightseeing and the affection he gave her was well overdue. The street they were walking on led them from the port to Placa de Catalunya, the center of old Barcelona.

"What a beautiful city, so vibrant and full of heart! Let's go into El Corte Ingles so we can say we've been in Spain's largest department store. I'll need to get a nice souvenir for my mum and Linda for taking care of Kristy and Joseph. I think I'll get Linda a leather bag and my mum a piece of jewelry," Carole said.

"Okay, then let's find a special place to have lunch and watch the world go by," said Charlie.

"That sounds perfect, and if we have time after lunch, let's goes over to the old quarters before we head back to the ship."

Carole did not have a problem finding a leather bag for Linda. Actually, there were too many to choose from. She chose a chocolate brown bag with beige tubing around the frame. "Linda will love it," she thought. She decided to wait until they got to Italy to buy a piece of jewelry for her mother.

Charlie asked one of the locals where to find an outdoor seafood restaurant; Merendero de la Mari was recommended. It had the perfect location, right on the waterfront, and they were seated at a corner table nearest the water. The waiter suggested trying the Catalan-style paella or the fresh mussels. Charlie ordered both as well as a pitcher of sangria. They spent longer in the restaurant than they had intended and decided to visit the old quarters on their return trip to the city at the end of the cruise. The restaurant was fairly close to where the ship was docked, and after they finished two pitchers of sangria, they set off to find the ship, giggling and laughing at each other's jokes.

When they arrived at the port, everyone was waiting in line to get their customary cruise photo taken with a life preserver that had the ship's name written on it. Once that was taken care of, they boarded the ship, found their room, and relaxed until the horns started to blow, signaling that they were leaving. They went out to wave at the well-wishers standing on the pier below as the ship slowly made its way out to sea.

That evening they got dressed for the Captain's Welcome Party. When Carole was putting on her finishing touches, her mother-of-pearl earrings and necklace, Charlie got a glimpse of her.

"Wow…you look gorgeous," he said.

She wore an elegant, form-fitted, short emerald-green dress with a little knit black bolero jacket, a pair of black satin scandals, and a black evening bag to match. Her red hair looked radiant, so long and shiny, and her makeup was perfectly applied. For the first time in nearly a year she felt beautiful and attractive again.

The next morning they arrived at their first port-of-call - Marseille, France. They booked a private tour for four hours, and then planned on heading back to the ship to enjoy some time by the pool.

"Bonjour, my name is Pierre and I will be your tour guide this morning," said their guide, in a lovely French accent.

Their first visit on the tour was the Notre Dame de la Garde, a 19th-century basilica. Pierre was wonderfully animated - a main ingredient for a good tour guide, and he took pride in his country's history. Carole took several pictures of the exceptional view of the city, the islands of the Frioul, and the castle.

This was the perfect tour for Carole and Charlie, as they didn't want to stay on the ship all day and miss out on sites of a city they'd never seen before, yet they didn't want to be touring all day either.

They continued on the tour passing by the historical monument Cite Radieuse of Le Corbusier, which lead them to the fishermen's villages of Callelongue and Goudes. This seemed the place to stop for a quick lunch. They asked Pierre for suggestions on where to eat and again they were not disappointed. This time, however, it was a quick lunch and off they went to see the Abbey of Saint Victor, which Pierre told them dated back to the 11th century and marked the entry into the Old Port.

Before he returned them to the ship, they followed the famous avenue of La Canebiere, and saw the stately fountain of the Longchamps Palace.

"I do hope you enjoyed your tour," Pierre said to them.

"It was absolutely lovely," Carole said, "and thank you for all your local knowledge of the area and the special stories you told us about the history."

By the time they got back to the ship it was nearly 2:30 pm and they quickly changed into their swimming costumes and headed for the pool.

"That was a fun day, wasn't it?" Carole said.

"Yes, I think it's great to have someone telling us what we're actually looking at and the history behind it, instead of just looking at something and saying 'That's nice'," said Charlie. "I think this is the way to see the other places we'll be calling into, what do you think?"

"Sure, the other thing I'm really enjoying is the company," she said with a smile.

"Yes, Pierre was nice…"

"Not Pierre - your company!"

"I know, I'm just playing with you. I'm enjoying your company as well. So what will be tonight's entertainment, my private cruise director…an evening show or are we going to the casino?"

"How about both?" Carole said.

"Are you trying to wear me out on our second day?"

"No, I just want to make sure we get to see everything at least once."

"Not to worry - we will do and see everything, and that includes just relaxing at least once, if not twice a day, so we don't go back home needing another holiday," said Charlie.

"On that note, I'm going to concentrate on getting a savage tan," said Carole.

"Good luck with your white skin,"

"You'll see…you'll be able to see my tan line."

"Is that a promise?" Charlie said with a smile.

"Only if you are a good boy," she said, smiling back at him.

Carole loved feeling pretty and desirable. "My God," she thought, "I probably haven't felt like this in years." The good news was she found the feeling again. It was always there, just hiding.

As they were relaxing, the horn blew to signal their departure, and it nearly threw Charlie off his sun bed in the middle of his power nap. Carole got the giggles and started to laugh uncontrollably. Every time Charlie tried to say, "Oh, so you think that's funny," the horn seemed to blow again with perfect timing, making Carole laugh even more. One thing was for sure: The ship was leaving, and if the passengers didn't return from the day excursions, they'd have to find their way to Genoa, Italy by 5:00 pm the following night.

The next day they took a private walking tour with Giuseppe to see the sights of Genoa.

"Ciao, Giuseppe! Buon giorno!" Carole said.

"Oh you speaka Italiano?" he asked.

"I wish I could say yes, but that is the extent of my Italian," Carole said.

"No problem, I speaka English, and since this is a private walking tour, we cana structure the tour however and whatever you'd like to see. We'lla start off from Ferrari Square, which is centrally located and itsa closeby to several sights of interest. Do youa like jazz music?"

"Yes," said both Charlie and Carole.

"Wella, then you are in for a treat: Apart from the usual art and historical museums that you might expect to find in a historic Italian city, therea is also a museum dedicated to jazz in Genoa. We'll go there. It'sa right off the Ferrari Square. We lovea jazz music, and it's been played in Italy for nearly one hundred years. You'll also enjoya hearing musicians playing in the Square, and anywhere they feel like playing," said Giuseppe.

"I know where I want to have our lunch today. Right here in the Square, at one of these outside cafes, with a bottle of wine," said Carole.

"The scenery is everything you would expect from an Italian city. They've got the Cathedral, art museums, and music. I'm becoming quite the cultural creature, and I just want to sit back and soak it all up. I've taken about 200 mental pictures," said Charlie.

"And I've taken about 100 actual pictures, so we definitely won't forget this place," said Carole.

"I'm glad*a* you are enjoying our city," Giuseppe said with a chuckle. "The Cathedral itself dates back*a* to the 12th century. It'*sa* called the San Lorenzo Cathedral. Let's go see the painting of the Last Judgment; it's a classic example of Christian art in Italy," said Giuseppe.

"Look at the size of those two lions," Carole said. "Giuseppe, can you please take a picture of us next to the lions?" asked Carole.

"Sure, the*ya* actually date back to the 19th century," he said.

The two lions sat at the top of the stairway, their eyes shaped like massive raindrops and appearing very deep. The art in the city was everywhere - on entrances into buildings, on buildings, in buildings, and on the streets.

"We'll*a* be heading for the Old City after this, once I point*a* out a few things and you've had a chance to get a feel of its maze-like structure, its alleyways and cobbled streets. I can see you don't want to leave here, but I promise we will come back*a*. I've saved the jazz museum for last, and then you'll be on your own to explore the Square, have lunch, and just listen to the music playing around you, if you wish*a*," said Giuseppe, "but the Old City is a must*a* see. It was built*a* mostly in the 16th century, at the height of the Renaissance, and it has some of the city's most*a* interesting art museums."

They took Giuseppe's advice and, after they toured the Old City and the jazz museum, they found a nice cafe, ordered lunch and a bottle of wine, and enjoyed talking about everything they had seen during their tour. Everything that day seemed like a beautiful piece of art to Carole. When they boarded the ship, the sky was picture perfect as well.

"Look at the sun's rays peeking through the clouds and bouncing off the sea. What a great photo to end a great day. Life is good," she said.

"Yes, life is good," Charlie agreed.

That evening they saw a comedy act and went to the dance club for a few hours. Carole dragged Charlie onto the dance floor, and he followed without too much coaxing. He was rather easygoing and proved to be a good dancer.

"I see I've dazzled you with my fancy footwork," he said.

"Actually, I'm pleasantly surprised," Carole said with a smile. "Now we are going to stay on the dance floor until we close the place."

By the time the last song was played, Carole's shoes were off and they were doing a chain dance with the other passengers around the dance club, grabbing others into the line as they made eye contact.

The next morning they were in Naples and knew a couple of hours' touring would be enough for them. They signed up for a city tour that would take them around in a minibus. There were only four other tourists on the minibus- their dancing friends from the night before.

Mario, their tour guide, assured them that he would look after them from the moment they stepped onto the bus, and he was a man of his word.

"Buon giorno! I'm going to give you a quick peek of what we will be seeing this morning. Stops will include the Cathedral to visit its charming baroque Treasure Chapel, and Saint Restituta basilica, which dates back to the fourth century," he said. "We'll also take a drive to Plebiscito Square to see the Royal Palace and the beautiful neoclassical Church of Saint Francesco di Paula. After a drive to the Town Hall Square and the New Castle, the tour comes to an end at the terrace at Posillipo, for a fabulous photo opportunity with wonderful views of the city. How does that sound?" he asked the six of them.

"Sounds good," one passenger grumbled.

"Mamma Mia! We need more enthusiasm so I know you are all awake to enjoy our beautiful city. Should we stop at a coffee bar for some espresso to wake everyone up? Let's try that again. *Sooo,* **how does that sound to everyone?"** he asked again, with his hands waving in the air and his voice raising up an octave.

"**Sounds g*ood*!**" everyone said.

"Bravo, much better!" said Mario with a smile. "Now let's get this tour started. On the right you'll see the Cathedral…"

It was a quick tour, but Mario gave them the highlights - exactly what they wanted.

After the tour, Carole wanted to do a little shopping. "Can I see those earrings, please?" she asked the saleswoman.

"Si, they are lovely heart-shaped cameo earrings and 14-carat gold," she said.

"They are beautiful, aren't they? I'll take them, please. Oh, can I see those pink pearl earrings as well? I think Linda would really like them," she said to Charlie. "I'll keep the leather bag for myself and give her these. I'll take these, too. Would you be able to tell me where to go for a nice pair of leather shoes?"

"Si, Signora, if you go out to the right - one, two, three. Si, three streets down and you'll see Ernesto Esposito's. It's a designer shoe store," the saleswoman said.

"Brilliant, just what I'm looking for. Let's go, Charlie," Carole said, with a twinkle in her eye and a smile on her face.

The shoes were exquisite and pricey, but Carole was in Naples and wanted to get just one pair of sandals.

"What do you think of these?" she asked Charlie as she pointed her toe and twisted her foot toward one side.

"They are very nice, very nice indeed," he said, sounding interested in her pending purchase.

However, after 30 minutes of trying on all sorts of shoes and trying to decide if she should pay $225 for the sandals, Charlie finally said, "Would you mind terribly if I paid for them so we can leave?"

"Oh, you don't have to do that," she said but thought it would be quite a nice treat.

"I was going to pay for them any way. Can I just pay for them so we can get back to the ship, eat lunch, and relax for the rest of the day?" he said jovially.

"**Absolutely,** I love being treated. Thank you. I'll wear them tonight. Thank you, thank you," she said again and again, as she gave him a big hug.

"You are quite welcome," he said with a big smile.

The rest of the day was spent lying around on the deck of the ship and going to their scheduled spa treatments. They both tried the hot stone treatment, and Carole got a facial and pedicure.

"I could get used to this pampering," she said to Charlie.

"Yes, it's quite easily done," he said.

They seemed to like the same things, and Carole felt comfortable in his company. That night she wore her new sandals and felt sexy in them, with her fresh French pedicure. They had a lovely meal and went to see the magician's show afterwards. Carole was picked from the audience to help assist the magician. He had her hold red, blue, and green handkerchiefs, and asked her to carefully mark each handkerchief with a black marker. He then asked her to place them in a bottle on the table. Once they were all in the bottle, he put a black cloth over it, and when he pulled it off, the handkerchiefs had disappeared. He then reached behind Carole's ear and, one by one, pulled out all three handkerchiefs with the same black marking. She thought that was pretty cool and tried to figure out how he did it, but gave up after a few minutes. After the show, they walked around the deck hand in hand, enjoying the view of the bright moon shining on the sea, the fresh air and the stars. They stopped and leaned against the railing for a little cuddle and decided to have an early evening that night.

That evening they were cruising towards Palermo, Sicily, and would arrive there early the next morning. The week was half over and moving rather quickly.

They were up early the next morning, ready for another dose of culture. "Do you fancy doing something different today for our tour?" Carole asked.

"What did you have in mind?"

"I was reading about a Wine Lovers' Tour in Sicily. It's an all-day tour and we wouldn't board the ship again until 7:00 pm. We'd learn about Sicily's culture through its food and wine. It sounds like fun, doesn't it?"

"Yes, it does. What time does it start?"

"We'll need to be there at 9:30. As it says in the brochure, 'Sicily is perhaps Italy's most fascinating wine destination and it has been placed in the avant-garde of the renaissance of Southern Italian wines.' Doesn't that sound posh? *The avant-garde of the renaissance*…very posh indeed," she said in a proper English accent. "It also says that the tour combines visiting the wine region with local history and cuisine of the area. That sounds good to me!"

They met their tour guide at 9:15 am that morning at the port and waited for the others who had signed up for the tour.

"Now that everyone is here, let me formally welcome you *all* to Sicily! My name is David, and our bus driver is Salvatore. We will make sure your visit to Palermo and Segesta will be one to remember," he said with a proud voice. "Palermo's history is marked by the multitude of conquerors and subsequent cultures that settled here. Even the Mafia are among those who have contributed to our collective cultural history. We are going to be driving to Segesta, one of the major cities of the Elymian people. They were one of the three native peoples of Sicily. Once we arrive, we'll visit the Temple and archeological park and spend some time there. We will continue on to a local winery to taste their wine, visit the wine cellars, and have lunch at their restaurant. Then we are off to Palermo to explore the lively Capo Market, a large, open-air street market. When we get closer to the Temple, I'll tell you more about it. In the meantime, enjoy the beautiful music and the sites," he said as he turned up the volume of classical Italian music that was playing in the background.

It was about seventy kilometers southwest of Palermo to the Doric temple. Carole thought the temple looked as if it had been built yesterday.

"Isn't it magnificent?" David said. "Would anyone like to guess when it was built?" he asked. "No? It was built before 430 BC. Every time I look at it I say to myself it's amazing how they did it. The temple is just over sixty meters long and twenty-six meters wide, and it's built upon four steps, with a total of thirty-six Doric columns. As you'll see when we get a little closer, there are fourteen columns on each side of the building and six columns across the front and back."

"What's amazing is how well preserved it is," said Charlie.

"Yes, this temple can make a valid claim to being the best preserved in the world, and the amphitheatre enjoys a hilltop position on Mount Barbaro, which is second to none. Although it's not very large, it's still impressive and has a high vantage point from which to view the surrounding valleys. That's one thing that never changed throughout the centuries - it's always about location, location, location. It's one of my favorite places to suggest a photo opportunity," David said. "Okay, I'm going to hand out little maps so you can see where things are in the park. Any questions before we move to the other side of the park?" he asked.

"What happened to its roof?" asked Carole.

"Ah, good question. It was never completed. The roof was never added and the pillars never fluted, nevertheless, still very exceptional, no?"

"Yes, very much so," said Carole.

"Okay, let's walk back to the bus and go to the amphitheatre and urban excavations," he said.

The park was extraordinary. To the right they saw the parts of the old city walls. Straight ahead was the fortress and to the right were the Church, the Mosque, and the Agora. They spent an hour walking around and then made their way back to the bus again.

"Did you all enjoy that?" David asked.

"Yes, it was fascinating," they all agreed.

"Fantastico! Our next stop is the local winery: the Tarantola dei Conti Testa. It's a working winery with a farmhouse that dates back to the 19th century. I'm sure you will be impressed. Relax and

I'll let you know when we are almost there. I have a little treat for you before we get there," he said.

When they were nearly 20 minutes away from the winery, David asked, "how many of you have been to a winery to taste their wines?"

All seven of them raised their hands. "Good, and how many of you knew what you were doing?" he asked.

One person raised his hand. "Thank you for your honesty. Would you all like to learn how to be wine snobs in one easy lesson, so when we get there, you too can have that sophisticated look?"

"Oh, yes, please," said the ladies.

"Ya. Why not, my pinky could stick out just as straight as the next wine snob," said one of the gentlemen as he chuckled at the thought.

"Looks like I am really going to be a wine connoisseur after all," Carole said to Charlie.

"Bravo, it's really very easy. Tasting wine starts with three basic senses: look, smell, and taste," said David.

"I've watched those food and wine shows at home and the wine taster always looks at the wine, but I was never quite sure what they are looking for," said one of the ladies.

"Good question. Let's start there. When red, white, or blush wine is poured into a glass, it comes out in a varying amount of colors or hues. Red wines can be ruddy, purplish, or maroon, while white wines can be goldish, pale yellow, brown, or straw-like. So to answer your question, you are looking for the color. And as you look at the color, you are also looking to see if the wine is clear or cloudy. I happen to have a bottle of wine to demonstrate," he said with a devilish smile, "but we won't be taste-testing just yet. The person at the winery will pour a little more than a mouthful of wine in a glass. By tilting your glass and swirling the wine gently like this," he demonstrated, "you'll notice the color and clarity, and you'll check to see if there are bits of sediment or cork floating in your glass. No big deal if there is - it won't harm you. Next you will smell the wine. Swirl the glass under your nose and take a deep inhale. You can stick your nose down into the glass if you wish like this, but try not to have your nose do a 'nose dive' into the wine, just smell it. After all, we are sophisticated wine snobs. Do I have a volunteer to smell the wine and tell us what you smell?"

"I will," said Carole.

"Great. Come smell the 'bouquet' for us," he said.

"Hmm…it smells a bit fruity to me," she said.

"Okay, good. A wine might smell fruity, or perhaps it will have a trace of vanilla or a spicy smell. Once you have smelled it, you'll get a hint of what it might taste like. Now it's time for the final step…tasting the wine!" he said very excited. "Would you like to be our taster, Carole?"

"Yes, I can do that," she said with a grin.

"I would like you to take a small sip of the wine and roll it around on your tongue. Next I want you to swirl the wine by inhaling an ever so small breath between your lips and allowing the air and wine to blend on your tongue. Remember, I said a small sip of wine and a small inhale of breath so you don't look like an amateur with wine dribbling down your chin. Are you doing it, Carole?" he asked with passion in his voice.

Charlie was looking at Carole with one eyebrow up and she was trying very hard to keep her giggles at bay. She kept on saying to herself, "Don't look at him, don't look at him because he will make you laugh and the wine will come down your nose." However, the way David was explaining the tasting of the wine sounded like an exotic dance was taking place in her mouth! She nodded and gave him a smile, wondering if she should be swallowing the wine now or was she to wait for another instruction.

"What do you taste?" he asked her.

"Well, it has a lovely fruity, berry taste to it," she said.

"Good! Another red wine might taste woody, or a white wine might taste citrusy or have a floral taste. You are only trying to determine what it tastes like to decide if you like it or not. If you like it, you can buy a case if you wish and they will ship it home for you. But if you don't like it, you have to make another decision, and this will be the last decision you will be faced with. To spit or swallow the wine, that is the question!" he said with expression. "If a bucket is available and you truly can not stand the thought of swallowing the wine, pucker your lips like you're about to whistle, keep your cheeks tight so they don't bullfrog out like a trumpet player and aim for the bucket. Easy, right?" David said as he saw seven sets of eyes looking at him, thinking they would not have to practice that technique because they would not be using a bucket.

"So that concludes your crash course in 'how to be a wine snob' in three simple steps….look, smell, and taste."

"That was brilliant! Thanks," said Carole.

"Yes, now I am not only going through the motions, I know why I'm doing them. Cheers," said Charlie.

"You are all very welcome. Now let's go test our new knowledge and do some wine tasting!" said David.

"How do you know so much about wines?" asked Carole.

"My uncle owns a company that manufactures the barrels that the wine is housed in. I work for him as well as do tours, so I've been around wine all my life," he said.

"Lucky you," said Carole.

"Si, I am very blessed," he said.

The countryside was lush with vegetation, and there was a smell of orange blossoms in the air as they drove through the village leading up to the farmhouse. As they got off the bus, they could immediately feel the warm ambiance of the farmhouse. Wherever they looked, they saw rolling hills of uniform rows of vineyards, and the smell of the wine they would taste was teasing them. In the far distance were steep mountains. They walked over to a wooden awning, which was open on all four sides so as to not block any of the beautiful views of the vineyard. There was a cozy wicker couch with puffy floral cushions that looked inviting, and it seemed to have Carole and Charlie's names on it. They sat there in silence soaking in the natural beauty that surrounded them until David walked over and told them that they would be starting their tour in 20 minutes, though it really meant 40 minutes. One thing they both noticed about the Italian culture was everyone seemed to move in one speed: slow…unless they were driving, of course. It was all about enjoying the experience and the company you were with, and relaxing. There was no need to rush through anything and if you ordered a meal and it wasn't served for an hour, it didn't matter as long as the food was good. Forty five minutes later, the tour began.

Their wine-tasting hostess, Rosa, explained to them that they were bottling two wines at the moment: Inzolia white, a Chardonnay, with the Gorgo del Drago label, and red Conti Testa Cabernet -Syrah- Nero D'Avola.

"You can taste both wines. We will have a tour of the wine cellar and then we will also be trying out different combinations of food at the restaurant," she said.

"Let's start with the red wine. It's very tasty," Rosa said. She gently poured the wine for everyone. They all looked at the wine to decide the color. Then they smelled it, and David was pleased that everyone's nose managed to stay out of the wine. Lastly, the moment they had been waiting for since they left the temple: They all finally got to taste the wine. Nobody in David's group dare put their pinky up, but they did feel more sophisticated than the other tourists standing around the small bar area.

Carole and Charlie both liked the red wine and decided to purchase a case. After they were done with the wine tasting, Rosa took them down to the wine cellar. Carole felt the temperature dropping as they reached the cellar and walked through an archway to the entrance of a large brick-walled room with built-in mahogany shelves. The lighting came from the top of the shelving, tilted upward towards the ceiling, making the room feel dark and perfect for a wine cellar. Carole had never seen so many bottles of wine at one time; Rosa was saying that at any given time there could be up to 500 bottles of wine in the cellar.

"Has anyone worked up an appetite taking in the views, tasting the wines, and walking down to the wine cellar?" Rosa asked.

"Yes. Is it time to mangiare?" asked one of the tourists.

"Oh, so it is. It's 2:30! Let me take you up to the restaurant," Rosa said.

The hostess led them through a half-moon archway into the intimate dinner area. Most of the tables were full and Carole could see that David was pleased that they were being escorted directly to their reserved table. The gold tablecloths brightened up the room of dark terracotta ceramic tiled floors and mahogany chairs. The waitress came over and introduced herself and took the wine order for the table. Carole looked at the menu and wanted everything. All their vegetables were harvested on site and used in their kitchen immediately upon harvesting. The waitress came back with their wine and went over the menu with them.

"If you want to start off with a salad, we have caponata, which is made with eggplant, olives, capers, and celery. Our soup is maccu, which is a creamy soup made from ceci beans. We've got crocché, a fried potato dumpling made with cheese, parsley and eggs; we have arancine, fried rice balls stuffed with meat or cheese; and my favorite, pasta con le sarde, made with sardines, wild fennel, anchovies, pine nuts, and sultanas," she said.

Carole's mouth watered from the descriptions of the appetizers. She convinced Charlie to share all their courses so they would be able to taste at least two of everything.

"Our seafood dishes are grilled swordfish or a snapper dish prepared in a vinegar and sugar sauce. Of course we have meat dishes that are made from lamb or goat and chicken dishes; we can prepare them the way you like if you don't see what you want on the menu," she said.

Carole was going to pace herself so she could try everything that was put in front of her. She asked the waitress what she recommended and ordered that. Carole was looking forward to sampling traditional Sicilian food with a delicious bottle of local red wine. Weight gain entered her mind for a millisecond, and then she decided she'd think about that once she got home to assess the real damage. More importantly, she needed to save some room for dessert, as she didn't want to have to miss out on a sweet treat because she was too full.

Dinner was served and the table talk went from a healthy chatter to silence in less than a minute. All you heard were sheer sounds of delight "Mm," "That is delicious," to "Taste this, it's gorgeous." As with most meals in Italy, they were at the table for nearly four hours. Surprisingly, they were not overly full and were looking forward to what was to follow.

"Are you ready to hear about the desserts?" the waitress asked.

"Oh yes, please," they replied.

"We have cannoli, which are my favorite, made with creamy ricotta and sugar filling; we have cassata, a sponge cake with ricotta cheese, nuts and candied fruits; and frutta di martorana, made with almond pastries colored and shaped to resemble real fruit. Oh, and of course, gelato…ice cream," she said.

"I'll have a cannoli, please," Carole said.

"And I'll have cassata, please," said Charlie.

After their meal they had a half-hour to walk around the grounds before they boarded the bus headed for Palermo and the Capo Market. Carole and Charlie found themselves back on the couch they started off on when they first arrived, wanting to soak up the sights as much as they could before they had to leave. Carole asked David to take a picture of them on the couch so she'd have a picture to remind her of the day. "I will come back here one day," she thought to herself.

The bus was waiting for them, and Salvatore had the inside nice and cool.

"So, did you all enjoy your visit to our local winery and your meal?" David asked.

"Do you even have to ask? It was brilliant!" said Carole. The sentiment was echoed by everyone on the bus.

"Great! I'm glad you enjoyed it. Our next and final stop is Palermo – the Capo Market. It's about 40 minutes away, and you'll have two hours in the city before your ship leaves," he said.

They were on the road for ten minutes, when Carole noticed that Charlie was being very quiet. She looked at him, and he was fast asleep. Carole thought, "When in Rome, do as the Romans do" and a siesta seemed like a good idea. Between the sun, wine, and food, everyone seemed to be following Charlie's lead.

"Okay, sleepyheads, we are ten minutes away from the Capo Market. It will be a much different experience from the one we just had at the winery, but, in an odd way, slightly similar, in that the open-air market is another way to soak up the local surroundings and culture, even if you choose not to buy anything. It's hidden from the main streets, so we will be dropped off at the Teatro Massimo," David said.

When they stepped off the bus, their surroundings looked and felt like organized chaos. David explained that almost every neighborhood had its own little market at least once a week. Carole felt like she'd stepped onto a movie set, with all the vendors engaged in conversation as their customers roamed through the winding stalls. The vibrant fruits and vegetables made her want to sample them, especially the blood oranges. There were several oranges cut in half and displayed on top of the whole oranges to give the buyers a look at the juicy fruit hidden inside the skin, and the meats were as fresh as they could possibly be without being alive. At first Carole thought the merchants were arguing amongst themselves, but David reassured her that they were just having a normal conversation, that the emotion and passion in their voices were the norm, and that gave the market the feeling of excitement. As they walked near the old city wall toward Piazza Beati Paoli, a man was selling sfincione.

"If anyone has room to try sfincione, I'd highly recommend it. It shouldn't be missed!" David said.

Carole and Charlie shared one. It was a form of pizza, prepared on thick bread with tomatoes, onions and anchovies.

"Absolutely delicious, but we'd best get on the ship before I'm the cause of it sinking," Carole said, holding her stomach.

There was no doubt about it: Food and wine were among Sicily's main attractions, and there was a good reason why; everything was scrumptious. Salvatore picked them up at the end of the old city wall and brought them back to the Palermo port to board their ship.

"So have you fallen in love with Sicily, our cuisine, and superb wines?" David asked.

"Yes, I will be back. I thoroughly enjoyed myself," Carole said.

"Grazie, then I have done my job successfully."

That night the last thing they wanted was to eat dinner. They had a late-night snack, which didn't come close to the food they had eaten during the day. That evening they had a quiet night and went to the movie theatre to watch *Bridget Jones's Diary*.

The next day they would be in La Goulette, Tunisia, and they decided to stay on the ship the whole day. Although the brochures looked inviting, the thought of lying on a sun bed, lounging around the pool was more appealing this time. They thought they'd try out the rock-climbing wall, but Carole's right side and arm were still a little sore from her operation, and she didn't want to chance it, so she just watched Charlie. Other than exploring every nook and cranny of the ship, they enjoyed their surroundings at pool side and rested up for the Captain's Formal Dinner that evening. Carole watched two children playing in the pool with their parents. Their mum was helping them get on their dad's shoulders one at a time, and their dad was springing them into the air, making a big splash each time they hit the water. Their little heads popped up out of the water laughing and asking for another turn. Each time their dad would say, "Okay, one more time," but twelve times later their dad was still saying "Okay, one more time." It seemed that he was having just as much fun as the children.

"I miss Kristy and Joseph," Carole said. "They would have loved the ship."

"Ya…I'm not into the kid thing…been there, done that," Charlie said.

Carole could feel her eyebrows go up; everything she was feeling towards Charlie came to a screeching halt. That was the first time she had heard Charlie's opinion on children, and it wasn't what she'd expected. Carole's children meant everything to her, and she wanted them to be accepted as part of her by someone she was dating. She stored that comment in the back of her head and thought it wasn't the time or the place to talk about it in depth, but as far as she was concerned, the next two evenings couldn't pass fast enough. She wanted to see her children.

That evening they got dressed for the formal dinner. Charlie wore a tux and his tanned face against the white shirt made his hazel eyes stand out even more. Carole walked out of the bathroom with her shoulders back, walking as if on a catwalk. Her black cocktail dress hugged her shapely body and the rhinestone accessories and black sandals completed her outfit.

"You look hot," he said.

"Thank you…you look quite handsome yourself."

"We are a fine-looking couple. If I may say so myself," he said.

"Yes, I'd have to agree," she said, but couldn't help but think, "Too bad this fine-looking couples' time together will be coming to an end."

The following night they left the port-of-call at 10:30 pm and cruised towards Barcelona for an arrival time of 8:00 am. Since their plane back home didn't leave until 2:00 pm, they had time to get a few more souvenirs and explore a little bit of the old quarter before they left. Carole saved the most important souvenirs- Kristy's and Joseph's - for last. Kristy got a traditional Spanish doll with a red dress, and Joseph got a lovely hand-painted yellow wooden truck with green frogs on it.

There was still plenty to see in the quaint city, but Carole was already thinking about being home with her children.

The flight got them home in time for her to see Kristy and Joseph before they went to bed for the night. As she came through the door, they both ran to her, singing "Mummy!" She got big hugs and kisses; all was well with the world as far as Carole was concerned. The thought of Charlie saying he wasn't into kids popped into her mind, and she thought, "His loss, because we are a package deal."

"How was your trip?" asked her mum.

"It was brilliant, but it's great to be home. I missed you guys."

BACK TO REALITY

Carole got right back into her work and family routine and, after a few months of part-time hours, she went back full time at work. She saw Charlie on the weekends every so often, but hadn't broached the topic of her children until he brought it up again one evening.

"I've meant to talk to you about that," she said.

"Talk to me about what?"

"On the cruise you said to me that you were not into kids. What did you mean by that?"

"Just that really, I'm not into kids. I've had my family and they are grown. I've been there, already experienced it, and had fun. I'm not saying you don't have great kids; it's just that I don't want to play daddy again."

"Yes, I do have great kids, and we're a package deal," she said.

Carole continued to date Charlie, but only to ride out the relationship until it ended. Oddly enough, she wasn't too fussed when it was over. Carole had gotten what she needed from the relationship. Her confidence was back - exactly what the doctor ordered. She not only knew, but she now felt, desirable, and that was the best gift Charlie could have given her. He helped her find the old Carole. The charming, beautiful, and desirable woman that she'd always been came back to life on their trip, and for that she was indeed grateful to him.

A few months after they had stopped dating, Carole asked Julie how he was doing, and she said he had gotten back with his old girlfriend, who was apparently pregnant with his child. Carole had to laugh and said to Julie, "If that isn't karma, I don't know what is." Carole explained to Julie what Charlie had said to her: that he wasn't into kids and that it was the main reason they stopped dating.

"I guess he's got to start getting into kids again, hopefully for his child's sake," Julie said.

Carole was now crystal clear on what she wanted: a man who gave her a lot of positive attention, and unconditionally loved her as well as her children. Carole knew such a man was out there and she'd find him, but for now she was content with getting herself back to full health, spending time with her family and friends, and climbing again.

After work she'd drive straight to the physical therapist to strengthen her right arm; the physical therapist was pleased with her progress. Carole felt ready to start climbing and scrambling again. She and Eve had plans to go climbing every Saturday, and Carole began to meet other people in the climbing club who were talking about climbing outdoors. It was then when she met Brenda, a petite, mature woman who was fit as a fiddle. She had short brown hair and wore a constant large smile. Brenda introduced Carole to a whole different world of climbing, trekking, and scrambling in the mountains (also known as Munros) of the Scottish Highlands.

"We are going up to do Ben Lomond next weekend. Would you like to join us?" Brenda asked Carole.

"Oh, I'd like that. I'll just have to ask my sister or mum to take care of Kristy and Joseph. How long is the drive up there?"

"It's just over an hour away. We would leave early Saturday morning and stay up at the Rowardennan Lodge Cabins. It's lovely up there. Have you ever been?" she asked.

"No, I haven't. How long does it take to climb?" Carole said.

"It's 3196 feet, to be exact," she said with a smile. "I've climbed it several times, and the views of the Loch are brilliant if we are fortunate enough to have a clear day. It should take us about five to seven hours to complete, depending on the route of ascent and descent we choose. So far there are four of us going up," Brenda said.

"I'll ring you as soon as I find out if my sister or mum can watch my children," Carole said.

They exchanged telephone numbers, and as soon as they got back to Carole's house, she asked Linda if she'd mind staying with the children the following weekend overnight.

"Not a problem," said Linda. It was never a problem for Linda or her mum. They were both very happy to support Carole and loved spending time with Kristy and Joseph. "Where are you going?" she asked.

"Brenda, a lady from the climbing club, has asked me if I'd like to join them to climb Ben Lomond, and we are going to stay in a cabin up there," she told Linda.

HER FIRST MUNRO

Carole enjoying her new pastime

The following Saturday, Brenda picked Carole up at 7:30 am, and they headed for the Munro. They were to meet the others in the car park at the end of the public road just beyond Rowardennan Hotel, which was near the cabins they were staying in. Their route of ascent would start there. Carole was excited about her first climb. She had met the others before, but was reintroduced once they arrived. Ian had the map and was eager to go over the route with them so they could get started.

"It looks like Mother Nature is on our side today. At least for the time being," he said as he squinted into the sun. The sky was a lovely shade of light blue; big, puffy white clouds were scattered over it. "We should get some beautiful views at the summit. So let's see," he said, looking at the map, "from here we'll follow a path through a forest northeast and then we'll come out onto an open hillside. Are we ready? Let's do it!"

Carole could feel butterflies in her stomach from the anticipated delight of saying she climbed her first Munro. It actually didn't look too challenging, but a small scramble up some slippery rocks quickly reminded her not to get overzealous on her first hike. She needed to mind the wet track just as much as she was keen to enjoy the forest and everything around her.

The birds were singing as they savored the morning sun peeking through the trees, and the sheer abundance of nature around her naturally put a smile on Carole's face for the whole climb up, as she thought, "I've truly found heaven on earth."

Ian explained to them that once they got out of the forest, they would stop and take in the views of the loch.

"How is everyone doing?" Ian asked. "We should be out of the forest quite soon, and then we will be in for a treat."

Carole could see the forest coming to an end in front of her. As soon as she got into the clearing, Ian said to her, "Turn around and look behind you." The loch became increasingly visible, with views of the lowland hills in the south and southeast.

"Wow, absolutely brilliant!" Carole said. The loch was so calm, it looked like a sheet of deep-blue sapphire glass cuddled by Munros. "We live in a beautiful part of the world, don't we!" she said to Brenda.

"We certainly do, and it's all God's gift to us. Free of charge. We just have to appreciate it, treat it with respect, and be grateful," she said.

"We are headed for the Sron Aonaich ridge now," said Ian. "The path will veer left around the corrie Coire Corrach, which will lead us to the ridge. Once the ridge is behind us, the incline eases for a while before we get to the final and steepest part of the climb. It zigzags up a long, fairly level track, with steep slopes to the left and, once we get past that, you'll see the last rocky slabs right below the summit. Stay to your right and, if for some reason you feel yourself falling, fall to the right," Ian said.

"Falling! Not an option," thought Carole. It was the first time Ian sounded serious since they had started their climb. Carole went into focus mode and listened to his direction. Ian reached the summit first and cheered everyone on to come see the breathtaking views they had all earned. He took out another map so he could point out all the peaks in the 100-mile panoramic view.

"This is indeed an incredible treat. For all the times I've climbed this Munro, I've never seen it this clear. That is Bens Cruachan, Lui, Nevis, More, Lawers, and Stobinian," as he pointed to his map and then out to the horizon, "with Ben Ledi and Ben Venue in The Trossachs. Beyond that, I can't tell you what we are looking at, but it's pretty much all of Scotland! Carole, you must be our good-luck charm. We'll need to take you with us more often," Ian said with sheer delight.

"That won't be possible," said Carole giggling, "because I am not leaving here. This is just spectacular! I just want to sit here and admire the views for hours, days, weeks, months. How long do we have?"

"How about another 30 minutes?" Ian said.

"In that case, Brenda, can you take a picture of me? That will have to do for now," Carole said.

"Sure, not a problem, Love. Smile pretty! There you go. One for the scrapbook that I'm sure you are going to start for all the Munros you'll be climbing," Brenda said.

"There are many to see and explore, but congratulations on your first!" Ian said. "Shall we start the trek down? We climbed it in good time, just shy of three hours. I thought we'd return via the northwest ridge to the beallach between Ben Lomond and Ptarmigan, we'll swing south to reach the summit of Ptarmigan, and then follow its south ridge that takes us to the lochside road just north of the car park where we started this morning," he said.

Halfway down, Carole felt herself getting tired. Her thighs were burning terribly, and with each step she held onto her thigh muscles to give them some support. Somehow she thought the descent would be easier then the ascent, but she was wrong. They took more breaks going down than they did going up, and drank whatever water they had left. The perspiration was dripping off Carole's forehead and down the sides of her reddened face. She was certainly getting her exercise for the day, but in no way was it deterring her from the joy she felt at having been at the top of the summit. Before long they were enjoying the view from the bottom again. She was pleased with herself and was already thinking about her next climb.

Time for a rest

"Which Munro would you suggest I do next?" she asked Brenda.

"That's up to you, but if you'd like, I have something to propose to you. I'll be starting to train for a climb I'm doing next year - the Matterhorn in the spring. Would you like to start training with me and perhaps climb it?" Brenda asked.

"What? The Matterhorn, in Switzerland!"

"Yes, the one and only!" Brenda said with excitement in her voice.

"I just climbed my first Munro, and my thighs are about to fall off my body!"

"That's okay, Love, no worries, but I know you'd be able to do it. Even if you decide not to climb the Matterhorn, you'll have climbed a lot of Munros in training for it. You don't have to decide now. Just have a think about it," said Brenda.

"Actually, my brother climbed the Matterhorn, I think, several times, if I'm not mistaken. He's more of an extreme climber. You know - 90-degree angles in winter conditions using ice axes to get himself where he wants to go. He was on an expedition to climb Everest, but didn't get to the top because of the weather. That's a shame, isn't it, to do all that training and not get to the top because of conditions out of your control? Oh well, never mind, I do know he got to the top of Mt. McKinley in Alaska, the Eiger in Switzerland, and Mont Blanc several times, and has some great stories," Carole said.

"Wow, I'm sure he does. Those are some great accomplishments. I'd love to hear about them one day. It does seem as if climbing is in your blood," Brenda said.

"Yes. Perhaps you're right. What is the climb to the top of the Matterhorn?" she asked Brenda.

"I believe it's…" she stopped in her tracks, "Maybe I shouldn't tell you right now, it might put you off,"

"No, you're all right, what is it?"

"I think it's approximately 14,000 feet," Brenda said, waiting for Carole's reaction.

"Oh, is that all!" she paused. "Are you having a laugh?" she asked.

"Shall we just go to the pub for a nice glass of wine and celebrate your first Munro?" Brenda asked.

"Yes, please, that sounds like a great idea," Carole said.

Although 14,000 feet took her breath away for a wee bit, she couldn't help but think about how brilliant it would be to climb the Matterhorn. She wondered if she could really do it as she massaged her aching thighs. One thing was for sure: She'd have to get into real shape before attempting it.

The other climbers joined them at the pub, and they talked about their climb, still amazed by how fortunate they'd been to see the spectacular views of the day. Ian was saying that the final section along the rim of the northeast corrie and the descent of the northwest ridge would require serious care in icy conditions. Carole knew she'd eventually be climbing in winter conditions, but for now continued to be pleased with her first attempt at hiking.

The next morning they got on the road after breakfast and were home by 11:00 am, so Carole had the rest of the day to spend with Kristy and Joseph before the weekend was over. Carole was on a high and was still thinking about the Matterhorn. She wondered if she was going mad even thinking about it as much as she had, but that didn't stop her from saying to Brenda as she got out of her car, "Count me in for the training part of it...for now."

TRAINING FOR THE BIG CLIMB

It didn't take Carole long to decide she would be climbing the Matterhorn. She actually knew that day, but her thighs had hurt so much that she could not commit until she had some sort of fitness plan in place. She talked to her brother, and he encouraged her to train by doing what she'd be doing on the mountain. Carole did her research and found out the type of terrain they'd be climbing, and she and Brenda tried to challenge themselves as much as they could with the peaks in their area. They obviously knew nothing would be as high as what they were training for, but it was a matter of building up their stamina and strengthening their leg muscles.

Carole enjoying her day out on a Munro

For the next year she got out and climbed a Munro as often as every other weekend, and when she wasn't able to, she made sure she did some form of exercise. The indoor rock climbing wall and her stepper became part of her alternative schedule. They climbed Beinn Ime at 3317 feet, Ben Lui at 3707 feet, and Ben More at 3852, and with each climb Carole felt herself getting stronger and stronger. Being out in the fresh air gave her a sense of freedom that she had never felt before. Even in inclement weather, they went out and, since that was the norm, it made the climbs more challenging. Sometimes the visibility on the Munros was so poor, they could barely see five feet in front of them. Carole was training, and nothing - especially a little rain and fog - was going to get in her way of reaching her goal. It wouldn't be Scotland if the days of rainfall didn't outnumber the clear days. Besides, she liked the rain and believed it was one of the reasons she had such a good complexion. Carole was also starting to believe when she put her mind to something, whether she was focusing on something good or bad, it would come to fruition. This time her focus was on a positive task: She would be fit enough to climb that huge mountain.

The following spring came quickly, and Carole confirmed with Brenda that she'd climb the mountain with them. Carole, Brenda, John, and Ian were confirmed climbers. Ian took care of all the necessary reservations and hired a mountain guide to take them up. Carole would be away for one week, and Linda and her mum agreed to watch the children. They would be climbing in June, and Carole was as fit as she had ever been.

Brenda and Carole had become rather friendly with all the training they did together, and she was aware that Carole was newly divorced. She also knew Carole would make a lovely, caring wife to some lucky man one day.

While Brenda was hill-walking with two other members of the climbing club, Jim and Fiona, she met Jim's cousin, who was visiting from America. Sean McGarrigle's parents had been born in Scotland, and although he was an American, he was probably more loyal to his Scottish roots than someone born there. He had sandy blonde hair, a tall slender body, and piercing green eyes. Sean and his mother visited his cousin and aunt at least once a year, and he always enjoyed his walks and bike rides in the Munros.

As they were walking, Sean said to Brenda that he wondered why he couldn't meet a nice Scottish Lassie. A light bulb went off in Brenda's head.

"Leave it to me, Love," she told Sean.

As soon as Brenda got home, she called Carole.

"Hello, Love, would you be interested in going on a blind date?" she asked.

Their First Date – Sunday, 19 May 2002

Carole and Sean met the following day at Linlithgow Palace. As Sean got off the bus, he walked up a lengthy hill toward the outer gate. They had planned on meeting inside the main gate. He had an idea what Carole looked like from a description that Brenda had given him. Sean hadn't been on many blind dates and felt a little nervous. He wouldn't call himself a social butterfly, but knew once he got chatting, he'd be fine. He got to the other side of the gate, looked around and didn't see anyone who fit Carole's description. He wandered around for a bit and then started to walk back towards the gate, where he found standing the prettiest redhead he had ever seen. As he walked towards her, a big smile formed on his face, and he prayed to himself that she was indeed Carole.

"Hi, Carole?" asked Sean with a shy smile.

She turned around and was pleasantly surprised. "Yes, I'm Carole, and you must be Sean," she said and gave him a soft smile back. "Did you have any problems finding the Palace?" she asked as they started to walk into the main building.

They had lots to talk about: where he lived in the States, what he did for a living, his family background, his hobbies. And he wanted to know all about her as well. There wasn't a moment of awkwardness. They talked about how they both loved to walk and climb, and she was impressed how knowledgeable Sean was about Scotland and the Munros. He told Carole that his favorite place was the Isle of Skye, and she commented that she'd never been there. He promised to take her there on his next trip to Scotland. "Looks like he wants to see me again," she thought to herself.

Sean told her that he had two brothers and one sister who were all married with children, and that his Dad had passed away several years ago. Carole mentioned that her Dad had passed away the same year. Both Dads had been the same age.

"So what do you like to do?" she asked.

"Besides looking at you? I like hunting, playing the bagpipes, cycling, and skiing."

"Would that be considered a typical American pick-up line?" she asked.

"I don't know, I actually enjoy looking at you," he said.

"Oh, thanks." At first she couldn't tell if he was being sincere or taking the Mickey, but she quickly learned that he was being genuine.

Sean told her that when he purchased his house, he had made the lower level of the house into an apartment for his mum. Carole liked that he took care of his mother.

Carole began to share her story and didn't hold anything back. She told him she had been married for eight years, but was newly divorced and had two lovely children who meant the world to her. Carole wondered how Sean would react to the next thing she was going to tell him, but she felt very comfortable with him and to her delight, he was very caring.

"And I am a breast cancer survivor. I was diagnosed in August 2000, and I'm feeling quite fit now," she said. She never felt so at ease talking to someone about her bout with cancer as she did with him, and he didn't miss a beat.

"You are? Well, congratulations! You must be feeling fit if you are climbing the Matterhorn in a few weeks," he said.

Her tenacity intrigued him, and he was eager to learn more about her. Carole shared with him that she had been working for PriceWaterhouse since 1984 and, during her free time, loved climbing, walking, and just being around her friends and family.

Sean mentioned that he had never been married and that he lived in New York, on Long Island, and was a detective in the local police department. They talked about her visit to New York when her brother got married, and Carole told him that her sister-in-law's family was from Long Island, though she couldn't remember the name of the town.

Carole wanted to see if Sean had a sense of humor and he passed with flying colors. She started slagging (making fun of) his pants.

"I can't believe you are wearing chinos!" she said.

"What do you mean? I'm wearing pants," Sean said.

"No, you are not wearing pants; pants go under your trousers. You are wearing trousers, and they are chinos!" she said and started to laugh.

He just smiled and shook his head back and forth. He was smitten and enjoyed listening to her laughter. Carole thought to herself, "If I do start a relationship with him, I'll need to get him to dress better, but that shouldn't be such a big deal I'll just take him shopping and help him pick things out." She smiled to herself as she caught her thoughts racing forwards the future.

As they continued to talk and walk around the Palace, they came upon the Great Hall and Gallery. Sean stopped to admire it. There were eight rows of chairs with a center aisle, and five chairs on either side of the aisle. At the top of the hall stood a dressed table situated in the middle of the hall with a lectern off center to the left. It was an open-air hall, the remains of a once-glamorous Great Hall and an upper gallery which was still in use. Carole could just imagine back in its heyday all the ladies-in-waiting sitting in the gallery looking down at the others enjoying a dance at a formal ball held by the Queen. The gallery was still very much intact, with its framed arch windows that once held glass panes.

"There is a Parish Church on the grounds, St. Michael's, and couples have the option of getting married in the Great Hall or the church," said Carole. "On that note," Carole continued, "hypothetically speaking, what would it be like if *we* were to get married, were would we live?"

"Hypothetically speaking," Sean said, "We would have to live on Long Island for several years until I'm able to retire with my full pension, then we could move back here, if you want, or live half the year here and the other half in New York," he said.

Oddly enough, it didn't even faze them that they had just met and were talking, albeit "hypothetically," about marriage.

Sean said he'd be leaving to go back home in a few days, and he would like her to meet his mum, aunt, cousin, and cousin's girlfriend before they left. Carole agreed and they arranged to meet at McDonald's the next day.

As they walked through the Outer Gate archway down the hill, Carole was wondering if she was going to get a good-bye kiss. He bent down and gave her a kiss on her cheek. "Thank you for a wonderful day. I really enjoyed your company," he said, as he gave her a hug.

"Yes it was lovely. Thank you as well...I'll see you tomorrow," she said. And as she got into her car, she added, "Oh, and don't wear chinos," she smiled, winked at him, and drove away. Carole was feeling excited about their first date and was already looking forward to seeing him again.

Sean watched her car go out of sight and, as he waited at the bus stop, he replayed everything they had talked about over their five hours together. He boarded the bus, and 15 minutes into the trip he noticed that he was traveling in the wrong direction. He had gotten on the wrong bus! Sean couldn't help but think that he had just met the woman he'd spend the rest of his life with...his very own, lovely Scottish Lassie.

TELLING HER FAMILY

On Monday she was getting calls from her sisters, her mum, and her brother, wishing her a happy birthday, but Carole didn't share with them that she had met an American whom she fancied, nor that she planned on meeting his *clan* that day.

As they sat chatting in McDonald's, Carole said, "This is the first time I've had a McDonald's for my birthday," and wondered what type of reaction she'd get from him.

"Oh!" Sean said a little embarrassed, "I didn't know it was your birthday. I would have taken you to a nicer place."

"No worries," Carole said with a soft smile.

His family was cordial and made her feel comfortable. Carole was surprised that his mother still had a Scottish accent, given she had lived in the States for over 30 years. At the end of their lunch, Sean walked outside with Carole and gave her his telephone number, and he made sure he got hers.

"How would you like to come over to the States for a long weekend next month?" he asked.

"I'd love to," she said.

"I'll call you when I get home," he said and gave her a kiss.

The following Saturday, Carole was with her family, celebrating her sister Christine's 30th birthday at the Jarvis Hotel in Gourock. On the drive to the hotel, Carole told Linda and Christine that she had met a lovely American named Sean and that he had invited her to come to New York for a long weekend.

"You're not thinking about going, are you?" asked Christine.

"Yes, I am. Why wouldn't I go?" Carole said.

"Oh, my God! What do you think you're doing? Have you gone mad?" Linda said, "You don't even know who he is! You can't go. Who is he? Where's he from?"

"No, no he's lovely...he's a sergeant in the police department. I met his mum, aunty, cousin, and his cousin's girlfriend as well."

"Wow, when did all this happen? Are you off your head, Caz? You don't know him! He is a stranger, and you are thinking about going to another country to visit him for a long weekend! Does that sound a wee bit crazy to you?" Christine asked.

"No, actually it doesn't at all. It sounds exciting to me," Carole said, "And let's just end this conversation now, before we all say something that we might regret later."

Based on their reaction Carole dared not tell her sisters that she and Sean had talked about marriage on their first date. They would have really thought she had lost her mind, but she couldn't explain it. There was just something different about Sean. She had an immediate bond with him, and she wasn't going to let her sisters get in the middle of how she was feeling, and she certainly didn't like their trying to make her doubt her gut feelings about going to the States.

"When will Michele, Deka, and Bradley be arriving?" asked Carole.

"They may already be there. Deka told me they'd be there by noon," Linda said.

Carole talked to Michele about her invite to the States, and told her that she had met a follow American who lived on Long Island, in East Islip. Carole was a bit relieved that Michele didn't have the same reaction as her sisters, but she knew she wouldn't, because Michele and Deka had met in Italy on a ski trip, and had had a long-distance relationship for two years. When Deka went to visit Michele in the States, Michele had hardly known him, and he had stayed at her parents' house.

"You're kidding...that is so cool!" Michele said. "Come on, then - don't hold back. Give me the scoop. What's he like, what's his name, what does he do for a living?" she asked eagerly.

"His name is Sean, he's quite tall, with blonde hair and stunning green eyes. I think he's absolutely lovely. He's a little younger than me, which makes for a change. We spent the whole day together last Sunday, and he's a detective in the police department. Were you nervous when Deka came over to the States for the first time?" she asked.

"I won't say nervous, but I do remember thinking, I hope this guy doesn't turn out to be a weirdo. I was more concerned about inviting him to stay at my parents' house and would have hated to think I put them – as well as myself - in harm's way. My old roommate said, 'Michele, if he turns psycho, just politely tell him he can't stay at your house anymore'." Michele couldn't help but laugh as she recalled the conversation. "I suppose that is your worst-case scenario as well - if he turns out to be a bit of a weirdo, but the good news is, he's a cop. Not that cops can't be weirdoes, but I'd like to think your odds would be better. At any rate, you can always call my brother or father if you start getting bad vibes, and they'd come pick you up. I'm sure they wouldn't have a problem with that - they live only 40 minutes away. I still can't believe you met an American and with 50 States to live in, he comes from the same area I grew up in. What is the likelihood of you meeting someone who lives that close to my parents? That is amazing!" Michele said.

Carole didn't have any doubts about Sean, but it did make her feel better that Howard and Michael, Michele's father and brother, would be not too far away.

"I did mention to Sean that you guys were relocating back to New York in the fall. You know, let me have your parents' telephone number. I'm sure I won't need it, but it would be nice just to have a contact number and perhaps we'll stop by to say hello. I haven't seen them since Bradley's baptism," Carole said.

Regardless of what her sisters said, Carole was going to New York, and she knew Linda would come around with time. She had really good feelings about Sean and was going to stick with these. However, she had to put them in the back of her mind for the time being and get back into her training, as the climb was only weeks away. She called Brenda to thank her for introducing her to Sean and wanted to know if she was going out climbing over the weekend.

TRAVELLING TO THE MATTERHORN

Linda and her mum took care of Kristy and Joseph while Carole was in Switzerland for the week. The evening before she was to leave, Carole double- and triple-checked that she had all the necessary equipment packed in her rucksack…boots, ropes, fleeces, gortex waterproofs, a harness, crampons, an ice axe, hat, helmet, gloves, sun cream, goggles, sleeping bag and, of course, a camera to capture the moment she reached the top of the mountain. She kept tossing and turning, trying to get herself to sleep, but her mind was racing, thinking of her pending climb and her torn feelings between being excited about the trip and anxious about leaving her children for a week. Carole went into Kristy's bedroom and lay next to her, looking at her beautiful long eyelashes and angelic face. She gave her a kiss and then went to see Joseph. His little body was spread-eagled over his bed, and she gently moved his legs to make room for herself. Joseph never stopped talking; during sleep was no exception. He was having a chat with someone in his sleep, which made Carole smile. She cuddled with him for a while, and when she woke up, she didn't know how long she had been sleeping. The clock read 1:30 am, and Carole knew she had to get back into her own bed to be well rested for her trip the next day.

They left from Glasgow International Airport the following morning and flew into Geneva. From there, their journey to Zermatt took four hours by train. It was all surreal to Carole. There she was on a train in Switzerland, watching the countryside pass her by like the speed of light. She was headed for the valley base to start her journey up a mountain, but it wasn't just *any* mountain. It was the Matterhorn - all 14,692 feet of it! The time had come to climb the mountain that she had been training to climb for nearly a year. Carole was confident in her abilities, but remained in awe of the sheer size of it. This little girl from Port Glasgow had come a long way…in more ways then one.

When they arrived at Zermatt, they met their mountain guide, a tall, trim man with sandy blonde hair and blue eyes. He had been climbing mountains for over 10 years and had reached several summits. This made him all the more eager to have his group summit the Matterhorn so they too could feel that awesome feeling of success.

"Hi everyone, I'm Sven, and I'll be climbing the Matterhorn with you. As you know, the climb is broken up into two days. Tomorrow morning we will hike to the Hornli hut; the distance between the valley base and the hut is 5,380 feet. I'd suggest that you get your rest tonight so you're ready to go bright and early."

They quickly learned that Sven was a man of his word. At 5:15 am they were awakened and asked to be ready to leave by 6:00 am. They left with their rucksacks on their backs, ready for an adventure. Carole had a skip in her step. She and Brenda were both comfortable with the pace of the hike and were eager to reach the hut by midday. They trekked toward the hut on a trail that wound along steep glacier moraines with metal stairways firmly implanted into the side of the mountain that led them towards the hut. At last, they could see the hut in the distance.

It's a beautiful day and life is good

"The hut sleeps fifty climbers, and five places have been reserved for us in an otherwise fully booked hut," Sven said.

Hornli Hut was nestled at the foot of the Hornli Ridge, which would be their starting point the following day.

As they got closer, Carole could see a two-story white building with gray shutters and was amazed how such a large hut had been built on the side of the mountain. More astonishing was the fact it had managed to remain standing through severe weather conditions year after year. As they approached the hut, they saw slabs of rocks scattered just below it, as if there had been an explosion of some sort. Carole was careful not to wrench her ankle on the rocks and, once they hiked past them, they were home free and could see the entrance to the hut and terrace. They sat on one of the fifteen picnic tables scattered about the terrace and looked back at the territory they had just hiked. The height of the hut made everything in the valley look like a miniature village, like a Christmas display on a dining room table. There was a small church with a tall steeple, stores, houses scattered about, and snake-like roads leading up the mountainside. Carole sat there enjoying the moment and soaking in the panoramic views.

"Good job, everyone," said Sven. "I'm going in to register us, and then we can all go in and set up our sleeping bags."

There were wooden planks along the walls of the hut. Carole followed Brenda's and Ian's lead, took her sleeping bag out, and rolled it onto the wooden slats, quickly realizing that the person who would be sleeping next to her would be inches away from her face. The quarters were indeed close, and although she wasn't expecting a five-star hotel, the mountain huts were indeed very basic. Sleeping bags were lined up next to each other row after row. There was definitely no more room at the inn.

In the communal hut were men and women alike appearing comfortable in each other's company, whether changing their clothes, eating, or sleeping. The hut satisfied everyone's basic needs for food and shelter, and as an added bonus, a toilet. Carole's group had their own food with them and had fun listening to the other climbers talk about their past experiences and how weather conditions could change rapidly on the mountain, which made the weather forecast the main topic of discussion.

THE CLIMB

The next morning they were up at 3:30. Sven gave them a briefing on the weather conditions while they ate breakfast. He also gave them his normal pre-climb pep talk.

"I'm not trying to frighten anyone, but every year there are accidents on the mountain; some cases end in death. As a matter of fact, since the first ascent of the Matterhorn in 1865, more than 500 climbers have lost their lives on the mountain, so when I give you a directive, I expect you to listen," he said.

Sven gave the same speech to all his climbers and always made sure they heard him loud and clear. He didn't want the fixed ropes, ladders, and huts along the normal routes to the summit giving anyone a sense of false security; much of the climb still required sound technical expertise. It was important for them to know that its death rate is one of the highest in the world. Sven said he thought the mountain's popularity was its own undoing, as every year around this time, large numbers of climbers ascended simultaneously, which guaranteed meeting and overtaking maneuvers.

"These sorts of maneuvers cause the increased likelihood of rocks being dislodged and falling onto climbers below. Dislodging of rocks tends to be caused by less -experienced climbers," he added. "But that won't be happening on my watch, because we won't be taking any unnecessary risks."

Not exactly what Carole needed to hear right before they were starting their ascent; nevertheless, she understood why he was saying it: They needed to keep on their game the entire climb. She could feel her adrenaline pumping and couldn't wait to start climbing the ridge. Carole was determined to get up the mountain and live to tell her grandchildren about it.

"The good news is, I have never lost a climber, and I don't intend to start now," Sven said, "The bad news, I'm sorry to say, is the weather conditions are looking a bit bleak. There is, however, a small window of opportunity here, so let's get out there before the other 45 climbers take the same opportunity. We'll meet on the terrace in five minutes," he said.

It seemed like a different mountain when Carole walked outside. The wind was blowing, the clouds were all around her, and the sky was pitch black. She and Brenda did a buddy check, making sure their helmets, harnesses, ropes, and crampons were tied and buckled up correctly. Her rucksack was comfortably situated on her back, and she was ready for the challenge. However, she couldn't help but feel that the mountain was sending out a message: "Climbers, beware!" She knew she needed to get her mind in a positive place. "Okay, Caz, you've trained for this and you can do it. Just follow Sven, use the techniques you've learned, and you'll be fine," she said to herself.

Sven led the way, followed by Brenda, Carole, John, and Ian. They all wore their head torches to help them see where they were climbing. Carole couldn't see too far in front of herself, but the ridge looked steeper than it had the day before. They walked towards the lower flanks of the mountain. Carole felt in awe of the sheer size of the rock piles. Everywhere she looked, each rock was bigger then the next.

A number of climbers were already out on the ridge, but all you could see were the lights on their head torches weaving back and forth as they climbed the mountain. Carole counted four lights in front of them and saw two other groups of climbers. "They must have been out here at 2:30 to have gotten that far up," she thought.

As they continued to scramble up the mountain, Carole felt as if the wind was pushing her around like a ragdoll. She kneeled a few times to try to get away from its gust. They had only been climbing for a little over two hours, when Sven turned to them and said the dreaded words, "It's too dangerous to go any higher at this time; we'll need to start going back down to the hut before we get ourselves stuck in a bad situation."

Carole now noticed that the climbers in front of them had already turned around and were on their way down. She was disappointed and felt a tear roll down the side of her face. All the preparation, the hours of climbing, hiking, and exercising didn't have the outcome that she thought she'd be rewarded with…to summit the Matterhorn.

As they sat in the hut, Sven tried to comfort them: Perhaps the weather front would change. But the forecast was predicting the same weather pattern for the three long days they waited around the hut. The weather didn't change, and their window of opportunity slipped by. It was time to leave the hut and make the descent to the valley base. Carole wanted a picture of herself and asked Brenda to do the honors. She made a disappointed face and held her hands up in the air, as if to say, "Oh well, I tried," and Brenda took the picture.

"I could now fully relate to how my brother must have felt when he didn't make it up Everest due to the weather conditions, and he was on that mountain 14 weeks! When he told me, I really couldn't sympathize, but now I can. He was obviously climbing at a different level, but nevertheless, it's still so disappointing," said Carole.

"Yes, but it is part of the sport, isn't it. Think of all the times we were able to summit during our training. Although it wasn't the Matterhorn, we made it to the top. It just was not meant to be this time," said Brenda.

"I suppose so. The fact of the matter is we just don't have any control over Mother Nature. What *she* says goes," Carole said with a little smile, trying to comfort herself. "Perhaps we'll be back one day," she added.

The trip home was a bit somber, but Carole had something else to look forward to…her trip to the States to see Sean.

TESTING THE WATERS

"Hello, how was your trip? When did you get in?" Sean asked, excited to hear Carole's voice. Sean knew he had missed hearing Carole's voice, but didn't realized how much until he was on the phone with her.

"It was great, up to the point when the weather conditions stopped us in our tracks, and Sven, our mountain guide, told us it was too dangerous to continue."

He could hear the disappointment in her voice.

"Well, at least you can say you **attempted** it. That is something to be proud of in itself. Heck, I don't know too many women who fall into that category, and I'm proud of you, if that counts for anything," he said.

"Yes, it does count. Thanks for that," she said as she felt a warm feeling of caring come over the phone.

"I miss you. When are you coming over?" he said, assuming she had accepted his invitation.

"How is the third week in July?"

As Carole predicted, Linda came around with the idea of her going to New York and agreed to watch the children. She flew out on

Thursday morning on British Airways and arrived at JFK International Airport by noon that same day. The weather for the weekend was supposed to be sunny and in the high 80s. Carole packed a few pairs of shorts, sundresses, sandals, and a bathing suit since she knew Sean had a pool and lived close to the beach. Carole loved the beach and found it to be just as peaceful there as it was on top of a mountain.

Her flight arrived on time and she was definitely looking forward to seeing Sean again. Other than the week she was in Switzerland, they had talked at least three times a week and she was certain that the long weekend was going to be fun. As she walked out of the arrival gate, Carole saw Sean standing against a pillar waiting for her with one long-stemmed red rose. Sean had been counting the days until he'd see Carole again.

"That's a nice way to be welcomed," she said, as she gave him a tender hug and a kiss.

"Oh it's so great to have you in my arms again," Sean said as he nestled his face into her neck and smelled her familiar scent. I missed you so much."

"I missed you too," Carole said as she held onto him even tighter.

"How was your flight?"

"Good, no delays, and a direct flight is definitely the way to go," she said.

The drive took nearly an hour and, as they drove up to Sean's split-level house, she noticed his address: 6 Carole Lane.

"You didn't tell me you lived on Carole Lane," she said. "And it's spelled the same way. Now that is a good omen, isn't it!" she said with a smile, shaking her head up and down.

They spent most of their days at Robert Moses Beach, talking and walking the shoreline, and their evenings were spent eating at nice restaurants and taking long walks around the neighborhood, holding hands. She noticed that there was a school just around the corner from where Sean lived and couldn't help but wonder if her children would be attending school there one day. Carole was amazed how quickly she felt close to him and loved learning all about him. Sean seemed to find peace and serenity by going out on his motorcycle, bike riding, and hunting. He'd sit in a tree for six hours straight, which wasn't something Carole ever contemplated as being enjoyable, but she said she'd like to try it once, just to experience it.

Sean seemed just as interested in hearing about Carole's interests and loves. She shared with him how Joseph's little stories and facial expressions would put a smile on her face, and how Kristy's intellect totally blew her away.

"She's such a smart little girl and sometimes just a wee bit too hard on herself, but when they are happy, I am happy," she said.

"Oh," she added, "and I love sharing a bottle of wine with friends and laughing until my sides hurt. I honestly believe that a lot of my misfortunes came from putting too much stress on myself. So I'm learning how to just let things go. It's such a freeing feeling!"

Carole continued to test the waters to see if they were right for each other; whether consciously or subconsciously, she knew she didn't fly over from the UK just for a tour of Long Island. Carole wanted to see if it was a place she and her children would be happy living in and, more important, if Sean was the soul mate she was looking for. She was happy that her mental checklist was being met, and was very pleased that she decided to stick with her gut feeling and take the trip.

Before she left, Carole managed to get a little shopping in and picked up a cute pair of shoes at the retail outlets in Riverhead. But then it was time for her to go home. Contacting Michele's father or brother had never entered her mind.

"I can't believe how quickly these four days went," she said.

"I know. When could you come back?"

"I'd have to check, but maybe next month. How does that sound?"

"The sooner, the better," he said.

As they drove to the airport, she dreaded the thought of having to say good-bye. She kept on telling herself, "Don't be silly, Carole, you'll see him again in a month." She was taken aback by the strong feelings she had for someone she'd known for merely two months. Carole's gut feeling was that God had answered her prayers, and had sent her the soul mate she had been waiting patiently for. "Why else would we both have such strong feelings for each other in such a short period of time?" she thought to herself.

The drive seemed quicker than she had remembered and, before she knew it, they were at the airport. They were both preoccupied with thoughts of having to say good-bye and were the quietest they had been all weekend.

"I really don't like good-byes," Carole said. "So when we get to the airport you don't have to wait with me."

"Yeh, right, are you kidding me? I'm spending as much time with you as I possibly can before they tell me I have to leave," he said with a silly grin on his face. "You are who I've been waiting for my whole life."

"How freaky is that?" thought Carole, "I was just thanking God for sending me the person I'd been patiently waiting for and he says the same thing to me."

She had never felt such a strong connection with anyone so immediately, and she was going to enjoy every bit of their new relationship and the future journey it would take her on. In the back of Carole's mind, she realized she had to think of the children and how Dick would react to their possibly moving to America, but she stopped herself before she got into a tizzy. For now she just wanted to enjoy Sean and the last few moments of his company.

"Flight BA2172 to London Gatwick with connecting flights to Glasgow and Manchester boarding at Gate 4," a voice announced over the PA system.

"That's my flight," Carole said, as the pit in her stomach ached a bit. She gave Sean a kiss and a hug and whispered in his ear, "I'll see you soon; it won't be long."

Sean felt an empty feeling come over him as he sat in the airport until he saw Carole's plane take off.

A Long-Distance Relationship

Carole couldn't stop thinking about Sean, and as soon as she got back home, she booked her flight to New York for an August visit. It would have to be the last weekend, as August 21 was Kristy's eighth birthday, and Carole wanted to be at home for that special day.

She was in need of some female bonding, and who better to contact than Fay, Jacqui, and Daryl. The Four Usuals were overdue for a reunion, and their meeting place this time would be in Scotland. They met at a restaurant in Edinburgh and went straight back to where they had left off at their last reunion, five months earlier. Carole spoke fondly of Sean and their relationship. In a playful way she told them all he really needed was a decent haircut, up-to-date clothes, and to wear his shirt outside his trousers.

"Oh, one more thing, all his checked shirts need to go in the bin or be donated to charity. Other than that, he's perfect!"

They could tell she was serious about this relationship, as she wouldn't really have cared about his grooming and sense of style if she didn't have thoughts of a future with him. After a few bottles of wine, she told them relocating to New York was a real possibility, but what concerned her was how Dick was going to react to their children moving.

"What if he gives me a hard time about taking the children to New York? What if he tells me they can't go? What will I do?"

"Why are you doing this to yourself? These are all 'what-ifs'. You won't know until you talk to him," said Jacqui. "Don't get yourself all worked up about something that might not be an issue," added Daryl.

"I know you are right; I'm just getting ahead of myself. He really shouldn't give me a hard time, but it seems every time he has a chance to make things harder, he does," Carole said.

"Well one thing is for sure: His name suits him perfectly," Carole added with a giggle.

They all had a good chuckle over that, and Fay suggested getting another bottle of red wine. Before they knew it, they had laughed and talked the night away, and one thing became crystal clear in Carole's mind by the end of the evening. One way or another, she would be going to the States with her children.

Carole and Sean spoke every Tuesday, Thursday, and Sunday, which fit into Sean's shift at work, but she wondered if it was too often because the extent of Sean's dialogue was "Hello, how are you?" Carole quickly put an end to that.

"Sean," she said playfully, but with a message that needed to be heard, "If you don't say more than 'Hello, how are you?' I'm hanging up!' "

"All right, lighten up, Francis," he said, laughing at her bold, upfront mannerisms, "How was your day, dear? Is that better?"

"A little, but not much. Who's Francis? It's Carole."

"No, it's from a movie. This guy Frank doesn't…"

Carole cut him off in mid-sentence, "I know, doesn't like being called Francis," she said with a chuckle, "I'm just busting on you. We get movies over here in Scotland, 'or I'll kill ya,'" she said, in her best American accent.

Carole had a lovely way of getting her point across and not hurting his feelings. It was so easy to talk to him in person, yet over the phone, it was hard work.

"When I come over next time, will we go out with your friends?" she asked.

"I don't have any, but my cousin Jim and his girlfriend Fiona, who you met will be over from Scotland, and we'll be going out with them," he said.

"Surely, he is just kidding about not having friends," she thought.

Carole was such a social person and thrived on building relationships with her friends and family. Although the more she thought about Sean's hobbies - hunting and cycling - she realized that he was probably telling the truth. As long as he didn't try to keep her from her friends and family, as Dick had tried to, they would be fine. She just marked her next project, which was to get him to become more comfortable with socializing.

Carole's second trip to New York came and went quickly, but she had a great time. This time she met Sean's sister, Ann, and her family.

Ann had two little girls and one on the way. Everyone seemed friendly towards Carole, but she couldn't help but notice that his family appeared to have the run of his house.

"Surely this can't be how it is all the time," she thought, but upon further reflection, it seemed a bit too odd, which lead Carole to make a mental note of it.

They continued to build their relationship; her next trip to the States would be in October - a big trip for everyone. This time Carole would be taking the children with her for a week. She and Sean thought it would be a good idea for Kristy and Joseph to talk to Sean over the phone, so when they met each other, he wouldn't be a complete stranger. Those conversations were shorter than short. Sean asked about their cat and their friends, and after that, it was, "Can you put your mum back on the phone, please?" Carole wondered how the children were going to react to Sean, but time would tell.

AN IMPORTANT VISIT – MEETING THE CHILDREN

JFK International Airport was becoming a familiar place for Carole. She was excited for the children to met Sean and see New York. As always, he was waiting patiently for the plane to land and for Carole to walk out, but this time with her children. He had a rose for Carole and two balloons for the children. This trip was bound to be different, Carole thought, but she just wanted the kids to have fun, get to know Sean, and love Long Island. The fun part Sean had under control…he had planned an exciting week for them.

October was a lovely time of year to visit New York, as the leaves were changing pretty colors of red, orange, and yellow. The next day they drove out to the North Fork of Long Island and took a tractor-drawn hayride out to a pumpkin patch. They each picked their own pumpkin; the rule was if they could carry it, it was theirs. Kristy picked a sensible-sized pumpkin, while Joseph was determined to pick the biggest pumpkin he could find. As he walked back to the tractor, holding his pumpkin by the stem, the pumpkin fell and landed on his foot, nearly breaking his toes.

"Ouchhhhhh!" he cried loudly.

"Oh, are you all right, little guy?" Sean asked. "You can still have the pumpkin if you want," he said as he picked him up and sat him on the tractor.

Joseph was in tears from the pain, but muttered out, "Yes, please."

That night at dinner, Sean asked if they'd like to go into the City the next day. They had been looking forward to seeing the big buildings their mum had been telling them about. They travelled into the City by train and arrived at Penn Station. Joseph loved the train ride and, during the trip, the questions were endless: "How fast are we going? How many times will the train stop? Why is the train so crowded?" he asked, in his sweet little Scottish accent. But before Sean had a chance to answer the questions, he riffled out a few more. "How much longer before we see the big buildings? Why did it go dark outside?"

"It's dark outside because the train is now in a tunnel, travelling under water. We'll see the big buildings in about 10 minutes," Sean replied.

Once they got up onto street level, Sean pointed out the Empire State Building to the children. Kristy observed everything with her big green eyes and didn't say much. The City was a big place for adults and an even bigger place for children. Everything seemed oversized to her -- the cars were longer, the buildings were taller, and hordes of people covered the entire width of the oversized sidewalks. She held onto her mother's hand like a security blanket, making sure she didn't get lost in the crowd.

Sean hailed a taxicab to take them up to Central Park. He sat in front with the driver, while the children and Carole sat in the back seat. The driver gave them a thrill ride up to the park, as he weaved in and out among the cars in front of him, muttering something under his breath in a foreign language. Nevertheless, they arrived at a part of the City far less hectic then Penn Station, in record time, safe and sound.

They walked over to the zoo, where their first stop was the polar bear pool. From a lower-level observatory, which looked like a large glass fish tank, they watched the bear swim. As it swam closer, it reared off to the left, pushing against the glass with its buttocks until it was able to swing its big paws around.

"Wow, that is a HUGE bear," said Joseph.

"Yes, and that is one very strong piece of glass separating us from lots of water and a *HUGE* bear," said Carole.

They moved on and watched the penguins being fed, saw little monkeys and pandas, walked through an indoor rainforest, and saw fruit bats and an anteater. Carole was pleased that the children were having a good time at the zoo and, more important, enjoying Sean's company.

Their next stop in the park was the carousel.

"You'll enjoy this, Carole, and so will the kids," Sean said, "There a great story behind it, too." He walked over to the ticket booth, got four tickets, and picked up a brochure.

"The carousel has been in operation at the park since 1871. The original carousel was powered by a blind horse and mule, which is pretty wild, isn't it? The current carousel was made for a trolley terminal outside Coney Island."

"Coney Island? I've been there," Carole said.

"Why would you have been there?"

"When I was in town for my first trip to New York, Howie, Michele's dad, took us to the wooden rollercoaster there. I can't recall the name, but we had some 'famous' hotdogs as well."

"Leave it up to you to have been to Coney Island! That would have been the Cyclone, and the hotdogs were Nathan's."

"Yes, that's right. I'm sorry for interrupting you...do finish what you were saying," she said.

"No problem. The carousel was moved to this park when a fire destroyed the first one. The other neat thing is, to this day the carousel and its hand-carved figures are still hand-painted. That's pretty cool, isn't it?" he said.

"Wow, look at the detail of the horses. They're gorgeous," Carole said.

Their features were intense. Carole imagined them running along a beach in full gallop, with their tongues hanging out the sides of their mouths, in desperate need of a drink of water and some rest.

"Come on, Joseph, I'll share a horse with you. Kristy, get on the horse in front of us, and Sean will ride alongside you," Carole said.

The carousel quickly picked up speed. "Oh, hold on, kids, here we go!" she said.

After they had seen enough of the park, they had lunch and then walked over to FAO Schwartz. Two human "toy soldiers," with tall black hats and red cheeks, welcomed them at the door as they entered the toy store. Carole could see Joseph and Kristy's eyes darting left to right, not knowing which way to look first.

"Oh, look at this! Can I have one, Mummy?" Joseph asked.

"Let's see what else is in the shop, okay? We just got here, but I will let you both get one thing each," she said.

"Yippee!" they shouted with glee.

As they went up the main escalator to the second floor, they could hear piano music. There was a huge piano keyboard on the floor, and each key was about 1 ½ feet long. Several children were lining up, looking forward to playing the piano with their feet.

"That's the piano Tom Hanks played in the movie *Big*," said Sean.

"Oh, that's brilliant! Mummy, can we play on the piano?" asked Kristy.

"Absolutely - let's get in the queue," Carole said.

When it was their turn, they took their shoes off, and Joseph ran off and did a Tom Cruise slide from the movie "Risky Business." As he slid across the keyboard, each key lit up as he came to a stop without falling.

"Well done, Joseph," Carole cheered.

Kristy, on the other hand, tried to compose a song and was getting distracted by Joseph's running.

"You have great kids," Sean said.

"Thanks, I'm very proud of them and love them to bits," she said with a big smile on her face.

Once they were done playing with most everything in the store, they walked down and across to Broadway, so they could see the lights and billboards before they headed back to Penn Station to catch their train to Long Island. The two very tired children fell asleep on Carole and Sean's laps as they travelled home.

The following night Carole and Sean went out to dinner with Michele and Deka, who had recently relocated to the States, and were staying with Michele's parents until they found jobs and a place to live. Other than Joseph and Kristy, these would be the first family members Sean would be meeting, along with nephew Bradley and Michele's parents, Rose and Howard. Sean's mother, Elizabeth, volunteered to watch the children for the evening, and they travelled to West Hempstead where Rose and Howard lived.

Michele had shared with her mother the good things she had heard about Sean, and they were eagerly waiting to meet him. They wanted good things for Carole and were praying he was her Prince Charming.

Finally, the doorbell rang. "I'll get it," Rose said.

Carole stood at the front door with a big smile, Sean by her side. "Hello, Rosie, how are you? It's been a long time," she said as she gave her a hug and kiss.

"Yes, it has been. I'm good. Please come in," Rose said.

"Hi, Caz," Deka said, giving his sister a big hug and kiss.

"This is Sean," said Carole, introducing him to Deka, Michele, Bradley, Rose, and Howard.

Sean seemed a bit quiet standing at the front door. "Come on in." Howard said, "Can I get you something to drink before you head off to the restaurant?"

They had a quick glass of wine so Carole could have a chat with Rose and Howard, and they could have a chance to talk to their fellow Long Islander. They asked him all the typical questions: "Where do you live?" "How long did it take you to get here?" And of course, the most commonly asked question: "Did you hit any traffic?" Sean cordially answered and joined in with their conversations.

"It's time to go, or we'll be late for our reservations," Michele announced.

They went to Dodici's, an Italian restaurant in Rockville Centre, and had a good evening, getting to know Sean over dinner and a few bottles of wine. Deka and he both liked climbing mountains, skiing, cycling, and motorcycles. As a result, the conversation flowed.

When Carole and Michele walked together to the restrooms in the back, Carole asked, "What do you think?"

"He seems very nice, but more important, what do you think?"

"Oh, I think he's absolutely lovely,"

"Well, that's all that really matters, isn't it?" Michele said.

Carole thought he was a wee bit more than lovely. She and Sean had been talking about their future together for weeks, but they hadn't shared this with anyone. Suffice it to say they were way beyond the "hypothetical" stage of speaking about marriage.

Two days before Carole and the children were due to return to Scotland, Sean had arranged for his mother to watch the children for a few hours in the afternoon, so he could take Carole to Robert Moses Beach one more time before they left. They sat on the highest dune they could find and enjoyed the sights and sounds of the beach. The seagulls were flying about without a care in the world, the waves were crashing against the shore, and the sun warmed their faces. Sean turned to Carole and gave her a smile, and she thought he was going to say something, but he stopped and looked away. He knew what he was about to ask her would change his life forever. Sean looked at her again and this time his butterflies went away as he said,

"Carole, will you marry me?"

"Absolutely! I will," she said and gave him a gentle kiss and hug.

There wasn't a doubt in her mind that this was the right decision. After the beach, they went back to Sean's house and enjoyed a bottle of champagne to celebrate their future union. They were in the middle of a magical whirlwind, and everything seemed so right. Sean knew Carole would want to pick out a ring, and he made an appointment with his jeweler the next day to design her engagement ring.

A CHRISTMAS PRESENT TO REMEMBER

Before Carole knew it, Christmas was upon her. There was a big wreath on her front door, an electric-light candelabrum was displayed on the inside window sill, along with a decorative shovel with Santa's face painted on it and a message saying, "Santa stop here." The tree was fully adorned with white lights and decorations handmade by Kristy and Joseph. Garlands draped the staircase leading up to the bedrooms, and there was a feeling of joy in the air. Carole was going to Glasgow International Airport to pick up Sean, who was arriving on an early flight. She had four days before Santa would be visiting their house, and she had a lot to do, but she was finding it hard to concentrate, knowing she would be getting her ring.

"I hope he just gives it to me when he gets off the plane," she thought. She couldn't wait to see it on her finger, and she had her nails manicured just for the occasion.

Jim and Fiona were at the airport, waiting to welcome Sean as well.

"Your ring is absolutely beautiful," Fiona said, "and I know how much it cost."

Carole just gave her a perplexed look, not sure how to respond, but thought it was cheeky for her to say such a thing.

"Thanks, I think," she said making a mental note to ask Sean why Fiona knew this and how she'd seen it before Carole did. But once she saw Sean, it was the furthest thing from her mind. She couldn't wait to be in his arms again.

"Hello, Honey. How was your flight?" Carole said as she gave him a kiss.

"Yeh, it was a good flight. Oh, I missed you," he said, as he gave her a big hug. "I have your ring - do you want it now, or should we wait until we get back to the house?"

"Oh, let me think…," she said, as she put her finger to her chin and looked up to the sky as if she really had to think about it - "Now, please. I can't wait to see it," Carole sang with excitement.

She had been trying to visualize it since they'd had it designed two months earlier. He took the small ring box out of his jacket pocket, opened it, and handed it to her. Carole's mouth dropped open with delight. Fiona was indeed right: It was absolutely beautiful. Three diamonds sat next to each other in a platinum setting. It was a trilogy engagement ring, representing past, present, and future. To Carole it also symbolized the three loves of her life: Sean, Kristy, and Joseph. Carole put it on her finger and stared at her hand for a few minutes, moving it from left to right to see the brilliance of the diamonds as they caught the light.

"Oh, my God, Sweet Pea, it is just perfect. I love it," she said.

"I'm glad, because it looks perfect on your hand," he said.

They were going to have a busy holiday session. The biggest news was to tell the children and her whole family that they were getting married and moving to New York with the children next year. And she'd have to tell Dick.

SURPRISE!

"Helllloooo, where is everyone?" Carole sang as she walked into her house.

The kids ran downstairs followed by her mum and Linda.

"There you are…Mum, Linda, this is Sean," she said.

Carole truly hoped this meeting would go smoothly and she was over the moon with her ring and just couldn't help but flash it at them. She had told Linda and her mum that she was getting married back in October, but when Linda saw her ring, her mouth dropped open.

"Nice to meet you," Linda said, "and your ring is lovely, Carole," she added.

"It's nice to finally meet you as well. I've heard a lot about the two of you," he said.

Everything was happening so quickly. Linda was happy for Carole, but still a little nervous, wondering if she was rushing into something. Not only did this mean that Carole would be moving to the States, but Kristy and Joseph would obviously be going as well, and the thought of not seeing her niece and nephew every weekend brought tears to her eyes.

Carole showed the ring to the children and explained that she would be marrying Sean, which meant they would be moving to New York. Joseph didn't seem too fussed by the announcement, but Kristy knew it meant she'd have to leave her best friend, Hayley, her Nanny, Aunty Linda, and Aunty Christine, and she got very quiet. Kristy was a deep little thinker for her age, and Carole let her sit with it for a bit.

"Are you all right, Kristy?" Carole asked.

"Mummy, I like New York, but my friends, Nanny, Aunty Linda, and Aunty Christine are all here," she said.

"I know, but our family will come to see us on Long Island, and we will come back to visit Hayley. You'll definitely be coming to Scotland on a regular basis to see your father and, when you do, you'll be able to see Nanny and Lindy. I'm sure Long Island will be a lovely place to live, and once you start school, you'll be making plenty of new friends - you'll see." Carole said.

As soon as Sean left to go over to Jim's house, Linda asked the question that was preying on her mind.

"Carole, he seems like a very nice guy, and you know we all only want you to be happy, but what is the rush?" she asked.

"There really is no need to wait, and this is what we want. We're planning on getting married in June of next year," Carole said.

Carole rang her brother and, although he was happy for her, he asked the same question. "You're getting married? I think it's great that you are moving over here, because you'll be close to us, but what's the rush? It's such a big move!" Deka said.

"It's what we want. Really, there is no need to wait. His family is apparently saying the same thing to him, but also adding, 'Are you sure you know what you are doing marrying someone with two kids?' " she said. "We are very happy, he's good with the kids, and we are planning on getting married in June at Linlithgow Palace. Will you give me away?" she asked her brother.

"Of course, I would be honoured," he said. "I only want the best for you, Carole," he added.

"I know…Mum, Linda, and Christine are concerned as well, but trust me, this is the right thing for me. I'm sure of it," she said.

"Okay, would you like me to wear my kilt?"

"Absolutely! I'd also like Michele to say a reading. Is she there so I can ask her myself?"

"Yes, hold on - I'll get her."

"Hi, from what I just overheard, it sounds like congratulations are in order!" Michele said.

"Yes, thank you. We are getting married in June, and I'd like you to read *Footprints* for me at the wedding," Carole said.

"Yes, I would love to," she said.

"That was the easy bit," thought Carole. Now she had to have a conversation with Dick. She paced the kitchen, trying to get her thoughts together on how to tell him the news. "No time like the present; let's just get this over with," she thought.

"Hi Dick, it's Carole. I need to talk to you about something. Is this a good time?" she asked.

"Sure. What's up?"

"Well, I've been dating someone and we've decided to get married," she said.

"Oh…," he said, sounding shocked by the news.

"The other bit is, he is an American, and we will be moving to New York,"

"What do you mean, you'll be moving to New York! You are taking the kids to America?"

"Yes, we're getting married in June, and we'll be moving over some time before the start of the new school year. I'd like to work out a schedule for the children to come over to Scotland and visit with you during their holiday and summer breaks," Carole said.

There was a pause and Carole was wondering if he'd hung up.

"Don't expect me to pay you the full child support that I'm paying now if you move to America," he finally said.

"How pathetic," Carole thought. "I'm telling this man that he won't be able to see his children on a regular bi-weekly basis, and the only comment he makes is about the child support he is going to cut."

Carole was dying to lace into him, but knew it was more important to keep the peace until she had the solicitor write up the new agreement and had Dick sign it. The agreement would reduce the children's maintenance to half, or he wouldn't sign the paper allowing them to live in another country. She should have known that his main concern wasn't his parental rights, but rather his financial responsibility, which he had no problem shrugging off. It was a relief, however, for Carole to know he wasn't going to fight her for custody.

Carole could relax a bit and start thinking about planning her fairytale wedding, but they'd have to get over a few hurdles before they would be able to enjoy their new lives together.

A CHANGE IN PLAN

Carole's job was to organize a wedding for June 20, and Sean's job was to get all the Immigration paperwork completed for their relocation. He was quickly finding out, however, that there was much more red tape than he had thought.

Carole asked Michele what the process had been like for her, and it had indeed been complicated and long. Unlike when Michele had relocated to England in 1998, when the only requirements were filling out some paperwork at the British Embassy in New York, an interview and a marriage certificate, and a year later, the Embassy making sure they were still married. Michele and Deka's relocation to the States, however, had taken eight months to complete and had cost about $1,000 in application fees, on top of a doctor's fee for a medical examination.

Sean was finding out firsthand that the process was, without a doubt, especially long if he filed the paperwork prior to their getting married. They wouldn't be able to enter the country for over a year.

"Oh, my God," Carole said; "there must be a quicker way."

There was, and upon further investigation, Sean found out that the process would be a little less cumbersome if they were married, as he would be able to complete all the paperwork as a married couple.

"Let's get married earlier and still have our reception and honeymoon in June," he said.

"That's a good idea, which also gives me a reason to buy a winter *and* a summer wedding dress!" Carole said, smiling.

VALENTINE'S DAY – 2003

It was their wedding day, February 14, 2003, and the frigid temperatures quickly reminded everyone it was the middle of winter. Carole came down the stairs in her house wearing a winter-white fur hat that sat perched down to the middle of her forehead. Her tailored above-the-knee winter-white dress was accompanied by a matching jacket trimmed with fur cuffs. She looked like someone out of "Doctor Zhivago."

"Carole, you look beautiful!" Linda said to her sister.

Stunning was more like it. She strolled down the staircase like a film star. Her life story was quickly becoming something out of a movie. A private hired car took Carole, Linda, their mum, and the children to the church at Linlithgow Palace.

"This is so romantic, isn't it…you're getting married in the church at the Palace where you had your first blind date with Sean, and you're getting married on Valentine's Day! I don't think it could get any more romantic," said Linda with delight and excitement in her voice.

"Yes, and I'm going to the chapel and we're going to get married," Carole said. "I feel a song coming on," and Linda quickly chimed in and before they knew it, so did their mum. They sang and laughed the whole way to the church.

As they drove up to the church, Carole felt a wave of excitement rush over her. She looked at the massive structure before her and saw its strength and beauty, similar to Carole's own character -- strong and beautiful.

Like everything else in Scotland, the church came with a wealth of history. St. Michael's Parish Church sat on high ground and had been built between the town of Linlithgow and Linlithgow Loch, with the Palace to its north. It was thought that there had probably been another church on the site dating back to 1138. As she walked up the long main aisle, Carole stopped counting the rows after she reached fifty-seven. Upon approaching the pulpit and the main altar, Carole looked around for her favorite part of the church: St. Katherine's Aisle window. It was a new stained-glass window with brilliant colors that lit up the side of the church on sunny days. They walked passed the choir benches, which were cordoned off with red braided rope that matched the red rug on the floor.

Finally, Carole saw Sean and felt butterflies in her stomach. "I've never felt so sure about anything in my whole life," she said to herself, and realized that her butterflies were caused by sheer excitement. Sean looked so handsome wearing his Stewart clan kilt, and wore it with the same pride as any other Scotsman.

He took one look at Carole, gave her a soft smile, and couldn't wait until he'd be calling her his wife.

Father McGulligan met them in the middle of the altar, welcomed everyone, and started the ceremony.

He asked, "Carole, did you come of your own free will to give yourself to Sean in marriage?"

"I did," she replied.

"Sean, did you come of your own free will to give yourself to Carole in marriage?"

"I did," he replied.

He continued, "Will you both honor and love one another as husband and wife for the rest of your lives, and will you both accept children from God lovingly and bring them up according to the law of Christ and his Church?"

"We will," they both answered.

"Please join your right hands as you declare your consent before God and the Church," he said.

The priest blessed the wedding rings as symbols of deep faith and peace, and Carole and Sean exchanged them with a promise of unconditional love and fidelity.

He turned to Sean and said, "Repeat after me, Sean: Carole, I give you this ring. Wear it with love and joy. I choose you to be my wife, to have and to hold from this day forward, for better or for worse, for richer for poorer, in sickness and in health, to love and to cherish as long as we both shall live."

He looked at Carole and said, "Your turn -- repeat after me." But before she started, she looked deeply into Sean's green eyes and then began her vows in a sincere and loving voice. "Sean, I give you this ring -- wear it with love and joy. I choose *you* to be my husband, to have and to hold from this day forward, for better or for worse, for richer for poorer, in sickness and in health, to love and to cherish as long as we both shall live."

As Carole heard someone behind her blowing their nose, she was pleased that she herself had managed to get through her vows without crying.

The priest blessed them, joined them together in marriage, and recited, "May the Lord in His goodness strengthen your consent and fill you both with His blessings. What God has joined together, let no man put asunder."

And at 1:30 pm, amongst twenty of their friends and family, Father McGulligan said to Sean, "I now pronounce you husband and wife. You may kiss the bride."

Sean smiled at Carole and gave her a long, gentle kiss on her lips followed by a tender hug.

CELEBRATE GOOD TIMES

Carole and her husband

To celebrate their marriage, Carole planned a lovely dinner at the Houstoun House Hotel in Edinburgh. The venue was perfect, with its wonderful Scottish history, which Carole knew Sean would love. It had been built in the 1600s and had been host to Mary Queen of Scots. Carole felt the warmth of the house, nestled among acres of private grounds. The dinner was spectacular, and as a special little touch, Carole arranged for each of their guests to receive a red-foiled chocolate heart lollipop to wish them a Happy Valentine's Day.

After their meal, they walked around the hotel and then the grounds.

"Why don't we just book our reception now?" Sean suggested.

They couldn't think of a better place to have it, and before they left it was all confirmed. Their wedding reception would be held on June 20, 2003.

Everything so far had gone off without a hitch. The next hurdle playing on Carole's mind was how quickly they would get their permanent visas, and would this be in time for the children to start their new school year? "Surely," she thought, "Sean will be able to get us over there before September, as it's only February now." However, only time would tell if her plans would work out the way she wanted.

RED TAPE – AND LOTS OF IT

As soon as Sean returned to New York, he started on a mission to get his new bride and his stepchildren permanent visas to live in the States. With their marriage certificate in hand, he started the process again, this time as a married couple.

First, he sent in the completed and signed Petition for Alien Relative form, a completed and signed Biographic Information form for both Carole and him, a passport photo of both of them, his passport (for proof of citizenship), their marriage certificate, and a gas bill with his address on it as proof of residence. And this was only the first step. It would take anywhere from three to six months to be notified of its approval, and then Packets 3 and 4 would have to be completed before they would be allowed to enter the country to live.

As the weeks and months went by, Carole was feeling a bit anxious and started to ask Sean on a regular basis if he had received the approved petition.

"I'm sorry, Sweet Pea, I know you would tell me if you had gotten any word, but I just feel the need to ask. I hope you don't mind," she said.

"Of course, I don't mind, but try not to worry. It will all work out. It's only the beginning of May. I'm sure I'll know before I come over for the reception and honeymoon," he said.

Sean always had a very calm way of handling things, and Carole found his demeanor very comforting. She knew he was right and everything would work out just fine.

On May 27 he received a letter stating the petition was approved, and so he could now send in Packet 3. Once Sean completed the Instructions for Immigrant Visa Applicants checklist and sent in the Application for Immigrant Visa and Alien Registration, they waited again until they were given their visa interview date.

"We should hear within five weeks' time, and then I'll complete Packet 4, which is the final stage," Sean said.

"Thank God for that! I didn't even have to do anything but sign the paperwork, and it was exhausting. Thank you for doing it all," Carole said.

"I'd do it again tomorrow, if I had to," he said "Good night, and I'll see you tomorrow. I love you."

"Good night. I love you too."

Carole knew that God had answered her prayers when she met Sean. She also knew that he would do anything for her...anything, and that she would do the same for him.

LINLITHGOW PALACE – TAKE TWO

For Carole, June 20 couldn't come quickly enough. Sean was arriving the following day. Carole was tying up the final details for the formal reception that her family and friends would attend. The invitations had been sent out weeks ago and everyone had replied. The Four Usuals would all be there, her climbing friends, friends from work, neighborhood friends, and family members. It took Carole over three months to put together a reception that would ordinarily take a bride twelve months. The flowers, photographer, reception hall, religious blessing, menu, a piper for the hall, and music for the reception were all confirmed for June 20; and the girls' dresses and Joseph's kilt had already arrived.

Her three sisters were in the wedding party and wore shimmery, pale-pink, strapless gowns with matching shawls that Carole had picked out. Small pink daisies adorned their updos, and everyone carried one large white lily nestled in large green lily leaves. Kristy wore a lovely white sleeveless, empress-cut chiffon gown with a tiny bow in front and another tied neatly in the middle of her back. Her hair was pulled up on the sides, and she had small pink flowers in her hair. She carried a small flower ball that had white and pink flowers with a loop of pink ribbon which she held onto like a pocketbook. She looked like a little princess and really enjoyed the excitement of the wedding. Joseph wore a kilt for the first time, including all the trimmings: a black bowtie, a black formal waist jacket, a crisp white shirt, and a white flower in his lapel. His black dress shoes had long laces that tied up his little legs and a sporran that he couldn't help but play with. Joseph looked very smart in his Stewart clan tartan, which matched Sean's kilt.

The whole Rodger clan was buzzing with excitement. Carole's other younger sister, Elaine, came up from England with her two children, and Christine travelled up from Wales. Linda and their mum had them staying at their house with Andrew, Deka's son, who came in from Northern Ireland. Deka and Michele flew into Manchester from New York and drove up with Mick and Sue. Everyone was there to celebrate Carole's marriage to Sean.

The day finally came and on Saturday, June 20, Carole and Deka arrived at the Palace in a black Victorian horse-drawn carriage. The two horses were jet-black, purebred Friesian stallions that could have been transporting royalty, for all they knew. Carole's white gown was strapless and straight lined, down to the tips of her white satin shoes. Her hair was parted on the side, and little white flowers crowned her upsweep hairstyle. Her long white shawl covered her shoulders, as she waited patiently in the carriage for everyone to make their way to the Great Hall.

"You look beautiful, Carole," Deka said to his younger sister.

"Thanks! I feel like a Princess, and I couldn't be happier," she said with a big smile.

"That's all I wanted to hear and truthfully all that matters. Now let's get this ceremony started," he said.

Carole and Deka at the Palace

Deka helped Carole out of the carriage and handed her a bouquet of three large white lilies with green leaves. They walked through the large walkway of the main entrance to the courtyard and headed towards the Great Hall. They met up with their sisters and Kristy and Joseph, all waiting outside the entrance of the open-aired hall.

The hall had twelve rows of six white folding chairs on each side of the red center runner. Marking the start of the center aisle were two four-foot tall black wrought iron candle stands decorated with white candles and green ivy. The piper started to play and everyone stood up and faced the back of the hall. As he started to walk up the aisle, Kristy and Joseph followed, and close behind were Linda, Christine, and Elaine. When the piper started to play the Wedding March, it was Carole and Deka's cue to enter the hall. She slowly strolled up the center aisle, making sure she took in every bit of the moment. Carole looked regal as she held her shoulders back and her head tilted up a wee smidgen, giving her an air of elegance and grace. Deka handed her to Sean, who was standing at the top of the hall with his best man, Jim, standing to his right, and Linda to Carole's immediate left. Father McGulligan welcomed everyone and began the blessing ceremony.

As Michele sat in her chair practicing the poem, she shivered from the northern wind.

"I don't think I've ever felt this cold in my life. I can see my breath and I only have this little suit on. It's June, isn't it?" she whispered to Deka.

"Yes, but you are in Scotland. Do you want my jacket?" he asked.

"Yes, please," she said through chattering teeth.

The temperature with the wind-chill factor was 45 degrees, yet nobody was wearing coats. Poor Kristy had goose bumps on her arms, as did all of Carole's sisters, but they didn't seem too fussed by it. Michele just hoped that she wouldn't stutter through the poem.

"Michele Rodger will read the first prayer," Father McGulligan said. She got up and caught Carole's eye as she walked toward the lectern and gave her a smile.

"One night," she said, *"A man dreamed he was walking along the beach with the Lord. As scenes of his life flashed before him, he noticed that there were two sets of footprints in the sand. He also noticed at his saddest, lowest times there was only one set of footprints. This bothered the man and he asked the Lord, Did you not promise that if I gave my heart to you that you would be with me all the way? Then why is there only*

one set of footprints during most of my troublesome times?"
The Lord replied, "My precious child, I love you and would
never forsake you. During those times of trial and suffering
when you see only one set of footprints, it was then I carried
you."

Michele looked at Carole again and gave her a wink. Carole
motioned back with a nod of her head and mouthed, "Thank you."
Whenever Carole heard *Footprints,* it reminded her that she was
indeed never alone and how blessed she was to have a higher power
always looking over her. Carole closed her eyes and said to herself,
"Thank you too, God."

After communion was served, Father McGulligan gave his final
blessings and the ceremony was officially over. It was picture time
at the palace, and then off to the reception for yet more pictures!

Pretty as a Princess

HOUSTOUN HOUSE - TAKE TWO

The grounds at the Houstoun House were perfect for wedding photos and every combination was taken…all females, all males, all relatives, all friends, and even one with all the men holding Carole as she lay across their arms.

One hundred twenty guests were invited to the reception, and one hundred and twenty guests attended. They waited in the courtyard and queued up to congratulate the happy couple before proceeding into the reception hall. Once everyone was in the hall, the maître d' announced Carole and Sean.

"Three cheers for Mr. and Mrs. McGarrigal," he said. Everyone stood up and cheered, "Hip, hip hooray! Hip, hip hooray! Hip, hip hooray!" followed by loud applause and whistling.

It was a typical Scottish wedding, with plenty of drinking, the traditional speeches, ceilidh dancing and singing. Carole and her sisters took the floor at one stage and performed "Runaway," as sung by the Corrs - this was Carole and Sean's song. The Rodger girls knew how to have fun and enjoyed singing together whenever they had an opportunity.

As the night was coming to an end, Carole sat back and realized she was living the fairytale wedding she had planned out in her mind hundreds of times. The day was absolutely perfect, and now it was time for her and her prince to ride away into the sunset. Their sunset, however, led them to a seven-day honeymoon in Italy. She had always wanted to return to Italy ever since the cruise she'd taken, but this time they went to Rome and Venice. So much had happened in the last year that it was truly hard to believe only a year had passed since she was on a cruise with Charlie. Not only had she gotten married; she was leaving for her honeymoon and relocating to America sometime in the very near future, she hoped.

ITALY IN FULL BLOOM

Spring was in the air and so were new beginnings and love. The flowers and trees were in bloom, and Carole couldn't think of a better place to spend her honeymoon than in romantic Italy with Sean.

They got off the plane in Rome and headed for their hotel. Sean had planned the whole honeymoon. They'd be spending three days in Rome and four days in Venice. The taxi pulled up in front of Hotel Majestic Roma, a five-star hotel, and Carole knew she was in for a treat.

As they walked into the hotel, Carole thought, "I don't think I've ever seen so much white marble in my life! It is absolutely gorgeous!"

The five marble steps that led their guests to the main lobby were covered partially with a red rug and stood between two tall, white marble pillars. Carole noticed everything on their way to the front desk. The brass hand guards, the black wrought-iron gates, the oversized chandeliers, and the mahogany antiques scattered throughout the lobby. It had such a welcoming, wealthy atmosphere. Carole couldn't wait to explore the rest of the hotel and then Rome.

"Buongiorno, come posso aiutarle?" the front desk clerk asked.

"Buongiorno," Sean said. "Do you speak English?"

"Yes, good morning. How may I help you?"

"We are checking in…our last name is McGarrigal."

"Yes, Mr. and Mrs. McGarrigal, your room is ready. I hope you enjoy your stay. I will have the bellman take your luggage to your room. He will meet you up there."

"Thank you," Carole and Sean said together.

As they waited for the elevator, Carole said, "That was the first time we've been addressed as Mr. and Mrs. McGarrigal in public…it sounds lovely, doesn't it?"

"Yes it does," he said, as he kissed his bride behind the closing elevator doors.

Sean opened the door and held it open for Carole to enter. The room spoke of wealth, from its high, white ceiling and long taupe drapes that were pulled back with large sling backs right down to the dark hardwood floors. It had a sitting area with two chairs and a table, a taupe settee with four purple throw pillows, and a coffee table with a fresh pineapple cut down the middle and stuffed with all sorts of fruit. Behind that, a wall table was chilling a bottle of champagne that Sean had ordered. To the right was one very large bed.

"Wow, would you just look at this room! It's brilliant, isn't it!" she said.

"Yes, and it's just fitting for my princess," he said in a shy manner.

Sean really wasn't a mushy sort of guy, but could be quite romantic when the moment struck him. Carole seemed to bring out a side of him that even Sean didn't know existed. He had never loved anyone the way he loved Carole.

"It's a wee bit early, but let's open the champagne!" she said with a silly grin. "Sure, why not? We are on our honeymoon, after all!"

"To us, and a long, happy marriage!" they toasted.

***

"Do you want to walk to the Spanish Steps and the Trevi Fountain later? Looking at this map, it seems to be quite close," she said.

"That sounds gooda. After I finish my champagne, I'm justa going to get unpacked and change and then we can explore Roma if you wisha, my lovely bride," he said, in a very bad Italian accent.

"Sounds like a gooda plan…" Carole giggled.

The concierge, Mario, helped them plan out their days so they were sure to visit all the must-see landmarks and monuments of Rome.

"If you like art," Mario said, "Villa Borghese is just around the corner. It is a beautiful art gallery. Even if you are not art lovers, I would recommend it," he added.

They strolled around the local sites, enjoying each other's company as they held hands, heading for their first stop: the Trevi Fountain, which seemed smaller than Carole had imagined it from seeing it in the movies. They held their coins, thinking about what they wanted to wish for. Carole closed her eyes tight and wished for continued good health for her family and herself, and a strong marriage. She threw her coin over her shoulder and turned around to see it flying in the air and hitting the water in slow motion. She was getting good at asking for what she *wanted* as opposed to what she *didn't* want in life.

"What did you wish for?" Sean asked.

"I can't tell you that. I'm a little superstitious when it comes to wishes. I know it's silly, but nevertheless I'm keeping it to myself."

"What did you wish for?" she asked.

"I've already got what I wished for. I'm just thankful for you."

"You *are* a good egg, Sean McGarrigal, and I am so happy I found you. I love you."

"I love you too," he said.

Sean bought two gelatos, and they walked over to the Spanish Steps and sat on the steps watching the world go by as they enjoyed their dessert.

"Come on, we can't come to the Spanish Steps and not walk up and down them all," she said.

"Are you sure you can climb them all?" he said sarcastically.

"Not only can I climb them, but I bet I could beat you up them," she said as she quickly got moving up the steps. Sean remained on her tail the whole 138 steps it took to get to the top and let her win.

On their way back to the hotel they went to the art gallery. They spent hours walking around the twenty rooms that were spread across two floors. There were paintings, classical and neo-classical sculptures, and lovely mosaics.

"Look up, is that three-dimensional?" Carole asked. Above their heads was an exquisite trompe l'oeil ceiling fresco.

"I don't know, but it is certainly beautiful, and if it isn't 3D, it is definitely tricking my eyes," Sean said.

A tour guide for the gallery overheard their conversation and praised them for their novice interpretation of the artwork.

"It is actually an art technique involving extremely realistic imagery in order to create the optical illusion which appears to be three dimensional, but it is actually a two-dimensional painting. However, an excellent observation on your part. Bravo," she said. "Let me know if you have any questions. I'd be happy to answer them," she added.

"Thanks, we'll come find you if we do," Sean said as he moved on to a nearby mosaic. "Look how old this is. It dates back to 320-30 AD!" said Sean. They were looking at a famous mosaic of gladiators found on the Borghese estate in 1834.

"How do things this old not disintegrate over time? That is absolutely amazing, isn't it!" Carole said.

They appreciated the artwork they were viewing, but what also caught their attention were the stunning park grounds that surrounded the villa. It was one of the largest public parks in Rome, designed as a formal English garden, with peacocks, ostriches, swans, and cranes milling about the grounds. The peacock turned its long blue neck around and opened up its fan of feathers in full adornment. Its lengthy feathers had a design near the tips which resembled an eye, and the colors were a brilliant blue and green. Sean took half a dozen pictures as the peacock proudly walked around them as if they weren't there.

That night they dined at the hotel restaurant, La Ninfa, and enjoyed delicious Roman cuisine, followed by a nightcap at the bar before retiring to their room.

"What a brilliant day this was," Carole said.

"What was your favorite part?" Sean asked.

"Waking up next to you," she said with a smile. "And a close second had to be the Trevi Fountain, the Spanish Steps, and the art museum."

"So in other words, you liked everything about the day. Good! Tomorrow will be another great day, since I'll be waking up next to you again," he said with a shy giggle.

"That's just fine with me. Let's have breakfast in the hotel and have a lazy morning before we go on the Vatican City Tour. This way we will have at least one meal a day in this gorgeous hotel," she said. "I love this place, but then, what's not to like? It's so elegant and the staff can't do enough for us. I just want to enjoy the stay here as much as the sites of Rome," she added.

They had their leisurely morning, as planned, and before they knew it, it was time to travel towards the Vatican for their three-hour tour.

They met Riccardo, their tour guide, along with a few of the other tourists they'd be spending the next several hours with, and by the look of the lines it would probably be longer.

"Ciao," said Riccardo. "As soon as I have everyone here, we'll go into the Vatican Museums. The good news is, we don't have to wait on these lines."

"Thank God for that," Carole said.

"Yes, and no pun intended, I'm sure," said Riccardo. "Our tour will take us through the 2000 rooms that stretch over almost nine miles, so I hope everyone has comfortable shoes on! I'll also share some insights on the artwork that you might not have noticed, had you decided not to take my tour."

As they entered the Sistine Chapel, Riccardo said, "This chapel will leave an everlasting impression on you. I'll be pointing out a few things about Michelangelo's famous 'Creation of Adam' fresco."

"What actually is a fresco?" one of the tourists asked.

"Good question - it's a painting done on plaster on walls or ceilings, and the Sistine Chapel is full of them," Riccardo replied.

"Take note of the positioning of God in this fresco…it is magnificent how Michelangelo depicts this image. Adam is at the right hand of God the Father, who is portrayed as an elderly, bearded man wrapped in a cloak, while Adam, as you can see, is completely naked. Keep in mind that this work was done between 1508 and 1512 - 495 years ago!" he exclaimed. "Look at God's right arm. It is stretched out to pass on the spark of life from his own finger into Adam, whose left arm is extended in a pose mirroring God's, which in essence is a reminder that man is created in the image and likeness of God. What else do you see?" he asked his group.

"Their fingers are not touching," said Carole.

"That's right…it gives the appearance that God, the giver of life, is reaching out to Adam and Adam is receiving. One more thing I want to point out is the pink backdrop behind God. What shape is it?"

Everyone was staring at the fresco, but nobody took a guess.

"It's in the shape of a brain! There are several hypotheses on why Michelangelo may have used this symbol. I choose to believe it was to show God's plan of creation which had not yet been revealed to the first man," he said.

Once he pointed out that it was in the shape of a brain, it was clear as day to Carole. "What a brilliant artist he was," she thought.

"Michelangelo painted approximately 12,000 square feet of the chapel's ceiling and stood on scaffolding while he painted, resenting the commission, because he believed his work was only serving the Pope's need for grandeur. Nevertheless, today the ceiling and especially "The Last Judgment," are widely believed to be Michelangelo's crowning accomplishments. Let's move down to

"The Last Judgment" and I'll show you Michelangelo's self-portrait in the painting," Riccardo said enthusiastically.

Carole smiled as she listened to the passion in Riccardo's voice, eager to share all the stories he knew behind Michelangelo's masterpieces. She didn't know where to look first, as the painting was massive and covered the entire wall behind the altar.

"I want you all to find the main figure, Christ, in the middle of the painting. To the right of his foot is a man with a beard, St. Bartholomew, who is holding a knife, and notice this flayed skin. Michelangelo did a self-portrait depicting himself as St. Bartholomew after he had been flayed, in other words, skinned alive. This was Michelangelo's way of conveying his feelings of disapproval for being commissioned to paint "The Last Judgment," he said.

"He was unbelievable, wasn't he? No need to ask him how he's feeling - he portrayed it for the world to see in his painting. Brilliant, really," Carole whispered to Sean.

"This was a very controversial painting," continued Riccardo, "and one that caused several disagreements between church personnel and Michelangelo. Since the painting showed naked figures with their genitals in view for all to see, the artist was accused of being immoral and obscene. Surely, they thought, this should not be the scene depicted inside the most important church of Christianity! So a censorship campaign, known as the Fig-Leaf Campaign, was organized to remove the frescoes. When Biagio da Cesena, the Pope's Master of Ceremonies, said, 'It was most disgraceful that in such a sacred place there were so many nude figures, exposing themselves so shamefully,' and also that such work belonged in 'the public baths and taverns rather than a papal chapels,' it was war! Needless to say, Michelangelo was out for revenge, and revenge he got! He put Cesena's face into the scene as Minos, judge of the underworld. Look at the bottom-right corner of the painting, at the figure with donkey ears, insinuating that he was stupid, and his nudity is covered by a coiled snake. The story goes that when the Pope's Master of Ceremonies complained to the Pope, he responded that his jurisdiction did not extend to hell; therefore, the portrait would remain. Obviously, Michelangelo was someone you would not want to differ with, as you could end up portrayed in a masterpiece with donkey ears, taking the idea of expressing one's anger to a different level! I'd say he used his creativity in his paintings in more ways than one! Does anyone have any questions?"

"He was quite a character. How old was he when he painted 'The Last Judgment'?" asked Carole.

"He was 67 years old, and lived to the ripe old age of 89," he said.

"Wow, given the time period, I thought you were going to say 45 or so - not 67. The man was absolutely amazing," Carole said.

"Indeed he was," said Riccardo.

The group walked over to St. Peter's Basilica to view another of Michelangelo's masterpieces, "La Pieta."

"What a perfect way to end the tour," Carole said. "Look at the ray of sun beaming down onto the marble floor of the Basilica. You can't help but feel you are truly in a special place."

She and Sean decided to stroll around St. Peter's Square for a bit and then return to their hotel as they chatted about all the awesome art work they had seen on their tour, as well as the great stories that came with it.

"I can't believe tomorrow is our last day in Rome. This has gone quickly," Carole said.

"Yes, but we have the whole day tomorrow, and a visit to the Colosseum, where we will listen to tales of gladiators!" Sean said playfully. "Besides, we can always come back if you want, and we still have four days in Venice to look forward to."

The next morning they had their usual breakfast and headed out to the Colosseum. As they approached the area, they saw a small crowd of people gathered around someone talking; they assumed it was a tour guide. When they got closer, the tall young man, who was actually a student, invited them to listen to the history of the Colosseum.

"You are looking at the largest amphitheatre ever built in the Roman Empire, as well as one of the greatest works of Roman architecture and Roman engineering," he said with great admiration and enthusiasm. "Its construction started between 70 and 72 AD and was completed in 80 AD. All 272 feet by 157 feet of it, and it was capable of seating 50,000 spectators," he said.

"Would you look at the size of that arena! It always fascinates me how people in early times were able to build such large structures without machinery to help them," Carole whispered to Sean.

"I'm sure thousands of slaves were probably used," he said.

"How many of you have seen the film *Gladiator*?" the student asked. "It was a brilliant movie, and the Colosseum was re-created using computer-generated imagery, which gave the audience a pretty accurate picture of what the Colosseum looked like in its heyday, back in the 2nd century. It also gives a good impression of what the underground *hypogeum* would have been like. Ah, what is an underground *hypogeum*? you are asking yourselves," he said with a giggle. "I'm glad you asked. The arena had a wooden floor covered by sand, which covered an elaborate underground structure called the *hypogeum,* literally meaning 'underground.' As you will see, little remains of the original arena floor, but the *hypogeum* is still clearly visible.

"The movie shows how the Colosseum was used for gladiatorial contests and games, but also for public spectacles, mock sea battles, animal hunts, executions, and re-enactments of famous battles. The animal hunts had wild beasts running about. Try to imagine rhinos, elephants, lions, bears, tigers, and crocodiles out on the arena's floor being hunted. These events were occasionally on a large scale, and it's been said that Trajan celebrated his victories over Dacia in 107, with contests involving 11,000 animals and 10,000 gladiators over the course of 123 days. It's also been estimated that about 500,000 people and over a million wild animals died in the Colosseum games," he concluded.

"Wow, that seems quite barbaric, not to mention a huge waste of lives for entertainment purposes. Shouldn't it be classified as a sacred burial area if 500,000 people died there?" Carole asked the student.

"You would think, but you have to realize we are talking about the 2nd century, and people didn't value lives the same way we do today,"

"I would hope that people in general value life – regardless of the century they are in. I'm sure the influential people who ran the games valued *their* lives and wouldn't be caught dead --no pun intended--in that arena," Carole said.

"I'm sure you're right. I can tell you something on a lighter note: The Colosseum is used for a much different type of entertainment these days. Paul McCartney used it as a backdrop last month for one of his concerts. We've come a long way in 18 centuries!" the student said.

"Thank God for that," Carole replied with a grin.

As much as it bothered Carole to think about the lives wasted in the games and contests, when she got into the Colosseum and saw the structure from the inside, she found it a sheer wonder how they had built it in the first place, and how it had withstood earthquakes and time. She and Sean sat in the arena, imagining the gladiators waiting in the *hypogeum* for the signal to enter the arena. It was a bit bone-chilling and sobering.

"Let's change the mood for the rest of the afternoon," said Sean. "Is it time for a glass of wine?"

"Yes, I do believe it's that time. Shall we go back and enjoy our hotel for the last night?"

The next morning they boarded the train to Venice; they would be arriving just in time for lunch.

"It was a great idea to take the train. The scenery is beautiful and the ride is quite relaxing, isn't it?" Carole asked.

"Yeh, I thought it would be kind of fun and adventurous to take the train in a different country."

The trip was quick, and before they knew it, they were at the Santa Lucia railway station and about five minutes from their hotel. Carole was hoping it was going to be as nice as the one in Rome and, if the lobby of the Hotel Luna Baglioni was any indication of what their room would be like, she was surely not going to be disappointed. As they walked into the lobby, the crystals in the large chandelier caught Carole's eye and pulled her attention toward the high ceiling that welcomed them into the hotel. A seven-foot portrait trimmed in a gold frame sat above the formal fireplace and a lovely, round mahogany table in the center of the room. The table had a large crystal vase of fresh-cut flowers, which set the tone for what they were about to experience, which was sheer elegance and luxury.

"Sean, I think you've outdone yourself again. This hotel is absolutely beautiful! You're two for two in picking out fab hotels! Let's go up to our room as soon as we can, unpack, and check out Venice. I think we are only a stone's throw away from Saint Mark's Square," Carole said.

The location of the hotel could not have been better. It took fifteen steps to get to the square (Carole counted). As they walked across the square to get a seat at an outside café, they saw two children running towards the pigeons that were minding their own business eating in the square. Seconds later came the sound of 40-odd sets of flapping feathers, as the pigeons took flight to escape the children's raid.

"Look at that! It's like a scene out of a movie, isn't it! Those birds are probably saying, 'Hey, this is my square and if you do that again, I'll pooh on your head,' " Carole said, making herself laugh.

Minutes later the birds returned to the busy square, which was full of tourists taking pictures and local Venetians going about their normal routine. Carole and Sean managed to get a front-row table on the square at Café Florian, which seemed like the place to be, to sit and sip a cocktail over a light lunch. Three hours passed as they sat enjoying the world go by.

"What would you like to do for the next couple of days?" Sean asked.

"Let's just relax today, and tomorrow we will get some of the sites in," Carole said. "It seems a shame to move, since we are really enjoying ourselves and we do have three more days."

"I'm with you. Tonight let's have dinner at the hotel and take a gondola around the canal," Sean suggested.

"Oh, that sounds like fun. Hopefully we'll be serenaded as well," Carole said.

They were in luck; their gondolier loved to sing.

"We will soon be going under the Ponte dei Sospiri, the Bridge of Sighs. It has been said that it got its name because it was a rendezvous for lovers; however, the bridge was really built to convey magistrates to the courts and prisoners to their fates," said the gondolier.

"Since we are on our honeymoon, I'd prefer believing it was a rendezvous for lovers," Carole said, as she gave Sean a kiss.

"That sounds good to me! There is so much romance in the air in our city that believing that to be the truth would be realistic," the gondolier added.

As they approached a woman selling flowers on the side of the canal, the gondolier asked her a question in Italian. Once they got close enough, she handed him a rose.

"Grazie," the driver said.

"Prego," she replied.

"Here you are, pretty lady. Congratulations on your marriage to this fine man," he said.

"Oh, thank you. It's lovely." Carole sank into Sean's arms and felt the happiest she'd ever felt in her life. "Life is perfect," she thought, as she savored the moment.

The next morning they woke up bright and early and planned out their day. They took a motorboat tour of the islands of Venice. The highlight of the trip was a visit to a glass factory on Murano, where they watched a glassmaker create a vase, but not just any vase - a vase that was part of the Golden Quilt Millefiori Collection.

"This unique technique of Millefiori was used in Roman times," said the tour guide. "Then, the secret to how it was made was lost, but later rediscovered in Murano in the 15th century. As you see, the glassmaker will go through a multi-step process which starts with a glass rod prepared in a special way and ending with it being placed in a special furnace two times before its process is finally completed and the famous millefiori pattern is created! Bella vista…it's a beautiful sight, no?"

"Yes, it is. The colors are brilliant," Carole answered.

Carole studied the vase, with its golden background and vibrant colors of green, blue, and red flowers. The long, thin neck of the vase stretched the shapes of the flowers, distorting them, and the top of the vase curled open, looking like a flower in full bloom.

"It's a fabulous piece of artwork," she said, wondering if they had a gift shop.

They took a tour of the glass museum, which showcased the famous Venetian glass, and then visited the gift shop. Carole bought a pair of earrings and a vase for her new home. She hadn't put too much thought into her relocation recently, not with all the plans for the wedding and the reception, but in a few months she'd be moving to New York. Carole didn't have any doubts, but it still was a big move, leaving her friends and family. The hardest part was definitely going to be saying good-bye to Linda and her mum. That started to make Carole feel sad - the last feeling she wanted to be dealing with while in Venice on her honeymoon. She'd have plenty of time to work through how she was going to handle leaving them, but for now she wanted to enjoy where she was and think about what was in store for them on the next part of the tour.

They were on their way to visit the island of Burano, where Carole bought a beautiful lace tablecloth. The last island stop on their tour was Torcello, where they went to see Venice's first church. Once they re-boarded the motorboat, Carole watched the pilot navigate through the lagoon and managed to stay in the moment as he took them back to where they started the tour. The lagoons and the structure of the island fascinated her, and she enjoyed watching locals getting on with their everyday activity, as if there was nothing special about where they lived.

That afternoon they had free time to explore the back streets of Venice. They walked around the narrow alleys hand in hand and went in and out of stores picking up souvenirs for the children. The streets were magical, and the gondolier was right: Romance was in the air in this City.

"Not that I'd mind, but are we lost? I feel like we've passed this shop a few times now," Carole said.

"How lost can we be? We are on an island that isn't that big! I'm sure our sense of direction will get us back to where we need to be," Sean said.

They had made so many right and left turns that once they passed the same shop for the fourth time, Carole asked a local to point them in the direction of St. Mark's Square.

"This is an amazing little place, isn't it? It's like a maze and hard to believe that the buildings are all constructed on wood piles. I wouldn't want to be here during a flash flood. I think I remember reading that the basilica is sometimes closed due to high water levels. Let's take a tour of the basilica tomorrow and maybe go to a palace," Carole suggested.

"I'm easy," Sean said. And that he was - the most easygoing guy Carole had ever met. He went with the flow pretty much all of the time.

The next morning Carole was happy to see that it was sunny, and the tour of the cathedral would not be cancelled because of rain.

They would be leaving the following morning and it was their only chance to see it.

From the outside it was a very busy-looking church. Carole didn't know which way to look first. The four upper arches of the basilica each had life-sized Warrior Saints adorning the tops, watching over the city, with St. Mark situated in the center, a large dome behind him, and a Winged Lion holding a book directly underneath him; in each of the lunettes in the arches were gilded mosaics. The lower part of the church had five arched entrances surrounded by marble columns with a gilded mosaic of the Last Judgment, and as Carole looked up, she saw in the center of the balcony large stone horses facing the square. Like most basilicas that date back to the ninth century, it had a long history of being moved, burned down, built up, and added onto. It was an impressive piece of artwork and Carole was soaking it all in.

"I've made reservations for us tonight to dine at a special restaurant, since it's our last night," Sean said, as they toured the basilica.

"Oh, that sounds nice. I know exactly what I'll wear!"

Sean had requested an outside table and a bottle of champagne to be chilling at their table upon their arrival. Carole wore a lavender silk sleeveless dress with a pair of black sandals and a black clutch handbag.

"You look very pretty," said Sean admiringly, as he gave her a hug. "Um, and your perfume is nice too."

"Thanks. It's the one I bought yesterday. And you look quite handsome yourself, all dressed up," she replied with a little smile.

They walked to the restaurant and the host took them right to their table, which was accented with one long-stemmed red rose in a simple vase and two glasses for champagne.

"Aaaah, champagne! My favorite..." she said.

"I'd like to make a toast to us and our lives together as husband and wife. May it be filled with long walks on Munros, and real moments of happiness, good health, and fond memories. To us," Sean said.

"Yes, to us. I'm sure our lives' journey together will be a special one," she said, as she leaned over to give him a kiss.

HOMEWARD BOUND

Their flight the next morning was early, and they landed in Glasgow at 10:30 am. Carole couldn't wait to see Kristy and Joseph and share with them all the wonderful sights they saw in Rome and Venice.

"Hellloooo," she sang as she walked in the house.

"Mummy," she heard them scream, and they raced into her arms, wanting hugs and kisses.

"Hi! How are you? Did you have a nice week with Nanny and Lindy-Lou?"

"Yes, we did, but we are happy you are home. Did you have a nice trip?" Kristy asked.

"Yes, it was lovely. We will have to take you there one day. It's an absolutely beautiful place."

Sean was staying in Scotland for another week before he returned to New York. He had called his mum to see if there was any mail for him from the American Embassy. There was: They finally got their interviews set and had to be in London in five days.

"Wow, that was lucky. We'll drive down and I'll book a hotel for us," Carole said.

They drove down to London the day before their appointment and walked over to the building the next morning. Carole would be interviewed first. Carole and the kids then had to go for their medical exam. She wondered when they would get clearance to enter the States, because September was just around the corner, and she wanted to be in America by mid-August to have the children all settled before they had to start a new school year.

The government officials seemed very serious and a smile was nowhere to be found. Carole was asked to follow the officer into the interview room. The interviewer asked her a series of questions, one being when she got married, to which she replied, February 14, 2003. Sean was then asked to enter the room once Carole was finished and he, too, was asked a series of questions.

"We seem to have a problem," the interviewer stated to them. "When I asked Mrs. McGarrigle when she got married, she replied February 14, 2003; however, when I asked you the same question, Mr. McGarrigle, you stated February 14, 2002. There seems to be a discrepancy on the year you got married, so which is it?" he asked.

Sean could feel his face getting red by the second. "I am so sorry- it is February 14, 2003," he said.

"That's a quick way to get yourself in the doghouse with your new wife," the interviewer said, grinning.

As they left the building, Carole was worried that giving the wrong date might delay their entrance into the States.

"I can't believe you gave them the wrong date! What's going to happen if they delay our entry or, even worse, they think we are lying and don't let us in!" she said with panic in her voice.

"Don't worry, it will be fine," he said.

And he was right. They received clearance a few weeks later. Carole pushed herself into fifth gear and started making lists of all the things that needed to be done: Call the realtor to arrange for the house to be rented out, sell her car, call a moving company and get quotes, resign from the company she had been with for 15 years, pack up her belongings, and ship them to New York.

Sean travelled over to Scotland again in July to help her pack up the house and they managed to fit in a quick getaway up to Skye with Sean's cousin Jim, and girlfriend Fiona to do some climbing.

It was the first time Carole had been up there and she was already missing the fact she wouldn't have time to enjoy the Munros again until she was back for a visit, which sounded odd to her.

"Oh my, the next time I come back here, it will be a *visit*," she thought to herself uncomfortably, as she felt her first twinge of being homesick, before she'd even left the country. This was the first time in her life that she was so excited about starting a new chapter, but also sad that the old chapter was coming to an end. She knew she would miss Linda, her mum, and her friends terribly.

"I love it up here," she said, "The feeling of peace and tranquility this place gives me is priceless, and here it was at my fingertips all this time," she said to Sean.

"Well, every time we come back, let's make it a point to come up here. We will be coming back at least twice a year just to satisfy Dick's visiting rights, correct?" Sean asked.

"That's right, and it will be a nice thing to look forward to, won't it?" she said; this gave her some comfort.

How could anyone **not** love Skye? Just the trip getting up there was pleasant as they travelled through quaint villages, and drove next to lochs and near riversides. It was making Carole appreciate her love for Scotland in a different way, as she was mentally starting to prepare herself for her pending relocation. She didn't spend too much time thinking about the move because her mind was preoccupied by all the things that had to be done. She was really more concerned about how the children would acclimate. As long as they were happy, she'd be happy.

Once they reached Mallaig, a 20-minute ferry ride brought them across to Skye. The weather wasn't looking too good, which brought back memories of her attempt to climb the Matterhorn, but ten minutes later, the rain clouds passed over, the mist cleared, and an impressive view of mountain peaks, forests and seascapes in their glory appeared, waiting to be admired.

"I wish the weather changed that quickly in Switzerland," Carole said. "What just happened in a matter of minutes, we waited for *days* to happen, but it never changed! Oh well, never mind."

"I'm sure Switzerland is beautiful, but this is nothing to sneeze at, and it's where you're from, which I think has more of a sentimental connection to it," said Sean.

Although he was American born, Sean had a sense of pride about Scotland that most Scotsmen didn't have. The first time he had met Carole, he told her that one day when he was able to retire, they'd live half the time in Scotland and half in New York, and that was still the plan. The views they were seeing from the hotel were of a lovely bay and rolling mountains. They stayed in Portree, the island's capital, at the Cuillin Hills Hotel. The town had quaint shops and charming restaurants that fit the atmosphere of the island.

The next day they headed six miles north of Portree, to the Trotternish ridge.

"We should be able to see the Old Man of Storr," said Sean. Sean could see by the look on Carole's face that she had no idea what he was talking about.

"It's a stunning black finger of rock pointing 165 feet up into the sky," he said with excitement.

"Oh, I thought you were talking about a person!" Carole giggled.

The climb through the woodland began quite gently, but this soon changed, into steep scrambles until they reached the base of the giant rock where they enjoyed fabulous views across to the neighboring island of Raasay.

"This is what I love about climbing…isn't this breathtaking! I feel like I'm on top of the world," Carole said to them.

"Yes, we lucked out with the weather this time. The last time I was up here it was very wet and cloudy," Sean said.

The following evening they drove back down to Linlithgow and continued where they'd left off, going through what Carole wanted to take with her and what she would get rid of. It was an easier task than she thought, because when she had downsized from the big house two and a half years earlier, she had gotten rid of a lot. Carole called the movers to confirm they would be coming on the morning of August 15. Kristy, Joseph, and she would sleep over at her mother's the night before they were to leave for New York.

The eve of the day she'd be leaving finally arrived. All night she tossed and turned in bed. "God I am dreading this," she kept saying to herself. Carole had been struggling with how she was going to say good-bye. They had been there for Carole throughout everything over the past few years, and had seen each other practically every weekend, and now she'd be living an ocean away. But by morning she had reassured herself that it would be okay and she'd have to focus on knowing that she'd see them in four months' time.

After breakfast Carole called a taxi service to pick them up and take them to the airport.

"Shall we get this over with? It's not good-bye…it's 'I'll see you in four months, for the holidays,' " Carole said, trying to convince herself that tears were not necessary. But as soon as she looked at Linda's face, she knew it was not going to be an option.

"I'm going to miss you, Carole," Linda said through her tears, as she gave her a hug.

"I'm going to miss you too. You are a great sister and I love you," Carole managed to get out through her tears.

Before they knew it, the whole family was crying, and they nearly didn't hear the doorbell ring through the commotion. It was the taxi driver.

"Mum, I love you, and we'll call you when we get to the house," she said.

"Okay, Hen, take care…love you too," her mum said.

Linda and her mum walked them downstairs and watched the car drive away, as Kristy and Joseph waved at them from the back seat of the car.

A New Beginning – Long Island, New York

Sean met them at the airport and took them to their new home. They had to wait four weeks before their belongings arrived on Long Island, but in the meantime Carole quickly got the children signed up for school while Sean helped them get acquainted with their new neighborhood. Joseph had already made his first friend, Steven, who lived next door, and Carole was feeling out how she was going to deal with living with her mother-in-law, Elizabeth. She knew when Sean originally bought the house, he had created an apartment for his mother on the first floor. It had always been just the two of them, but now the family dynamics were changing drastically.

Something was nagging at Carole, but she couldn't put her finger on it until, after months of being in her own home, she realized it just didn't feel like her own home. In fact, she felt more like an intruder.

"Why is your sister and mum always up in our part of the house?" she asked Sean.

"I don't know," he said. "I guess that's just the way it has always been."

"But that has to change, because it's not their house, and I don't feel like they are respecting our privacy," Carole said.

"I'll talk to my mum," Sean said.

Months went by and Carole didn't feel any different. His sister would still come over unannounced, jump in the pool, and go into their refrigerator without asking.   Carole thought, "Isn't that cheeky! I would never go into her home and act as if it were mine, so why is she doing it here?"

Carole had been looking for a job for a few months and finally found one where she'd be able to use her marketing experience, but now she'd be working full-time for United Way, and God knows what would be going on in her house in her absence, which made her anxious. Carole went back to Sean to continue their now-ongoing discussion: "Look, I'm starting my new job in a few days, and the last thing I want is your sister and mother going through my things when I'm at work. I would like you to put an end to this or I will ask them to stop. They are not respecting us as a new family and as a newly married couple."

The following weekend Carole went to visit Deka and Michele, who lived in New Jersey, and she spoke to Michele about how angry she was getting every time she went home and they were in her house. She even felt that his sister didn't like her and couldn't understand why, but she was making an effort because of Sean, nevertheless.

Hanging out at her brother's house

"I wouldn't say she doesn't like you, but if I had to guess what the problem is, it would be that your mother-in-law and sister-in-law were used to having the run of Sean's house prior to your coming into the picture, and for some reason they didn't think things would change once you guys moved over. I don't know how they could think that, but obviously they do. In other words, you upset their apple cart. They need boundaries, and I would suggest that it should be Sean who puts those boundaries in place," Michele said.

"I've tried that. I've asked Sean to speak to them and I know he has, because I heard him speak to his mother, and I do believe he supports me 100 percent, but they arrogantly ignore his requests."

"Why don't you say to your sister-in-law, 'You are more than welcome to come over, but I'd appreciate a call before you come'?"

"I've tried that too and the answer I got was, 'I don't have to call to come over to visit my mother'."

"Oh...she sounds like a piece of work - one who's got not a clue on how she's intruding on your privacy. At least you've got one good sister-in-law," Michele said, which made them both smile. "Honestly, don't stress about it; it will work itself out."

Carole and Sean had decided to leave Michele and Deka's house earlier than normal that morning and traveled back to Long Island. Depending on the traffic, it would take them two hours to get home, but the traffic was quite light that day, and they got home in record time, only to find her sister-in-law and her children in their pool.

"I've had it. I need you to get them out of the pool and out of this house now. This is not their house, and I don't know why it's taking them so long to figure this out. They don't respect me and they don't respect you," Carole said firmly.

Within minutes they were gone, leaving behind a tense atmosphere in the house amongst the in-laws. Carole went into the other room to let off some steam.

"Well, you were right...it worked itself out," she said to Michele. "They obviously thought the coast was clear, because we normally don't get back from your house until later in the afternoon, but when we got home, they were in the pool."

"You have got to be kidding me - the nerve!"

"I know. I just lost it and told Sean to get them out of the pool and house. I don't think I'll ever feel like this is my house. It's time we look for another house, and I don't want his mother living with us anymore. Why doesn't she just go live with her daughter!"

***

Carole's first year of marriage and living in the States didn't go as smoothly as she had hoped, between her new in-laws, getting used to the culture, and Sean's getting used to being married and having two children in his life 24/7. And she missed Scotland. She had started to wonder if she had made the right decision, moving her family to the States and began talking to Sean about possibly moving back. There was always one thing, however, that remained consistent, and that was her love for Sean and his love for her. He would support anything she wanted to do, even if it meant having a long-distance marriage until he was able to retire from the police force. The other consolation was her frequent visits back home.

"I'm really looking forward to seeing Mum and Linda, and I could really use my fix of Scotland right about now. I'll be having some of Mum's homemade soup as soon as I get there," Carole said.

"Only two more weeks, and we'll be climbing in Skye again. I think Brenda, your climbing buddy before I came on the scene, will be joining us this time, as well as Jim and Fiona. I'm looking forward to seeing my cousin. I can't believe it's been just about a year since we were last there," said Sean.

A Visit to Paradise - Skye

"I'd like to get the Four Usuals together for another reunion as well. The kids will be with Dick for two weeks, so we should have enough time to get everything in," Carole said.

Just the thought of going back home put a smile on Carole's face. She hadn't anticipated missing home as much as she did, but it was comforting knowing when her next visit was planned and that one day she'd return home to live.

As the months went on, Carole started to adjust to her new culture and seemed to get over the obstacles that had been stressing her out. One thing was for sure: She loved the summers in New York and quickly started to enjoy the distinct seasons and made sure they all took advantage of each of them. They enjoyed the beaches in the summer, apple- and pumpkin-picking in the fall, skiing in the winter, and bike rides and long walks in the spring. She was also pleased how well her children acclimated themselves to the States.

They both made friends quite quickly and got used to the American culture overnight, which concerned Carole at times. She didn't want her children to be spoiled, but on the other hand, wanted them to have things she hadn't had. The balancing act was not to give them everything, while giving them much more than she had had.

Their next trip back to Scotland was in December, and Carole had a doctor's appointment for a check-up, and on December 16, 2004, she said to Linda, "I've just got the best Christmas present I could have ever asked for. I got an all-clear report from the doctor," Carole said. "Happy Christmas!"

***

The following February, Carole and Sean went skiing for a long weekend at Hunter Mountain with Michele and Deka. As they sat in the lodge next to a blazing fire, Carole shared with them that while at physical therapy two weeks earlier, the therapist had felt something and had stopped working on her.

" 'I don't want to touch that, and I'd go see your oncologist,' she told me."

"Okay, where is it?" Michele asked.

"On my chest. I can feel it…it's hard. Look - you can see it."

"Hmm, I'm sure it will be fine. When are you going to the doctor?" Michele asked.

"I have an appointment next week."

Carole dreaded the thought of going to the doctor, but the hard, round mass in her chest was concerning her. She was trying to be calm; after all, she had just gotten an "all clear" two months earlier.

When the doctor felt the lump, he ordered a chest x-ray and a CAT scan to be done immediately.

"Have you been feeling any pain?" he asked.

"It feels sore in that area, and sometimes I feel pain. Almost like a feeling of pressure, but I thought maybe I pulled a muscle, or the muscle got caught in a stitch from my last operation," Carole said.

He didn't say much, other than, "I'll put a STAT on the test so we can see what we are dealing with sooner rather than later."

"I'm glad to hear that you'll put a STAT on it so I'll get the results quickly, but what will the x-ray and CAT scan tell us?" she asked.

"It will give us an idea of the size, density, and shape of the growth, and it's also used to diagnose what it is."

"So how long before I get the results? Are we talking days?"

"It depends on the timing. If the test gets read by the radiologist on the same day, and they see STAT on the test, it's possible that I can have the results within a couple of hours. As soon as I get the results, I'll call you."

Carole left the doctor's office with a hollow feeling in her stomach. She was happy that the doctor suggested putting STAT on the test, but also wondered if he had other reasons for wanting to see the results quickly. She was able to get an appointment the following morning and tried to keep her mind off her pending exam by stopping into DWS, her favorite shoe store, and picked up a new pair of winter shoes on sale.

The following morning Sean went with Carole to get the CAT scan done. The technologist brought her into the room where she saw the familiar doughnut-shaped machine. She was asked to lie down and make herself comfortable; it was very important that she not move during the test, which took 15 minutes.

As Sean and Carole were having lunch a few hours later, Carole's cell phone rang. It was the doctor's office, asking her to come in to see the doctor. Carole lost her appetite.

THE RESULTS

Carole tried to tell herself it was going to be okay: "It doesn't necessarily mean it will be bad news," she said to herself. But she didn't have a good feeling about the whole thing. Within the hour they were in the doctor's office, waiting to get the results.

"Come on in," Dr. Hoffman said. "We've got the results back, and I wanted to go over it with you," he said.

The amount of time between saying that and opening his mouth to continue seemed unbearably long. Carole took several deep breaths trying to prepare herself.

"Unfortunately, the cancer has come back," he said and paused. "Here's where it is," he said, pointing to the scan. "We don't have the tools today to eradicate this disease once and for all, and I know, when you started your treatment in Scotland, it was with the hope that the cancer would not come back. But the good news is, many women with advanced breast cancer do very well."

Dr. Hoffman went into detail about the results: There was an abnormality, and the CAT scan had zeroed in on the location and size of the tumor, which gave him some information about what type of abnormality it could be. The tumor, in the chest wall, was a secondary tumor, which meant it had originated elsewhere in her body and had spread…or metastasized…to the chest wall.

"It's malignant and it's stage 4," he said.

The hair on the back of Carole's neck stood up: This has to be a bad dream. She sat there shaking her head in disbelief. "The cancer is back and it's malignant" was all she could hear him say. Nothing else entered her mind as he continued to speak. "How could this be happening to me *again?*" she thought.

"Are you sure?" she interrupted him. "How could that be? I just got an 'all clear' two months ago," she said.

"Unfortunately, I'm sure. It's a deep, rather than wide, tumor," he said.

The drive home was very quiet. Sean tried his best to comfort her, but he, too, was shocked by the news. When they got home, Carole went into the bedroom and lay down. "I can't believe I've got to live through this nightmare again. Why me? Why is this happening to me again?" For the next couple of days, she flipped back and forth between anger and shock. "This just is not fair. I just got my life back, I'm newly married to a great guy and have two great kids…why again!" she thought. Then, suddenly, something clicked in her head. "I'm wasting valuable time and need to educate myself on what the doctor told me. If it's back, I will get through this just like I got through it the first time," she thought. The Internet became her main source for researching the disease and what metastatic breast cancer meant. She had a lot of questions, now that she had time to think about what the doctor had said, as well as things she wanted to share with him.

The first thing she wanted was to make sure she had the right group of doctors looking after her. What she learned was even though the cancer was back and on the wall of her chest, it was indeed the breast cancer that had spread. She would be going for another opinion and would definitely be part of the decision-making on her treatment plan.

Once she was able to talk about it, she started to tell her family and friends. She called Linda several days later, and as soon as she heard her sister's voice, Linda knew something was wrong.

"Are you all right? How did the doctor's visit go?"

"Well, the cancer is back. They found a tumor on my chest wall," she said, "and they can't cure me this time...they can only control it," she said through her tears.

Linda was speechless, and after a few seconds of silence finally was able to say, "Why can't they cure it?"

"It's stage 4, which means the cancer that started in my breast has spread to the chest wall; it's the most advanced stage of cancer."

"But you just got an all-clear report. Are they sure?" Linda asked.

"Yes, I know. I said the same thing. I will be going for another opinion, but it's metastasized, which means the cancer that started in my breast has spread. But they can control it," she said with hope in her voice. "I've been doing a lot of research, and I can tell you one thing: I am going to be very involved in my treatment and learn everything I need to know about this disease and my treatment options."

"I know you'll be fine, Carole; they'll just have to figure out how to control it and they will. They have to," Linda said. "Did you tell the kids yet?"

"No, but I'm feeling better about things because I have a plan, so I will probably tell them this weekend. Sean has been great. At first he was in shock, too, but he's been very supportive, and I know we will get through this together. He was talking to someone he works with who suggested trying a certain tea that stimulates the immune system to fight disease. He's been brewing it for me daily, and I've been drinking it three times a day."

"That's good. Did you tell Deka yet?"

"No, I've got to give him and Michele a call. I'll need to talk to Christine and Mum as well," she added.

Carole eventually spoke to everyone one by one; shock was the top reaction from all her friends and family. But they also knew what Carole was made of, and had great faith and hope that her strength and will to live would get her through this. Kristy and Joseph's reactions were true to their personalities. Joseph said in Joseph style, "Okay," as if to say, "No big deal, Mum, you'll be fine," and Kristy asked her, "Are you going to die, Mummy?" Carole looked into Kristy's eyes and said, "Not if I can help it, no; I am not..." and that was what they both believed to be the truth.

DOING HER ONGOING HOMEWORK

Carole spent hours weeding through the information on the Internet on metastatic breast cancer. It was a bit overwhelming, but one thing was for sure: She was quickly becoming her own advocate and was prepared to do what it would take to learn everything there was to know about the disease. She started to think about putting together a magazine for women going through the same thing to help them navigate through it all.

"I've got to get on Oprah," she said to Michele. "Just being on her show will help promote the magazine, and it will surely help millions of people!" she said with excitement in her voice.

"Sounds like a great idea! Start collecting the information you've already got and think about how it could be formatted," Michele said. "Can I go with you to the Oprah Show?"

"Absolutely!" said Carole with a giggle.

After completing her research and meeting with a few doctors, she decided on a medical team that had offices both on Long Island and New York City and were affiliated with Sloan Kettering. "I guess if I have to have this again, I'm in the right place for treatment," she thought and quickly started focusing on getting better again.

Carole felt comfortable with her doctors. At her following appointment, they explained to her that the next step would be to have a biopsy done. Carole was prepared for every appointment with questions and with simply writing down what they were saying. As soon as she got home, she would thoroughly research what they had told her. The doctors were very impressed by her knowledge and the suggestions she was making on her own treatment plan. Every visit, she entered their office armed with a pen and note pad with additional information she wanted to share, in hopes that it would be a viable treatment option available to her.

Carole made an appointment for the biopsy, and once the doctor removed and examined a sample of the tumor, he was able to speak to her and Sean about a plan: "We were able to fully diagnose the tumor from the cell samples, and we'd like to start radiation therapy and chemotherapy to try to shrink the tumor. At this stage, surgery to remove it is not an option because of the size and depth," Dr. Dryfus said.

"How much time do I have?" she asked.

"Let me tell you what we *do* have…we do have a lot of tools to help women with advanced breast cancer live long and very productive lives. And we're going to start implementing these. We're going to start using these one after another for as long as that drug is effective or that treatment is effective, and for as long as you tolerate it well. If it's not effective and if you don't tolerate it well, we're going to find something else. And we're going to go through these treatments one after the other for as long as we can."

Carole felt confident and full of hope when she left the doctor's office, but she didn't leave it all up to the medical profession. She needed to keep her mental health intact, which meant keeping her stress level down. Visualizing and relaxation became part of her daily routine.

"I listen to a tape before I go to bed," she told Michele on the phone. "It's relaxing - my favorite visualization is when I'm in a garden. It's a bright, sunny day, I'm taking deep breathes, and with each exhalation, I am getting rid of all the bad cancer cells in my body. So it's in with the good and out with the bad, and as I'm sitting under some sort of glass gazebo, I can hear children laughing and playing in the distance...it's Kristy and Joseph, and I'm sitting there with my eyes closed, soaking up the sun and enjoying listening to them have fun. It's a lovely place to be and I go there as often as I can."

"It's important to keep your stress levels down as much as possible," said Michele. "On that note, have things calmed down with the in-laws or should I say out-laws?"

"We've decided we will be moving, but probably not until next year. I just don't feel like this is truly my home, and I really could do without the stress of them right now, so the sooner the better. We definitely love the area, and I want the kids to be in the same school district. I'm sure we'll find something we like in this neighborhood," Carole said.

***

Carole was on chemo and radiation through the fall of 2005, and there was a report of good news: The treatment was shrinking the tumor, and the doctors were confident that they would be able to operate in the new year. The other good news was she was an aunty again. Michele and Deka had another baby boy, Cameron James, who had beautiful red hair and blue eyes. Carole felt an immediate kinship with Cameron and was very pleased when they asked Sean to be his godfather.

Everyone was excited about Carole's good news, but one of the side-effects from her treatments that she was dreading started to happen: Carole was losing her beautiful red locks.

"I could deal with the nausea and the pain, and even the fatigue, but losing my hair is just horrible. This disease is just cruel; it strips a woman of her beauty. First I lost a breast to it and now my hair. I know it sounds vain, but you know what…I didn't want to lose my breast, I don't want to feel sick all the time, and I definitely don't want to lose my hair. There has got to be a better way to treat this. It's just barbaric, isn't it? I mean they cut my body parts off and inject me with toxic medicine in the hopes that it will kill the bad cells, but in the meantime it's killing all my cells," she said to Sean.

He was at a loss for words, but listened and agreed with a nod of his head. "One thing is for sure," he finally said after a few minutes of silence: "You are beautiful and I love you inside and out…with or without your hair, and we will get through this."

"Thanks, you always know how to make me feel better, and I know we will get through this, but sometimes I just get so frustrated. I just want to be well again, I want to feel well, and I want to have my energy back. I'm tired of feeling sick. These chemo cycles wipe me out, and as soon as I get my strength back, I have to go back for another cycle. I know I'm whining, but sometimes I just can't take it. All I ever hear is, 'You look really good,' and I know I put up a good front, but I just want to feel as good as I look, and I want it for a long period of time. Is that too much to ask?"

"No, it's not too much to ask. Let's hope and pray that all these horrible side-effects are going to give us a good result, for a very long period of time, like 40 years of cancer-free living," he said.

"Yes, from your lips to God's ears, but for now I know I just have to soldier on through this, and I have to build my strength up for this operation come February. Enough of that. It's just a pure waste of my energy."

"It's okay, Carole.

"I know I have to visit that place now and again, but I also know I can't stay there very long. My frame of mind is just as important as the treatment the doctors are giving me. So when my sister comes over for Christmas, I'm going to go wig shopping with her. My hair will grow back," she said.

CHRISTMAS – 2005

By Christmas all Carole's hair was gone, and she wore a scarf to keep her head warm when she wasn't wearing the wig. The first wig she bought was nice, but the wig she bought when Linda was over looked really natural, so she decided to call it Alicia.

"What do you think of Alicia?" she asked Kristy.

"I like it, Mum; it looks like your own hair."

"I like it, too, and it doesn't itch as much as my other one."

Christmas Day they were invited over to Michele's parents' house. Michele's brother, Michael, his wife, Paula, and their three children were there, as well as a bunch of aunts, uncles and cousins. Rose put on her annual Christmas Day pageant after dinner. Carole smiled as Bradley and Joseph pranced down the stairs into the living room as two reindeer with red noses, brown turtlenecks, and tights with white cotton-ball tails. Michele's three nieces were in it too: her brother's youngest daughter, Sophia, was Santa Claus; Kristy was Mrs. Claus (they gave out gifts to everyone); and Gillian, her brother's eldest daughter, was the MC and took care of the music.

The second act was a nativity - Kristy played Mary, Joseph was Joseph, Bradley was a shepherd, and Sophia was a king. A doll was used as a stand-in for Cameron, who was supposed to play baby Jesus, but he'd fallen asleep before his acting debut.

Every year there seemed to be some sort of technical difficulty, which added to the humor of the show. This year was no different. The music didn't play at the right time, and the kitchen tablecloth/stage curtain went down too soon. The actors were not in their places, but they remained calm as their parents, aunts, uncles, and grandparents kept their giggles down, listening to the commotion in the upstairs bedroom. Carole was laughing at Michael's jokes - he kidded about this being like waiting to see the production at Radio City Music Hall. Everyone had a good time; Sean had the video camera going as usual capturing it all. Carole had a constant smile on her face and was enjoying having her family around her.

***

Throughout the next months, Carole started to choose healthier meals, still drinking her homemade brewed tea religiously, and began to exercise a little when she wasn't too tired. She needed to keep healthy, because the last thing she wanted was a low white blood-cell count. This would mean her immune system wasn't as strong as it could be, and she'd be at an increased risk for infection. She knew that the fewer white blood cells she had, and the longer she remained without them, the more at risk she'd become for developing an infection.

Carole continued to work at United Way while getting her treatments and needed time off only if she didn't have enough time over the weekend to recover from the Thursday afternoon cycle. Her friends at work became very close to her and helped keep her mind on other things. When it was time for Carole to go out on short-term disability for the operation, they gave up their vacation time and donated a total of 124 days towards her leave.

"Wow! That is unbelievable," Michele said. "And very generous."

"I know! It's brilliant, isn't it? I don't think that would ever have happened in the UK," Carole said.

"No, I'd have to agree with you on that one," Michele said. "What day do you actually go in for the operation?"

"Next Tuesday, January 17, the doctors have been talking about possibly taking out a rib when they are in there, and they will be removing the reconstructed breast before they operate. They won't know about the rib until they are actually doing the operation. The good news is, while I've been on the chemo and radiation, my doctor has done routine blood tests, just to make sure the white blood cells, red blood cells, and platelets in my blood are at the right levels, and they are quite pleased with my blood count."

"Well, that's good news. I'm sure it will be successful. I know you know this, but as your brother says, 'You'll have to keep your pecker up,' " Michele said with a crooked grin, as the translation in the States didn't quite mean the same thing in the UK.

"I know, and I will, but I have to say I am upset they are taking the implant out. I feel like a guinea pig, and I hate the thought of being dismantled after each operation. I also feel like this disease just continues to try to rob us women of our femininity. I'll have to use one of those silicone bras again and constantly check to see if my breasts are lopsided."

"I'd be upset, too. I understand what you mean by feeling like you are being robbed of your femininity, but it really can't rob you of how you feel about yourself, because you have control over your state of mind. You are a beautiful woman, inside and out, and always will be, with or without a breast or rib."

"Thank you, Michele."

"You're very welcome. Anytime, Carole."

"How are those nephews of mine?"

"They're good. Bradley has stopped asking me when Cameron is going back to the hospital. I guess he's finally figured out his little brother is here to stay. As a matter of fact, I'm looking at little Cameron now, and he's saying, 'Tell my Aunty Carole to get well real soon.'"

"Well, you tell him to rest assured, because I plan on it, and give him a kiss for me."

THE OPERATION

Carole and Sean arrived at the hospital on Monday, January 16, completed all the necessary paperwork, and had the pretests done prior to the operation scheduled for the following morning. The doctors again discussed the possibility of removing a rib, and Carole had been mentally preparing herself for this, but regardless of what they had to remove, she wanted the tumor out. Carole was glad Sean's mum was taking care of the children so Sean could be with her. She was feeling anxious and had mixed feelings about the operation. Carole obviously wasn't looking forward to her chest being pried open with clamps; yet she couldn't wait until the tumor was out of her body so she could begin her recovery. The morning of the operation, Carole said a prayer, asking God to be with her during the procedure, and then read her favorite prayer, "Footprints." It was always a nice reminder to know that she was never alone. This was going to be one of those times when she'd be relying on God to carry her. Sean walked with the nurses and Carole as they wheeled her gurney towards the operating room.

"This is as far as you go," the nurse said to Sean.

"I'll see you in a few hours. You are going to be fine. I love you," Sean said.

"Okay. I love you too," she said, as she felt a tear run down the side of her face. Carole remembered being wheeled into the operating room, chatting with the anesthesiologist, and taking a few deep breathes before she was out.

The operation was longer than Sean thought it would be. He waited patiently for the doctor to come and talk to him. After four hours, every doctor who walked toward him in scrubs he thought was Dr. Dryfus. Finally, the sight he was waiting for was in view, and Sean was trying to read his facial expression. Was it going to be good news or bad? Sean felt himself holding his breath.

"Sean," Dr. Dryfus said. "The operation was successful. We took out the tumor and didn't have to remove a rib, but we shaved a bit of it and removed part of the sternum."

"That's great news. When can I see her?"

"As soon as she is back in her room. Just as a reminder, she'll be sore for a while, because the ribcage was opened with clamps, but she is doing well. We'll talk about this more in detail with Carole, but we will be recommending soft-tissue replacement as a follow-up procedure, to help restore normalcy to the chest's structure and appearance. But one thing at a time. I'm pleased, and I'll come by tomorrow morning," he said.

"Thank you, doctor."

A sigh of relief came over Sean. The worst was over, and now it was up to Carole to recover at her own pace. He knew how strong his wife was, and it would only be a matter of time before she was back to her normal routine.

Sean stood watch over Carole's bed, waiting for her eyes to open. Finally he saw her big brown eyes fluttering a bit and opening, trying to focus on something familiar. "Where am I?" she thought, until she heard Sean's voice.

"Hello," he said softly. "Your operation was a success. How are you feeling?"

That was exactly what she wanted to hear.

That weekend the kids came to the hospital to visit, which gave Carole a boost to get out of the hospital and back home as soon as it was physically possible.

"I'll be home soon," she said to them, as they heard the announcement that visitors' hours were coming to an end.

***

The doctor was right: Carole was very sore for months, but that didn't stop her and Sean from purchasing a new home. It had been nearly two years since she and Sean had made the decision they'd be moving, but they never really started looking for another house until her operation was behind them. After just a few weeks of looking, they found the one for them. It was a corner house in Great River, blocks away from the water and in the same school district. The house was bigger, and so was the built-in pool in the back yard. Carole loved her new house; it finally felt like *her* home. Her mother-in-law moved in with them and had her own room and sitting area. It was a temporary set-up until a spot became available in the local adult living community in town.

Carole picked out paint colors for the bedrooms and had a couple of swatches hanging in almost every room to make sure they were right, while Sean methodically worked on the to-do list for the house.

"I love our new house, and I know we will have many happy memories in it," she said.

"I'm glad you're happy," he said. "I like it too."

TURNING THE BIG "4-0"

That spring Carole turned 40, and Linda came over to help her sister celebrate her special milestone. They went upstate and stayed at the Mohonk Mountain House. Michele, Deka, Bradley, Cameron, and Michele's brother, Michael, sister-in-law, Paula, and their two girls, Sophia and Gillian, were there as well. When Carole walked into the dining room she saw the balloons, a birthday banner, and a few bottles of champagne chilling. They had two round tables and, once everyone was seated, Carole took a little piece of paper out of her pocket and announced she wanted to say a few words.

"First I'd like to thank you all for helping me celebrate my 40th birthday. I'd also like to thank you for supporting me through some difficult times over the past year. I could not have done it without you, your support, and prayers. Linda, thank you for coming over and looking after me and the kids. Sean, you continue to be my rock and I love you. You all know how important family is to me and I'm very happy to be here with you celebrating my birthday. So, Paula and Michael, thank you for driving up here. Michele and Deka, thanks for all your support. I love you all from the bottom of my heart."

Michele and Linda caught each other's eyes and, as much as they tried not to cry, all the blinking and looking away just wasn't working. Between Carole, Paula, Michele, and Linda, there wasn't a dry female eye at the table, but as soon as the champagne was opened, they got back to being merry and celebratory.

After they finished lunch, they went outside and enjoyed the sunny day by taking a brisk walk up the mountain. Carole was feeling good and wasn't going to let the burning sensation in her chest interfere with her celebration. She was wearing a V-neck shirt and Michele could see the middle of her chest was red and looked very sore.

"How did your chest get so red?" Michele asked.

"It's from the treatments," she said, as she blew on her chest to cool it off. "The medicine is so harsh, it's burning my skin basically from the inside out, and it's blistering."

Michele fanned her chest with a piece of paper, trying to help cool it down. But Carole was not complaining…she had her family around her and was very happy on her special day.

After their walk, they all sat out on the Adirondack rocking chairs that overlooked the lake. They had high tea and homemade cookies at 4 pm. Carole was itching to hold Cameron, but wasn't sure if she was strong enough yet, so she sat and had Deka put him on her lap. She held him and kissed the top of his head.

"I love the way you smell, Cameron James," she said to him as he cooed to the sound of her voice. "There is something about you. You are an old soul, aren't you?" she said to him. Cameron smiled and giggled for his aunty.

"Thank you for my birthday gift," she said to him.

The following week Linda left to go back home, and although Carole always dreaded the good-byes at the airport, this time it wasn't as bad, since she knew she'd be seeing her in three months time in the UK.

***

One of Carole's childhood friends, Caroline, was also turning 40 and was planning a big party in Scotland. She gave Carole a call to see if she'd be able to make the party.

"Oh, I'm really sorry. I'd love to be there, but I've already committed to come over for my friend Julie's wedding in the fall," she said.

"That's okay, Love; I know you'll be here in spirit," Caroline said, but couldn't help but feel disappointed. They had known each other since they were seven years old, and had shared their dreams and secrets throughout the years. Caroline had been around Carole's family for as long as anyone could remember, and she had quickly become Carole's confidante.

But Carole really wanted to be at that party, and several days later called Caroline's husband, Ian, and told him that she'd be there.

"Oh, that's brilliant - she was gutted when she got off the phone, thinking you weren't going to be able to come. We're doing a 'This Is Your Life' for her, and we're putting the Red Book together now. This is going to be good fun! You'll be our special Guest of Honour."

"That sounds great - I can't wait to see her face when I walk in!" said Carole.

This was the first trip the children were spending two weeks with Dick, so Carole started making plans to get the Four Usuals together again; to see her other friends, Eve, her old neighbor from Linlithgow, and Julie, one of her other work colleagues; and, of course, to take a trip up to Skye, one of her favorite places on earth.

Carole was in a positive state of mind, felt good, and would be going home for 16 days. August came around quite quickly, and before she knew it, Dick was meeting them at the airport to collect the children. Carole kissed them good-bye and told them she'd call them that night to say good night.

Sean spent time with Jim, while Carole booked an overnight stay and a table for four in Glasgow. The following day she met Jacqui, Fay, and Daryl, and they all fell right back into reminiscing about the days they worked together, got caught up on what was happening in each other's lives, and eventually got around to just telling jokes, laughing, drinking fine wine, and shopping. As usual, Carole purchased another pair of shoes, and the weekend was truly a perfect girly reunion.

"You look fabulous, Carole. How are you feeling?" Jacqui asked.

"Yeh, I'm doing good. I've finished my treatments and I feel good. It's *soooo* good to be home and to see you guys. I really miss you all and I miss this banter," she said.

"Ugh, I'm sure you are making friends in the States," Daryl said.

"I am, but they are not my people, if you know what I mean. The humor is different. The only one I tell jokes to over there are the kids, Sean, and my brother, because I know they'll get them. I could really do without the stress my new sister-in-law and mother-in-law have given me, but now that we've moved, it's gotten better. My sister-in-law doesn't come and go as if it's her house anymore and if all goes to plan, my mother-in-law should have her own place soon. I really love our new house! When are you guys coming over? You'll need to come when it's nice weather, so we can swim in the pool and go to the beach."

"Next year, for sure," Jacqui said, "But in the meantime, let's get another bottle of wine to celebrate our wee Caz being home."

"Here, here…" they all said in unison.

***

There was plenty of British banter going around for Carole to enjoy while she was home. The following weekend was her girlfriend, Caroline's, 40th birthday party. Carole stayed in the hallway out of sight, until they presented Caroline with her *Red Book*. There were nearly 30 friends and family crammed into Caroline and Ian's house, which was decorated for the occasion with multi-colored bouquets of balloons and *Happy 40th Birthday* signs hanging in all the rooms. The music was playing, the bottles of cheer were flowing, and Caroline was wearing a pink fairy birthday tiara and dancing merrily around the living room. Ian was trying to get everyone's attention and the guests in the living room quickly quieted down when they heard him say for the second time, "Can I have everyone's attention?"

"Caroline Mitchell!" he announced with excitement, "***This Is Your Life!***" Everyone cheered with applause and whistles.

He walked towards her with the *Red Book* in his hands, which was inscribed in gold lettering "*Caroline Mitchell – This is Your Life.*" He spoke about when and where she was born, who her parents and siblings were, and then talked about the first school she attended and who her childhood friends were. This was Carole's signal to get ready to enter the room. She was carrying Caroline's cake with all 40 candles lit. It looked like a small inferno. Carole was tingling with anticipation and couldn't wait to turn the corner to see Caroline's face.

This would also be the first time everyone would see Carole sporting her new short hairstyle that had been growing in nicely since her chemo treatments ended. She looked fabulous, dressed in a black-lace, short-sleeved French polka dot blouse and trendy jeans.

"Right, now let's talk about Caroline's first childhood friend," Ian continued as he flipped through the *Red Book* that had pictures of her childhood and special life events. "She has many friends from all stages of her life…as you can see from the crowd of ya here tonight, but let's see if you can guess who this might be."

A voice came from the hallway and it was right on cue.

"Hellloooo," Carole sang, "I might live far away, but we've known each other since we were seven years old, and I would not have missed this party for the world!"

"Oh my God, Carole, is that you!" Caroline said, as she held her mouth with her hands. Carole turned the corner and came into the room holding her birthday cake.

"I can't believe you're here!" she said, giving Carole a big hug, as she handed off the cake. "I can't believe you're here!" she said again through her tears. "How are you? You look great!" she said.

"I'm good, I'm good," Carole said with a big smile.

"But I thought you couldn't come because of Julie's wedding."

"Well…I told a wee white lie. Julie's wedding is next weekend. I had every intention of coming to your party," Carole said.

"I'm just over the moon that you're here, Carole!" she said, as she gave her another hug.

Carole Surprising Caroline!

Carole looked around the room, and everyone seemed to be just as touched by her presence. It was a great party, full of reminiscing, laughter, dancing, and good old-fashioned Scottish partying…just what the doctor ordered. The next morning Carole's head hurt a little, but it had been worth every bit of the fun she had the night before. At least she had one day to recoup before they left for the Isle of Skye.

This time Carole and Sean had a trip planned to the Cuillins for a few days on their own. She was hoping that they'd get a glimpse of the mountain range and, although it was overcast, they were able to see the loch and mountains in the distance. It would not have mattered, however, if she hadn't been able to see two feet in front of her, because what was important was that she was home: She was once again in Skye, breathing the fresh air, and she was enjoying time with Sean.

Childhood Friends

"How are you feeling?" Sean asked.

"I'm feeling good…a little out of breath, right enough, so I think it was a good idea to do some of the Red Cuillin Hills this time," she said.

"Not what you are used to, huh? They are lower and less rocky, so we'll have fewer scrambles and climbs, but still, it's not a walk in the park either. Glamaig is 775 meters!" he said.

"Considering where I was a few months ago, I thank God I'm here, and think I've made a decent recovery. Knowing I was coming home helped keep me focused on my recovery. I love it up here…the peace and serenity. I wish I could bottle this up and take it home with us. It's better than any medicine a doctor could give me," she said to Sean.

"You're a strong lassie," he said in his best Scottish accent. "And one day we'll live half our time in Scotland and half in New York."

"Only if you promise me when we move here, you won't try speaking with a Scottish accent," she said with a giggle as she picked up her pace.

"What...you don't like my accent?" he said, as he grabbed her around her waist.

"Well let's just say you'll need to work on it...a lot," she said as she gave him a kiss.

Their time together in Skye seemed like a blink to them, as they were in the car heading back to Port Glasgow before they knew it. Dick was dropping the kids off at Linda and her mum's house that afternoon, and she wanted to be there when they arrived.

"Did you have a nice time?" Carole asked her children as she gave them both big hugs.

"Yes, we did, but I missed you, Mum," Kristy said.

"I missed you too," she said.

That was the longest period of time they had been away from their mother, and although Carole enjoyed seeing her friends and getting up to Skye, she also missed having her children around her.

A Photo opportunity at Julie's wedding

The following weekend, after celebrating Julie's wedding, Carole said her good-byes to her mum and Linda, but she knew it wouldn't be long before Linda would be visiting them for Thanksgiving. Carole loved knowing when she'd see her family again…it made the good-byes much easier.

GETTING BACK TO NORMAL

It was a busy fall…Carole continued to be monitored by her doctors, and she returned to work part time in September. She had been out since January and decided to start off by working two days a week until she got herself back into the swing of things.

Carole's friends at work organized a team to walk in her honor at The American Cancer Society's Making Strides Against Breast Cancer Walkathon that was being held on Long Island, at Jones Beach, in October.

"Do you think you guys can come to a Breast Awareness Walkathon next weekend? It'll be an early start for you, because I believe you'll have to be there at 8:00 am, which means you'd probably have to leave your house at 6:30," Carole said to Michele.

"We'll be there…Cameron gets us up at the crack of dawn anyway. We'll just get them in the car and bring his stroller. What do we need to do?"

"I know we have to register once we get there. So let's meet at the registration area," Carole said.

It was a lovely, brisk, sunny day, but most visible was a sea of pink on the boardwalk. Carole wore a light-pink jacket with a banner across her chest that said **SURVIVOR**. She was thrilled with the turnout. Fifteen coworkers were there with their family and, of course, her family was there. Sean, Kristy, Joseph, Deka, who wore his kilt, Michele, Bradley, Cameron, and Michele's sister-in-law, Paula, who was there with two friends, all came to support her. She was touched that her colleagues at United Way had organized the whole thing and couldn't have been more gracious.

"Thank you again to my United Way coworkers for organizing this. It was brilliant…and thank you, everyone, for coming out," she said at the end of the four-mile walk. Carole then went to everyone in turn and gave them a hug from her heart.

"We'll be here next year for you, too," her boss, Theresa, said.

"It's a date," Carole said with a smile.

The event gave Carole a chance to see massive numbers of fellow survivors, which couldn't help but give her a dose of hope that she, too, would remain a survivor. All these people shared a goal: to end a disease that threatens the lives of so many people they loved.

"With all the millions of dollars raised each year, surely a cure has to be just around the corner," Carole thought.

TIS THE SEASON – 2006

Carole and Sean were invited over to Paula and Michael's house for Thanksgiving; they were joined by Michele, Deka, the boys, and Michele's parents, Rose and Howard. Carole knew Linda would enjoy this holiday, and she wanted to make sure they spent it with Michele's family. Paula and Michael bought a sampler case of champagnes from around the world, and they sat in front of the fireplace tasting all the different types of champagne, talking about what they were thankful for.

"I am thankful for my improving health, my family, and this lovely champagne," Carole said as she held up her glass.

"Hear, hear!" said Linda and Deka.

"I'll drink to that!" said Paula and Michael, and everyone else raised their glasses in agreement.

The holiday came and went quickly, as did Linda's trip. She wouldn't be back until the summer at the earliest, but their mum would be over for Christmas for one month, and Carole couldn't wait to spend time with her.

Carole's doctor visits remained regular and, although her blood counts were not getting any worse, they weren't getting any better either. Still, she was up to working three days a week. Every time she had blood work done, she'd be a little uneasy until she got the results back, but this time she received great news. Her numbers had gone down significantly, and she was over the moon with the news and needed to share it. As soon as they got into the car, she called Michele and Deka.

"Hi, I just got out of the doctor's office and he went over the results of my blood work," she said to Michele and Deka.

Michele crossed her figures and whispered, "Please, God, give us good news…"

"And I've got *great* news! My numbers look really good! The doctor is very pleased."

"*YESSSSS*!!! That is awesome," Michele said.

"That's *brilliant*, Carole. That is *absolutely* brilliant. Let's go out and celebrate!" Deka said.

"Thanks! I'll give you guys a call when we get home. Sean and I are just leaving the city now. I wanted to tell you the good news," she said with excitement.

As she hung up the phone, Carole took a deep breath and relaxed her shoulders. She always knew it was anxiety-provoking getting the tests done and waiting for the results, but she could actually feel the tension running out of her body.

From that point on, Carole busied herself decorating the house for Christmas, buying gifts for everyone, and getting things ready for her mother's visit. She was really feeling good; the transition of returning to work was getting easier; the kids and Sean were doing well; and she was finally on the road to a full recovery. Her mother was arriving on the following Thursday, December 14, and Deka would pick her up at Newark Airport.

Michele and Carole made plans for everyone to come out to Michele and Deka's house that Friday to celebrate her mother's birthday. Michele and Margaret went Christmas-shopping during the day, and Michele kept in contact with Carole on their whereabouts, so they'd be able to meet up at Wegman's Supermarket on their way back to the house. Margaret had thought she wouldn't be seeing Carole until Christmas Eve. As Michele drove through the parking lot, she spotted Kristy and Joseph.

"Oh, look who it is!" Michele said.

It took Margaret a few seconds before it all registered, "That's Kristy and Joseph, isn't it!"

"Yes, they've come out for the weekend to celebrate your birthday,"

"Oh…that's great, isn't it!" she said.

"Hi, Mum," Carole said, as she gave her a big hug.

"Hello, Carole. What a nice surprise. How are you?" she asked.

"I'm good. Let's get what we need in the shop and go back to Michele's for a cup of tea," Carole said.

That evening the whole family went out to the Union Hotel restaurant. The kids played together, and the adults enjoyed a glass of wine, celebrating Margaret's birthday. Cameron started to get tired, so as soon as they sang "Happy Birthday," she opened her gifts and they went back to Michele and Deka's house for a nightcap before retiring for the evening. The plans were that Margaret would stay at Michele and Deka's house, and then she would be back to Carole's house for the remainder of her stay, having spent Christmas Day at Rose and Howard's house with the whole family.

Carole had another doctor's appointment on Friday, December 22, and was thinking about postponing it until after the holidays, since she was feeling so good, but thought, "I'll just go in and get it done and have more good news for Christmas."

Carole and Sean sat in the waiting room, as they did for every visit they'd been in for the past year, until a nurse asked them to go into the doctor's office.

Carole could feel something was different, and when she saw the doctor's face, she knew something was wrong.

"Unfortunately, I've got some distressing news to share with you…your numbers are going up, and we are going to have to start the treatments again. I also want you to go for a PET scan," he said.

"What? Four weeks ago everything was good. Are you sure?"

"I'm sure. We'll need to begin right after the holidays, but first we'll obviously talk about your treatment options and then get you started," he said.

Carole was devastated. Not only was she not ready to hear that news, but the thought of starting treatment again made her sick to her stomach. The drive home was a silent one, as her mind raced, trying to make sense of it all. "I can't take this emotional rollercoaster," she thought. "This disease continuously plays with my head, as if it's a game and it's trying to break me down so I give up."

"I don't want to tell anyone until after the holidays," she said to Sean before they got out of the car. "I don't want their holidays ruined by this…this disgusting disease," she said as she cried.

Sean nodded his head in agreement. He, too, was shocked by the news.

Christmas Day came, and nobody was the wiser. Rose and Howard had 22 guests at their house, and everyone was in good spirits, including Carole. Once again, she was able to successfully mask what was going on inside her mind. She was determined that her holidays would not be affected in any shape or form, but what was really preying on her mind was the lack of a plan, not for herself, but for her children.

After dinner and a few glasses of wine, Carole and Paula were the only two remaining at the far end of the long dining room table.

"How is Lisa doing?" Carole asked.

***

Lisa was a childhood friend of Paula's who had been diagnosed with cancer in 2000 as well. Carole had met her several times - the first time, at the American Cancer Society Walkathon, and then later, up at the Mohonk Mountain House when, what started as a sister-in-law spa-tacular weekend, turned into a friends and sisters-in-law event. Paula and Lisa roomed together; Michele and Carole stayed in the same room; and Michele's friend, Janet, and her friend, Angel, had a room as well.

Paula, Michele and Carole at Mohonk Mountain House

Although not a topic of discussion while they were enjoying their massages, it dawned on Carole as they drove home that out of the six ladies up there that weekend, two of them had cancer, and

Angel's sister had it as well. "Something is wrong with this picture," she thought.

***

"She is doing well," Paula replied.

"Has she made any arrangements for her children in the event, God forbid, something happens to her?" she asked.

"No, she doesn't really want to go down that path, because she truly believes she is going to beat this."

"That's not really good… shouldn't she be making a plan? What kind of mother leaves that out there without a plan in place?" Carole said with a disturbed and almost annoyed tone to her voice.

"Well, I think everyone deals with this sort of thing differently, and she doesn't want to think it's going to happen, so she's not ready to do anything."

There was a long pause as Carole contemplated if she should share her news with Paula.

"I had a doctor's appointment on Friday," Carole finally said, "and he gave me very disturbing news. He told me my numbers shot up and I have to start treatment again. I can't tell you how much I regret going there right before Christmas. I just wasn't expecting bad news. I left the doctor's office in such a state of shock…I have to start making a plan for my children," she said, as she felt her eyes fill up with tears.

Paula completely understood why Carole was so passionate about Lisa's decision not to make a plan for her children. It was where Carole was in her mind and she was still trying to work through it all.

"Carole, you are a fighter, and you'll come back from this," she said as she got up and sat next to her.

"No...this is very important. It would be...I don't know...bad mothering if I didn't have a plan. I need to know that they will stay in the States."

Sean came and sat down next to Carole.

"I've shared the news with Paula," Carole said.

"It's another hurdle," he said. "We'll get through it."

Deka walked by and saw that his sister had been crying.

"What's up?" he asked Carole, as he headed for the sofa to get a good seat for the kids' Annual Christmas Pageant that was due to start.

"Nothing. I'm just talking to Paula about Lisa," she said.

Deka caught Paula's eye and had a gut feeling that something else was the matter. He knew Carole and Lisa had met in the past and they both had cancer, but what would bring her to tears?

"I'm sorry I'm bringing this up on Christmas Day," she said to Paula.

"Don't be...if there is anything I can do, just let me know."

"Maybe we can get together for a cup of tea or come over my house and we can finish this discussion."

"That's fine. Just give me a call," Paula said.

With that, the pageant was about to start, and they left the dining room table and moved into the living room to see the show. Like every year, it was full of confusion, as Rose tried to organize the kids upstairs in her bedroom; reindeer were prancing around the living room, and this year, they had an additional cast member. One-year-old Cameron was a shepherd, who took his role very seriously, holding his staff with one hand and his sheep with the other. Carole smiled as she looked at him and watched her children singing Christmas songs with their cousins.

Carole watched the show, but was haunted by an internal battle of mixed emotions. She was feeling very angry that she had gotten this news *three* days before Christmas. Yet, she was determined that she didn't want herself or her family to be robbed of enjoying the holiday that she loved. Watching all the cousins playing with each other, sharing a meal with everyone, and having a happy family around her was what she wanted for Christmas, and what she managed to get.

Deka, Michele, and the boys went over to Carole's house for Boxing Day, the day after Christmas - another holiday in the UK. After dessert, Carole decided to share the news with them, which also confirmed Deka's feeling that something was wrong.

"Do they know why the numbers are going up?" Deka asked.

"It's usually an indication that the cancer is back, which is why they'll be doing a scan and putting me back on treatment."

What concerned Carole was, there were only a handful of treatments available to her, and slowly she was going through them.

"I know once I sit down with the doctor and have a plan, I will feel better about this, but I don't have that right now."

"You'll get through this, Carole, just like you've gotten through all the other setbacks…after all, you're a Rodger," Deka said.

"I think you're right, Carole - once you've got your plan and have done the research on the treatment, like you normally do, you'll be able to focus on getting through it again," Michele said.

Michele and Deka were pretty much used to the drill. Throughout the past year, if they hadn't heard from Carole after a few days of getting her results, it usually meant the report was not favorable, and Carole was working through a plan to move forward, and once she was able to talk about it, she reached out and gave them a detailed update. Michele would tell Carole to speak slowly because she would take notes so she'd be able to give Deka an accurate update on her health.

"I just didn't see it coming this time. Quite honestly, it hit me like a ton of bricks," she said.

Carole knew she'd bounce back from this bit of bad news and had no intentions of giving up, because she had too much to live for. Why this was happening to her again was just overwhelming her at the moment. She decided not to share her need to have a plan in place for the children with Michele and Deka, as she didn't want to hear them say, "Why are you going down that path?"

The reality was, she felt she had to go down that path, and it made her heart sink. She really didn't think it was going to happen, but in the same breath, she didn't feel comfortable not having some sort of plan for her precious children.

"This has got to be every mother's worst nightmare," she thought. "I can't believe I have to even think about this. How do I even begin trying to sort this out?"

It was time to start talking to Sean and explaining her wishes ...she just needed to know her children would be looked after by anyone but their father.

AN EMOTIONAL ROLLERCOASTER

Carole took Paula up on her offer and invited her over two weeks after the holidays. Sean was home and the kids were running around, so they didn't have uninterrupted time until later on in the day. They sat at the kitchen table having a drink until Carole felt ready to talk about her children.

"How do I make this plan?" she said to Paula. "What will happen with the kids?"

Paula knew this had to be the hardest conversation a mother would have: Who would care for her children if she were no longer here?

"I just need it settled in my head. I'm not saying it's going to happen. Believe me when I say I have no plans on going anywhere; I'm just saying, I need a plan in place, just in case."

"I understand…if that's going to make you feel at ease, then start planning. Have you talked to Sean about it?"

"I've just started…it's a hard thing to talk about without starting to cry. He said not to worry…that it will all work out, but I need more than that. I want them to stay here in the States," she said.

"Well, you've spoken your peace, and he knows what your wishes are. Perhaps you just need to let it sit for a bit before you try discussing it again," Paula said.

That didn't last very long, and a few days later, while talking to Linda, Carole ran the situation by her as well. Although Carole didn't actually say to Linda, "Please take them," she wanted to know if she would be willing to take on the responsibility of raising them.

"Yes, of course, I would take care of them," Linda said.

"I don't think Dick would ever let that happen. He would fight for them if they were in the UK," Carole said.

"I don't understand that. It was eight months before he showed his face after he left you, wasn't it? He didn't see them for eight months. Why would he fight for them?"

"Do you remember, I actually called the attorney and asked him to write a letter to Dick, asking him to get in contact with the kids, because they missed him? The attorney thought I wanted him to ask Dick to stop seeing them when he wasn't supposed to, and here I was, asking him to see his children. The attorney said to me, 'I've never heard that before in my life.'"

"I know, so why fight for something that you didn't want in the first place?" Linda said.

"I don't know; all I know is he'd give you a hard time."

Carole continued to have conversations with Sean about the children staying in the States, and he was reluctant to commit to anything, which concerned Carole. She couldn't understand why he didn't see it quite the way she did.

"I don't think I can do this without you," he finally said to her.

"What do you mean? They are my blood, my everything. How could you say you don't want them?" Carole said.

"I'm not saying I don't want them. I'm saying, I don't think I can do it without you. Let's not talk about it anymore; we will work something out between Linda, Deka, and Michele…," he said.

Carole called Michele and shared what Sean had told her.

"Sean doesn't think he could do this without me. How could he say that...those kids are me!" she said through her tears.

"Maybe he is just scared of losing you. You are a planner, Carole, but the thought of your not being around scares the heck out of him."

"I know, it scares the heck out of me as well, but I also know it's the way I work things through in my mind. I need to have something in place. Would you be Kristy's mentor?" Carole asked.

"Her mentor? What do you mean, her mentor?"

There was a long pause.

"I don't know what you mean by mentor. But yes, I can be her mentor, if you help me mentor her," Michele said.

Michele understood a bit of where Sean was coming from, because the thought of agreeing to be Kristy's mentor gave her a sinking feeling.

"Where do you think you're going? You are not checking out, are you?" Michele asked.

"No, I just need to know they will be looked after."

Carole wondered why they weren't getting it. All she was saying is, she needed something in place...not that she was giving up on life.

"God forbid, it ever comes to that, and I know it won't, because I am getting that miracle, right?" Carole said.

"That's right, and I believe that...I know you are getting that miracle. I can see us in our golden years, just chilling out on a porch somewhere, reading a book, so you have to get that miracle."

Carole believed that as well and was incorporating everything into her healing. Anything that gave her hope, whether it was spiritual, news on up-and-coming treatments, a book, support groups, drinking her tea daily, visualizing...you name it, she was trying it.

Her main goal was to get that miracle and never have to put a Plan B into effect. Eventually Sean did say to Carole that there would always be a place for the children with him if that was what they wanted. That was all Carole needed to hear.

ONE MIRACLE TO GO, PLEASE

"I normally wouldn't do this," Michele said, "but I've shared your health issues with Eric and Debbie, two colleagues at work, and asked them to start praying for you. They are both quite religious, and my thought was, the more people praying for you, the better. Eric was telling me about Padre Pio, a priest who performed miracles while on earth and after his death, but the thing that really interested me was, he lived during our time…he didn't pass until 1968. Eric also mentioned that there is a National Centre for Padre Pio located right next door, in Pennsylvania, probably an hour away from my house. We need to go there and get you that miracle we've been praying for…what do you think?" Michele asked.

"Sounds good to me…maybe we can do a day trip from your house," Carole said.

She was starting to be prayed for from all over. From the day Michele shared Carole's story with both Eric and Debbie, they both would ask on a regular basis about her progress.

"Carole's in my daily prayers, and I like knowing if they're working," Debbie said to Michele.

"I've asked my sister, Maria, to pray for Carole, and her prayer group will pray for her regularly," Eric said.

"That is awesome! I can't thank you enough," Michele said.

A few days later Michele found two Padre Pio prayer cards on her desk. When she read the words of Padre Pio, she knew he was the Saint they needed to pray to for help.

"Listen to this, Carole...do you remember when I told you about Padre Pio? Well, Eric, the guy I work with, left me two prayer cards. I'll give you one when we see each other, but listen to his words for a minute:

...Pray, hope, and don't worry. Worry is useless. God is merciful and will hear your prayer...Prayer is the best weapon we have; it is the key to God's heart. You must speak to Jesus not only with your lips but with your heart. In fact on certain occasions you should speak to Him only with your heart...

"Isn't that powerful?! I love it. 'Pray, hope, and don't worry. Worry is useless.' That's working for me; how about you?" Michele asked.

"Lord knows, the worrying definitely creeps into my mind when I wake up at 2:00 in the morning. I'll need to start telling myself that: 'Pray, hope, and don't worry. Worry is useless.' That's a keeper," Carole said.

Every night, from that day on, Michele recited the same novena Padre Pio would say for all who had asked for his prayers and would ask Carole on a regular basis if she was praying to PP, as they affectionately had nicknamed him.

By early February, Carole was on chemo and radiation again, and the scan came back showing fluid around the lungs, which made sense to her, as she had been having a hard time catching her breath the last time she was up on Skye. She found herself saying the words of Padre Pio: "Pray, hope, and don't worry...worry is useless." However, as far as Carole was concerned, her life didn't stand still because she had cancer. Carole just went on doing what she liked doing and booked a family ski trip to Canada with her big brother, who had made the same trip with their friends every year.

ROAD TRIP…CANADA HERE WE COME

At the end of February they all drove up to Canada and shared a condo at the base of Mt. Saint Anne, 45 minutes north of Quebec City. Carole arranged it so she wouldn't be on her treatment the week they were away. Breathing seemed to be a little more difficult for her, but she still took skiing lessons. Michele's friend Janet and her family and friends went up as well. There were 20 of them in all.

"How do you like skiing so far?" Michele asked Carole.

"I'm enjoying it, but I wish I was better at it, quicker."

"You'll get there, Carole," Deka said.

"I can see how it gives you a freeing feeling, when you're headed for the top of the mountain on the gondola lift and then coming down the slopes on a nice wide, freshly groomed trail. I'm sure it's similar to how I felt when I took my flying sessions," Carole said.

"I didn't know you took flying lessons! When was this?" Michele asked.

"It was a gift from Dick for my 21st birthday. It was pretty cool flying a plane… quite freeing."

"I bet!" Michele said. "Leave it to you to have flown a plane! What was it like?" Michele asked.

"It was absolutely brilliant. The pilot briefed me on the aircraft, and I was in the pilot's seat from takeoff to landing for about 40 minutes. I highly recommend it," Carole said, with a smile on her face.

Carole taking flying lessons

Carole took private ski lessons for the first four days, but also made sure there was enough time to enjoy some Canadian pampering at the spa with Michele, Janet, and Angel.

"I think I'll have a facial and a hot rock treatment," Carole said.

"That sounds good, and I think I'll have a Swedish massage," Michele said.

"Shall we meet in the outside hot tub after our massages? I dread walking out there, but it's brilliant once you get into the water," Carole said.

They were surrounded by white mountains and a blue sky. The sun was shining bright, but it didn't melt a flake of snow that was piled up around the hot tub. The four of them (Carole, Michele, Janet and Angel) walked outside in their white robes and slippers. The air temperature was 17 degrees F and the Jacuzzi was 80 degrees F. They all picked up their pace, threw off their robes, and jumped into the water as quickly as possible.

"Ahhhhh, that was worth the cold, wasn't it?" Carole asked.

"I'm always cold," said Michele. "And the thought of going out in the winter's air with a bathing suit on was making my skin crawl, but I have to say, it's lovely in here. On that note, I'm not getting out of this tub...feel free to leave me here. I'll be just fine until springtime," she said, as she closed her eyes, tilted her head back, and sunned her face, which had a silly grin on it.

As Carole stood up, and her warm body made contact with the chilly air, she found herself surrounded by a cloud of steam. They quickly made a dash for the sauna before the warmth of the hot tub wore off.

"There's nothing better than being pampered now and again. Are we going back to Mohonk Mountain House this spring for our spa-tacular girls' weekend?" Janet asked.

"Count me in," said Carole.

"Me too," said Angel.

"Me three," added Michele.

Carole liked looking forward to getaways and was pleased that she fully enjoyed her vacation in Canada. She was able to compartmentalize her health issues until they were on their journey home, and by the time they were on Long Island, she had a plan in place.

A HEART TO HEART WITH THE "BIG GUY"

Carole went right back into her cycle of treatment upon her return. She couldn't help but wonder what she didn't get, or hadn't learned, the first time she had dealt with having cancer, that she again had to deal with such a horrible disease.

"Why is God putting me through this again?" Carole kept asking herself, and then verbalized it to Michele.

"If you are looking for someone to blame, I definitely wouldn't be blaming God. I'd be asking him to heal you. I really don't think God is *doing* this to you," Michele said.

"Okay, but what didn't I learn the first time that he wants me to learn? There must be something. What am I doing wrong? I mean, I've forgiven all the people who have wronged me throughout my life, so I'm not holding onto any toxic anger…I have even managed to forgive Dick for all the things he did to me which, believe me, wasn't easy."

"Have you asked Him? I mean have you prayed, asking Him to heal you, or are you mad at Him? This is only my opinion, but I don't think you are doing anything wrong, and God is someone you want rooting for you. Ask Him for help…'Pray, hope, and don't worry,' right?" Michele said.

After speaking to Michele, Carole thought perhaps she had a point and truly wanted "The Big Guy" in her corner because her miracle would be coming from him. She started to pray to Padre Pio daily and asked for her cancer to leave her body and then thanked him for healing her. She would not waste any more energy on asking why this was happening to her; instead, she focused her mind on getting better, knowing it was not an option to leave this world just yet...she had too much to do.

Spring rolled around quickly, and Easter was celebrated at Michele and Deka's house with Paula, Michael, their kids, Rose and Howard, and Carole and her family. Carole made her signature carrot and coriander soup, and Paula brought the appetizers that looked too good to eat. They both helped Sean organize an Easter egg hunt for the kids, as Michele was busy sorting out the main meal and Deka was serving cocktails to everyone.

"You look great, Carole. How are you feeling?" Paula asked.

"I'm doing well," Carole said as they walked outside to help Cameron find a few eggs before the older kids got them all.

"You'd never know she had any health issues just by looking at her," said Howard, as he saw Carole walking with Paula. "She always looks good and her spirits are always up."

"I think it's that positive attitude and spirit that helps her get through all the ups and downs she's been through over the last year or so. After all, she is a *Rodger* and a true survivor," Deka said, with a stronger-than-usual Scottish accent.

Easter Sunday – Paula, Michael, Howard, Deka, Rose, Sean and Carole

***

Deka was right: She was a survivor, and every night Carole continued to go on the Internet, seeking new treatments as well as researching which ones were at the point of human trials. She came across an article about a man named John Kanzius, who was diagnosed with cancer and took it upon himself to build a machine using radio waves to kill cancer cells and leave the good cells alone.

"Did you read the article I emailed over to you?" Carole asked Michele in a very excited voice.

"I did…that is awesome news, isn't it?"

"Finally, someone has invented a machine that has the potential of treating cancer without chemo and radiation. And no side-effects! He actually used pie pans and hot dogs from his wife's kitchen to test his theory and now has created a machine, which is in his garage that targets the bad cells. Isn't that the best news! Now all I have to do is hang in there until it comes to human trial."

"And you *will* hang in there. I can see it now. You'll be their poster person."

"Yes, because I *know* it is going to work, and I'll be the living proof! I'll be on Oprah helping to spreading the word of hope to everyone."

"Can I come with you to the Oprah show?"

"Absolutely," Carole said with a surge of hope in her voice.

Carole was so excited by this news and the national television coverage it was getting. Although it was still some years away from being used on humans, there was indeed another alternative to treating cancer patients out there being researched. She prayed to God that she would be able to be here long enough for the machine to be used on her so she'd get the cancer out of her body once and for all.

BREATHE IN, BREATHE OUT...
DON'T EVER TAKE IT FOR GRANTED

As Carole's breathing became more uncomfortable, her doctor's appointments were becoming more intense as they discussed her options.

"Where is the fluid coming from?" Carole asked the doctor, knowing what the answer was going to be.

"It's a secondary cancer that spread from your breast cancer to the lung, and we will continue to treat it with breast cancer treatments. We are going to try Herceptin again, and since the fluid is causing major discomfort, we are going to have to drain it by inserting a tube."

Even though Carole knew what he was going to tell her, the words still came as a shock, and she couldn't comprehend anything he said after she heard him say in what seemed to be slow motion, "...*s-e-c-o-n-d-a-r-y c-a-n-c-e-r t-h-a-t s-p-r-e-a-d*..." Carole instinctively held her stomach as she heard the news, feeling as if someone had just punched her in the abdomen. The emotional rollercoaster she was on was forcing her to hold on tight for yet another downward turn.

"I'm sorry, but can you repeat what you just said?" she asked.

The doctor recapped what he had just explained, and this time, Carole was able to hear everything he said.

"Will I be totally out for this procedure?"

"No...the tube is inserted under local anesthesia," the doctor said; "after the area is numb, a small incision is made through the skin and muscle into the chest. We'll then place a tube through the passage. Once the tube is in place, it is sutured to the skin to prevent it from falling out and we'll put a dressing on the area. The tube will stay in for as long as there is fluid to be removed."

"It doesn't look like we have a choice," she said to the doctor as she looked at Sean. "When can we do it?"

The thought of the procedure sickened Carole, but she was feeling as if she had run a marathon when she walked up and down the stairs in her house. The difficultly she was experiencing breathing was the worse of the two evils, and although she was feeling like a pincushion, with all the tests and operations she'd been through over the past year, she really didn't have much of a choice. "When will it stop?" she started to ask herself. "How many more times will I have to go through this before I am done with it all?" She took as deep a breath as was physically possible and continued her internal chat. "Don't go there," she said to herself. "It's only a dangerous, slippery path that leads to thinking, woe is me, and I need to be as strong as possible to get through this with no complications."

"I can schedule the procedure for next Thursday," the doctor said.

"Let's do it," she said.

The following Thursday the procedure was done, and when it was over, Carole was very sore and vowed never to go through it again, but she was relieved that she was able to breathe easier.

"They drained two litres of fluid from my right lung, and the procedure was very uncomfortable," Carole said to Deka.

"Two litres! That's a large bottle of soda," he said. "Is your breathing better, I hope?"

"Well…yes, but my lung partially collapsed. The doctors feel it may slowly re-expand without treatment. The good news is, since it affected only a small part of the lung, it hasn't closed off any of the airway…thank God."

"Wow, thank God, is right," said Michele.

"I never want to go through that pain again. Enough of that…did I tell you Linda is coming over next month, and that Stewart is coming with her?" Carole said.

"Stewart? Who's Stewart?" asked Deka.

"Linda's new boyfriend! Where have you been?" Michele asked.

"Nobody tells me anything," he said.

"I met him the last time I was home," Carole said, "He seems like a nice guy and she is happy. They'll be here in July so you'll get a chance to meet him. Jacqui and her husband are coming in August, Caroline was here in May for my birthday, and we will be going to Scotland in December. That's what I call a great flow of visitors, isn't it? I love when we have visitors from the UK," said Carole.

"Yeh, I wish I had people visit us….I don't have any friends," said Deka, with a crooked smile.

"Oh, if I hear that sad line one more time I'm going to scream. He's been saying that to our friends ever since we moved back here five years ago and our friend Howard keeps on saying 'I'll be your friend,' " Michele said laughing.

"Never mind - it's just a little Scottish humor…he's just playing, right, Big Bro? I forgot to tell you guys. I finally got the book *The Secret* you've been talking about. It really makes you think about what you might be attracting into your life without even realizing it, doesn't it?" said Carole.

"You said it. What you think about, you bring about," said Michele. "What part are you up to?"

"I'm kind of jumping around, but I read the chapter that talked about health, and it was very powerful, especially the part where the woman spoke about being diagnosed with breast cancer. She truly believed in her heart and with her faith that she was already healed, and three months after being diagnosed there was no sign of cancer…at all! How brilliant is that?"

"Absolutely brilliant, if you ask me," Michele said, "She was the one who watched funny movies, right?" she added.

"That's right. What she was saying was, she couldn't afford to put any stress in her life, because stress is one of the worst things you can have while you're trying to heal yourself, and I truly believe that. That's why I changed a few things in my life. I needed to de-stress my family life as much as possible, so we moved to sort out the in-law issues we were having, and we've actually started to watch funny movies with the kids as well, which is a fun thing to do anyway," Carole said.

"I totally think laughter and joy have some sort of healing power attached to them," Michele said.

"Yes, what I found fascinating was her ability to get her mind to the point where she believed cancer was never in her body, and she was cancer free within a few months without the use of chemo and radiation. That gives me great hope that all the visualizing I'm doing before I go to bed is going to give me the same result."

"That's great. It will, Carole…you will get your miracle. I do believe that," Michele said.

"Yeah…from your lips to God's ears. The other thing I've just started doing is writing in a gratitude journal. Sean actually bought me *The Secret* journal, and every day I write what I am grateful for. It's great to see all the things I'm able to write, and the list gets longer each day."

"Would you mind if I asked you what are some of the things you've added to the list that have surprised you?" Michele asked.

"No, not at all. Take today, for example…the actual day. Most people think this is *just* another day in their life. It's not just another day, it's another day given to them, and it's a *gift*. If you take this day, this gift, and treat it as if it were the first day in your life, but also treat it like your last day, you will have had a *great* day. It's so unfortunate that I only realized this once I got sick. Now, when I open my eyes in the morning, despite my pain, it's another day with my children, Sean, friends and family, and that means so much to me. Here's another thing I'm grateful for. I can look at the sky, and you know, we rarely really look at the sky, but when *I* do, I now truly appreciate all the nuances I see. The clouds coming and going, the change in color at dusk, the hundreds of stars at night…it's brilliant. I am literally grateful for everything: I have a roof over my head, and I have heat when I'm cold, and air conditioning when I'm hot. I can go to the refrigerator when I'm hungry, and I can have cold or hot water by the turn of a knob. Millions of people will never experience that luxury that we take for granted. So I am *truly* grateful for everything. I just wish I had realized it earlier, but better late than never, right?"

"Yes, you said it. I will take that on board myself, and I'm sure I'll be looking at the sky, and everything else for that matter, in a very different way. Thank you," Michele said.

"You're very welcome," Carole said.

SUMMER DELIGHT – 2007

By the time Linda arrived, Carole was on the mend, and her breathing was better, although not yet back to normal. She and the kids were very happy to see Linda, and Sean took everyone into the city to do the tourist thing, showing Stewart the main attractions. They then drove out to Michele and Deka's house for a barbeque and a sleepover. It always seemed that Linda's visits went too fast for Carole, but she said, "Not to worry, Linda - I'm planning on coming over earlier than Sean and the kids on my next trip…probably around the middle of December. It's Jacqui's 50th birthday, so I'll be spending some time with Jacqui, Fay, and Daryl in Manchester and then I'll fly up to Scotland."

Once all of Carole's UK visitors had come and gone that summer, Sean arranged a family vacation for Carole, Kristy, and Joseph. They drove up to Saratoga Springs, New York, where Sean's brother lived, and rented a cabin at Lake Desolation.

"This place looks absolutely brilliant, doesn't it?" Carole said as they drove up to the cabin.

"It looks more like a ski chalet, with its steep pitched roof, than a cabin. Let's go check it out," Sean said.

It was just as charming inside as it was outside, with its rustic furniture and spiral wrought-iron staircase leading up to a loft with a king-sized bed. The supporting beams on the first floor were in their natural oak state, complete with knots. At the far end of the living room, a pair of French doors led them out onto a deck that had a breathtaking panoramic view of the lake, and a lower deck with four Adirondacks chairs was waiting patiently for someone to sit in them.

"I just found where I'll be relaxing everyday around 4:00 pm...right there on that chair, with a good book," Carole said.

"Look how calm the water is...it looks like a mirror. Look, you can see the reflection of the trees on the lake," Joseph said. "Can we go for a swim, Mummy?" he asked.

"Let's get unpacked and take a walk around first," said Carole. "We'll have plenty of time to enjoy the lake while we're here."

"I found my room," they heard Kristy saying from downstairs.

On the lower level there was one room decorated perfectly for a girl, with its canopy bed and pink furnishings. Kristy was in heaven and quickly made the space her own. The room across the hall was Joseph's room; he wasn't too fussed about how it was decorated, as he just wanted to get his clothes into the drawers as quickly as possible so they could go and explore their surroundings.

The cabin was surrounded by a forest and was in the foothills of the Adirondack Mountains. Sean's brother lived about 12 miles away; they had planned on visiting him and his family a few times during the week and joining them for dinner.

Carole loved the peaceful surroundings, and the kids liked playing in the lake every day. They went on a few short hikes, rented bicycles built for two, and took a canoe out on the lake a few times.

Every evening Sean opened the French doors and they watched the sun set over the lake.

"This has been a lovely holiday. Thanks for finding this place," Carole said to Sean, as they sat holding hands and enjoying the views.

"Maybe we should come back next year," he said.

"I'd like that," Kristy said.

"Me too," said Joseph, "Can we have movie night tonight?" Joseph asked.

The house came with a stereo, TV/VCR/DVD, and a well-stocked library of books and movies.

"That's a good idea. Why don't you and Kristy go and pick out a funny movie, get in your PJs, and we'll start movie night in 15 minutes," Carole said.

They all sat around the living room settling themselves in for the start of *Daddy Day Care*.

Carole sat back and treasured every minute of seeing Kristy and Joseph laughing at the movie. Joseph especially liked the part when Eddie Murphy went to see how one of the kids was doing in the bathroom, only to find a big potty mess all over the place, including the ceiling. Once Joseph got tickled by a good potty joke, he'd giggle for quite some time, which made Carole laugh, and before they knew it, they were all laughing just to laugh.

The next day it was cloudy so they decided to go horseback riding in the morning. Carole was able to keep up with everything they had planned for the week and, even with all the activities, she and Kristy still found time to read together on the porch before they'd start getting ready for dinner.

At the end of the vacation they all agreed that one day they'd be back.

FALL – 2007

As the summer came to an end, Carole started getting Kristy and Joseph ready for the new school year. They went to the store with the list of supplies and one by one ticked off what they needed.

Although Carole always pushed herself and would not allow the cancer to stop her from doing what she needed to do for her children, work started to become more difficult each week and, by the middle of September, she decided to speak to the doctor about going out on full disability. It was a hard decision for her, as she enjoyed her job and really didn't like the thought of leaving, but she felt it was more important to think solely about getting better without any outside distractions.

Her colleagues still organized the American Cancer Society "Making Strides in Honor of Carole" walkathon, but this time they had made signs that all Carole's supporters pinned on their jackets. It had two pictures of Carole on it and read *"Making Strides in honor of Carole: an inspiration to us all in spirit, love and life".* As promised, her old boss, Theresa, showed up, as well as everyone else who had been there the year before. The four miles seemed a bit harder for Carole this year, as her breathing was becoming an issue again.

"It feels like I've run the New York Marathon, and this is the same feeling I had prior to the doctor's draining two litres of fluid from my lungs," she said to Sean.

"I think we'll have to discuss options again with the doctor when we see him next week. What do you think?" he said.

"Yes, but I really don't want to get that tube put in me again. It hurt like heck," she said.

"Let's just see what the doctor has to say," Sean suggested.

The doctor ordered a scan to be done before deciding whether to drain the lungs again, but what he found was more alarming than he had expected.

"I know how you feel about going through getting another drain, but we are going to have to do it again," the doctor said. "From what we can tell, there is a substantial amount of fluid buildup around both the lungs and heart, which can cause some serious complications if we don't drain it," he added.

'*Oh, my GOD, please give me a break,*' Carole said to herself. She sat there in silence, looking at Sean, shaking her head in disbelief until she was able to collect her thoughts and words.

"Okay, then, when can we do it?" she asked.

By the beginning of the following week, she found herself with a tube in her side, being drained again, but this time she knew what kind of pain to expect and, unfortunately, it was a carbon copy of the first procedure.

As soon as Carole shared with Michele and Deka that she now had fluid on her lungs and heart, Michele started to ask Carole on a regular basis when she wanted to go to the Padre Pio Shrine in Pennsylvania. Although Carole wanted to go, she didn't have any immediate plans to travel over to New Jersey and then onto

Pennsylvania, so Michele invited her parents out, and she and her mother would go together.

THE PILGRIMAGE

At the last minute, Michele's father offered to drive them there, which came as a pleasant surprise to Michele. Although her father believed in God, he struggled with the politics of the Roman Catholic Church, and she wondered how he was going to handle the whole experience. Off they went on their pilgrimage in honor of Carole to pray for a miracle.

Once they arrived at the shrine, they visited the chapel, which was empty except for Michele and her parents. There was an area to the left where they were able to leave their requests in writing. Michele read a few of the requests and then sat in the pew, writing her own letter to Padre Pio.

Dear Padre Pio,   *10/27/2007*

    I ask that you intercede on Carole McGarrigle's behalf. She is desperately in need of a major miracle and since you have been known to perform many of them in the past, we really, I mean really, need one now. She was diagnosed with breast cancer in 2000, it came back in 2005, and she now has fluid on her lungs and heart. Carole is a 41-year-old wife and mother of two children (ages 10 and 13). She has so much to live for and still has so much more to do. Her children need their mother, as do her husband, sisters, brother, mother, sister-in-law, nephews, and friends. Please grant her a miracle.

I thank you for your prayers and your intervention on Carole's behalf.

Love, Michele

She had brought with her one of the signs she had worn on the last cancer awareness walkathon at Jones Beach, and put the letter in the same clear plastic folder, on the opposite side. She attached her request to rosary beads her mother had in her pocketbook, so she could easily hang it on the wrought iron gate that enclosed the confessional booth that was once Padre Pio's. It hung among the hundreds of other rosaries holding requests people had made for Padre Pio's intercession. As they sat together praying, a man entered the chapel from behind the altar, wearing a robe and holding something in his hands the way a person would hold an infant: with the utmost care and protection. He stood at the front of the altar and instructed them to come up and pray with him as he asked them who they'd like him to pray for. ,"This is the glove Padre Pio wore, and is a first-class relic," he explained. "You will want to hold it and pray for your request."

Michele was clueless, as was her father, but her mother knew what that meant as she let out an "Ohhhh!" when he shared the information.

"I wonder what that means," Michele whispered to her father.

"I'm not sure, but I think the class of the relic has to do with whether it was part of the saint's clothing or part of his body. We'll ask your mother once we leave the chapel," he said.

After they were done praying, the man went in the back behind the altar, returned to the chapel without the relic, and sat in the pew in front of them. From nowhere came a treat none of them were expecting. The man in the robe started to sing the "Ave Maria" in a voice that gave them goose bumps. The acoustics in the chapel were brilliant.

"I think that was the most beautiful, angelic sound I have ever heard," Michele said. "And most unexpected...thank you for the gift," she said to him.

"You are very welcome," and he continued to sing another three songs.

After Michele was done listening, she left the chapel and met her father in the hallway, waiting until her mother was done. She mentioned to her father that her colleague at work, Eric, had told her to ask the clerk in the gift shop to see the ten-minute video.

When her mother came out of the chapel, Michele asked, "What is a first-class relic, and why did you respond to that man with an '*Ohhhh*'?"

"Well, there are three types of relics, I believe. A first-class relic would be part of a saint's body, a second-class relic would be an item that the saint wore or owned, like a shirt, a sock, or a glove, and a third-class relic would be a piece of cloth touched by a first- or second-class relic. That was a first-class relic, because Padre Pio's blood was on the glove from the stigmata," she said with excitement in her voice.

"But what does all that mean?" Michele asked, as if she was missing something.

"People claim that relics...even those that merely touched a saint... can perform miracles if you pray to them or touch them, and are said to possess mystical powers as well," her mother said.

"Wow, I wish I had known all that before touching the relic; however, since you did, that's good enough for me," Michele said.

As they walked toward the gift shop, Michele made mental notes to herself so she'd be able to tell Carole all about their experience. Michele bought two small pictures of Padre Pio in gold frames...one for her and one for Carole, and then asked the clerk if they could see the video.

The video started with a clip from the television show "Unsolved Mysteries," and it blew Michele and her mother away. It even gave her father something to think about.. Michele couldn't get home quickly enough to share their experience with Deka and Carole.

On the way home Michele kept on saying to her parents, "Was that an unbelievable experience, or what?" as she spoke about the man who sang, the video, and the meeting she had in the church.

"Honey," Michele said to Deka as she entered their house, "You are not going to believe what we saw today. Let me get Carole on the phone so I can tell you both at the same time."

After telling Carole and Deka about the chapel, the relic, and the singing gentleman, she told them about the video and who she met.

"Do you remember the TV show "Unsolved Mysteries"? They featured Padre Pio's miracles on the show, and they interviewed a lady named Vera Calandra. I'll try to summarize as best I can, but **YOU HAVE GOT** to go to this shrine. It was an awesome experience, and for my father to think the same, you know something special happened there...it gives hope! Okay," she continued with excitement in her voice. "This lady, Vera, had a very sick little girl named Vera Marie, who was born with some sort of dysfunctional bladder, and the little girl had gone through many operations to try to fix it. Her mum became acquainted with Padre Pio through a friend and then started to read about him. He was known as the priest who worked miracles. One night Padre Pio came to her in a dream, and said, come and don't delay. She and two of her children got on a plane and flew to Italy to see Padre Pio. When she got there and saw the line of people waiting to see him, she walked right up to the front of the line and said, 'He came to me in a dream and said I was to come to see him, and so I am here with my daughter.' Now that was a mother with a mission…you've got to love it!"

"They allowed her to cut into the line to see him, and as Padre Pio went by, he didn't say a word and only touched little Vera Marie on the head. Her mother felt a bit disappointed that he didn't say anything, but as they were leaving, she was asked to come back the following day.

Oh…I forgot to mention, prior to their leaving Pennsylvania, little Vera Marie had had another operation and the doctors at Children's Hospital of Philadelphia removed her bladder and basically said there was nothing else they could do for her except to go home and prepare for the worst because, as you know, you can't live without a bladder.

So while they were still in Italy, her mother made a promise to God that if her baby girl were to live, the whole world would know of Padre Pio. The next day they went for their second audience with Padre Pio, and this time he blessed her and both her children, and placed his hands on their heads. When they returned home and had another consultation, the doctor's report changed significantly. Now the family was told that Vera Marie had made 'great improvements' and that her prognosis seemed good. This is the part that is going to blow you away: The doctors discovered upon her return from her visit with Padre Pio that a rudimentary bladder was growing in place of the one they had removed. She was growing another bladder! If that is not a miracle, I don't know what is!"

"Oh, my God!" Carole said.

"You said it," Michele said. "Oh, my God!"

"Wow," Deka said.

"And…I'm not done. Mrs. Calandra held up her part of the promise and began spreading the word in her community and eventually opened the National Centre for Padre Pio. She has since passed away, but her daughters, Vera Marie being one of them, have kept her promise alive."

"I have got to get there," Carole said.

"It was such a powerful message of hope. I'm probably not even doing it justice. After seeing the movie, I wanted to speak to Vera Marie. I can't tell you why…I think I just wanted to be close to someone who received a miracle, so I could rub it off onto you. When I asked the clerk in the gift shop if she was there, she explained that she wasn't in, but her sister was and asked if I'd like to speak with her. I said, sure, and we met in the Church over in the main building."

The woman escorted her into one of the pews in the church. "I really can't tell you why I had the need to talk to you or your sister, except I just needed to be close and touch someone who had actually received a miracle or, in your case, someone dear to you who had received a miracle, because that is exactly what my sister-in-law needs."

Michele went on and explained Carole's situation and that she had two young children. The woman asked for Carole's full name and said she would pray for her. "See if you can get her here for a visit - that would be best, and don't forget Padre Pio has a soft spot for children, as does the Virgin Mary, so continue to pray, hope, and don't worry they'll be with her."

"I will, and thank you for your words of comfort," Michele said, as the woman gave her a hug.

"Is that wild?" Michele said to Carole. "Oh, and this miracle happened in 1968. I was 7 years old and you were 2. Padre Pio was actually alive during our lifetime, which to me is just the icing on the cake! He was a twentieth-century priest who worked miracles while on earth, and after his death...truly amazing...the hope for a miracle is very, very real. When are we going?"

Although it would be another five months before Carole was finally able to physically make her own pilgrimage to the Centre, she did get there, but not before a few more surprises came her way.

PRE-HOLIDAY COMPLICATIONS – 2007

Carole's recovery from the second draining was taking a little longer than she had thought, and she had to cancel a trip to the island of St. Thomas she had been planning for the end of November with her friends Angel and John.

"It would have been a great place to recuperate after this procedure, but the flight was worrying me, with my breathing and all," she said to Michele.

"Don't worry about it. You've got a big trip planned in four weeks that you'll want to be feeling good for."

"Yes, I was just saying to Linda, I'm getting a little concerned about my trip home as well. I'm supposed to leave by myself mid-December, but I think I'm going to have to change that. I don't want to leave the kids any more than I have to, so maybe we can all leave together. I'm also a bit nervous about being on a plane and struggling to breathe…I'd like to take an oxygen tank on the plane, but the airlines won't let me take my own," she said.

Although Carole was not using oxygen on a regular basis, she knew she'd feel more at ease thousands of feet in the air if she had oxygen nearby.

"Your breathing will improve, and we've got a few weeks before we go," said Sean, trying to encourage her as she got off the phone, "and this way we can all travel together, and you won't have to worry about dragging your luggage over there by yourself."

Carole heard what he was saying, but she was in a distant place, thinking about how she was going to get well again. The fluid seemed to be building up more quickly than before and, although the doctors were not telling her not to get on a plane, she started to think, perhaps it wasn't the best idea at this time.

"What's the matter? You know it's no big deal if we don't go to Scotland for the holidays this year," Sean said. "We can have a nice quiet holiday at home with the kids."

"I know, but I'm so disappointed. I was really looking forward to going home."

"It's okay. We'll go over when you're feeling better."

"I think that's what's concerning me about not being able to go home: I'm just not well enough to make the journey."

"You'll get there, Carole. It's just taking a little longer, but you will get there."

"You continue to be my rock, Sean, my confidant, and just in case I don't say this often enough, I love you and thank you for all you do for me and the kids. I know I'll get there, but I'm just not there in my mind yet. I'll need to give Linda a call and tell her that the plan is probably going to change."

"Hi, Linda," Carole said, with a disappointed tone in her voice.

"Hi...how are you?" Linda asked.

"I'm okay..."

"Are you sure?" she asked.

"Well, I don't think I'm going to be well enough to travel home for the holidays, and I was so looking forward to seeing everyone."

"That's okay...your health comes first. What's the doctor saying?"

"The fluid must be building up in my lungs again, because it's hard to even talk on the phone now without feeling out of breath. We have another appointment next week. I don't want to...," Carole started to say but couldn't get the words out.

"You don't want to what?" Linda asked.

"I don't want to die."

"That's good to hear, because I don't want you to die either. You'll get your strength back again...I know you will. I can come over in March if you want," Linda said.

"That would be fab," Carole said.

But Carole still was wondering just when her strength would be back. Her inability to breathe properly was starting to physically exhaust her and affect her spirit. Carole called Michele as well to let her know that they were probably not going to Scotland.

"That's a bummer, but you know you always have an invitation at my parents' house for Christmas."

"Thanks! I'll let you know what we end up doing; we haven't cancelled the plane tickets yet," she said.

"It's better to wait until you can really enjoy yourself over there, right? And being on a plane with air that doesn't circulate well probably isn't a good idea either. The last thing you need are other people's germs."

"Yes, I suppose so."

After they hung up, Michele thought Carole could use another big-brother pep talk, as she could hear that Carole's voice sounded troubled.

"Hi, Carole…how's it going?" Deka asked.

"It's going…"

"Are you all right?" he asked.

"I'm a bit upset, actually, I don't think I'm well enough to travel home and, more importantly, my breathing is becoming more difficult every day…"

"It will get better."

"I know - that is what everyone is saying, but when?"

"I don't know when, but just remember…you are a Rodger, and Rodgers are fighters, and it doesn't matter how many times you get knocked down; you *will* always get up again. Listen to me, Carole, it's absolutely not in my future that I'm going to your funeral today, next week, or next year…I don't see myself burying my baby sister. What I do see is us going on holidays again…sharing a bottle of champagne. You're just going through another rough round, and I know you will come out the other end and get through this. Now, if I know that is what's going to happen, then you have to be in the same frame of mind. Carole…you have to know you'll get through this."

Carole heard this regularly from Sean, her sisters, her mum, her sister-in-law, friends, and fellow survivors at the support group she'd been going to every Wednesday since last year, but sometimes when she heard it from her big brother, it just picked her up.

"I just have to get over this hurdle, as Sean calls it," she said.

"That's right. And you will, because you are a strong Rodger. Now come on...you can do this," he said, as if he was coaching her.

"Thanks...," she said with a little giggle.

"Anytime, Carole...anytime," he said.

As the holidays got closer, the decision not to go to Scotland turned out to be the right one, as Carole found herself back in the hospital in the city again on December 20, with problems breathing due to the fluid buildup on her lungs and heart.

"I think we should give the kids the option to go to Scotland without us," Carole said to Sean.

"I'm sure they are not going to want to go, but yes, let's give them the choice," he said.

It was an easy decision for Kristy and Joseph, and without hesitation they told Sean they wanted to stay with their mother for the holidays. Dick was informed of the change of plans and was not happy, as he had already purchased the kids' tickets. Sean called the airlines to cancel his and Carole's flights and went out to buy a turkey for their Christmas dinner as well as a few gifts.

"I want to be home for Christmas Day," Carole told her doctor.

"Okay, as long as you are back here the following day and if there are any problems, you get yourself to a hospital immediately," he said.

"I will...oh, and Doctor, Happy Christmas,"

"The same to you Carole, Merry Christmas, and may it be a very happy and healthy new year for you," he said.

They had a quiet Christmas together. Carole was grateful to be home. The following day they stopped by Rose and Howard's house to see Michele and Deka and to drop off the kids before they went back to the hospital. Kristy and Joseph stayed at their aunt and uncle's house during their holiday break, and Michele or Deka would take turns visiting and taking the kids into the city to visit their mother. Sean stayed at the hospital until visiting hours were over, went home to sleep, and then returned to the hospital. Carole had lost some more weight, and sitting upright was starting to hurt her buttocks.

"Look, I've lost my bum," she said to Michele. "I'm not filling out my pants anymore."

Carole's appetite was diminishing and she was finding it hard to swallow, so eating was uncomfortable.

"Once you get your appetite back, you'll gain the weight back," Michele said.

"Yes, I suppose you're right."

This was the first time Carole looked as weak as she felt. She knew the doctors had to do something because she couldn't breathe properly and when she swallowed, she felt like something was in her throat. "What the heck could that be?" she was wondering fearfully.

Once they arrived at the hospital, and back into a room, the medical staff quickly started medicating her again. The doctor had Carole on very strong drugs that had her stupefied. The doctor was becoming increasingly concerned with the amount of stress on Carole's organs.

"Carole," the doctor said, "We need to talk about DNR, in the event your organs fail."

"What are you asking me?"

"Do you want us to bring you back?"

"Bring me back from where? You'll need to talk to my husband, because I'm basically out of it and don't want to be making any decisions without him."

The doctor explained to Sean that it was the hospital's policy to discuss DNR (Do Not Resuscitate), especially since both her lungs and heart were under stress. Carole was clearly upset that the doctor was even discussing DNR, but once Sean explained to her that it was hospital policy, she calmed down a bit.

"We won't be signing that form, because we want you to do everything possible to keep her alive," Sean said to the doctor. "And please, don't have those sorts of conversations with Carole without my being here."

Sean was doing a good job keeping Carole's concerns at bay and making sure he kept her mum and Linda updated on her progress. Once the phone was set up in her hospital room, Carole called them herself.

"Big Bro just walked in," she said to Linda. "Let me go, and I'll talk to you later."

"How's it going, Caz?"

"Yes...all right. The nurses have been pestering me to get up and walk."

"Well, let's go then," Deka said. "If they think you are fit enough, we'll give it a go."

The nurse helped Carole out of the bed and took one of her arms, as Deka took the other. She took baby steps, and after a few steps, the nurse became concerned.

"We need to get you back into bed," the nurse said. "Wait here - I'm going to get you a wheelchair."

"Why?" asked Deka.

"Her pulse is 200...60 to 90 is normal."

Carole was at risk of having a heart attack and would remain in the hospital for another week before she was able to go home.

"I need to get out of here and be with my kids," she told the doctor.

"I know it was longer than you had anticipated, but we should be able to sign you out tomorrow morning. I would recommend being on oxygen while you're home. We can arrange for you to take a tank home with you tomorrow. It's best if you don't struggle for each breath you take. Just use it when you feel the need."

"I don't want to become reliant on it," she said.

"I've had patients who used it all the time for a short period and then didn't need it anymore. Just because you start using it doesn't mean you'll need to use it forever. If you feel the need for it, it makes sense to use it, right?"

"Yes…it's definitely more frightening not being able to catch your breath."

"I'm home," she sang as she entered the house to see a big sign that read "*WELCOME HOME MUM*".

"Mum…." the kids sang back as they ran to the door to welcome her home.

Joseph was surprised to see the oxygen tubes in his mum's nose. "What's that?" he asked.

"It's an oxygen tank to help me breathe easier."

"Oh, okay…," and that was all he needed to know.

"Mum, it's so good to have you back home," Kristy said. "We missed you," she added as she gave her a hug.

"I missed you too, and I'm very happy to be home."

Just being home put Carole into a better frame of mind, and once she got settled in, she called Deka and Michele. Bradley answered the phone.

"Hi Bradley, it's Aunty Carole. How are you?"

"Good. How are you feeling?"

"I'm feeling better. Did you have fun playing with Joseph and Kristy during the holiday break?"

"Yes, we played FBI agents...it was fun. Do you want to talk to my Mom?"

"Yes, please. Love you."

"Okay hold on… I love you too."

"Hi, you're home?" said Michele. "How are you feeling?"

"I'm good. We got in a few hours ago. It's so good to be out of that hospital and home with the kids. The doctor suggested that I bring home an oxygen tank to help me breathe, so I have one with me now. I just don't want to have to depend on it all the time. Although I have to say, it does make me feel better when I feel I can't catch my breath. It gives me instant relief, and I don't have that panic feeling anymore."

"Well, then it sounds like that's what you need for now. I'm sure it's not an indication you'll always need it."

"That's right. The doctor did say he's had patients who used it for awhile and then weaned themselves off it once they felt comfortable breathing on their own again."

"There you go…whatever gives you the relief you need, Carole, is what I'd be doing."

"Yeah, I'll just wean myself off it," she said as if she was convincing herself. "Oh, guess who flew in for a long weekend to see the kids?"

"The kids? Who?"

"Dick…"

"Dick? That's odd. It's the first time he's done that, right?"

"Yes, he surprised the kids and picked them up at school. I guess because he didn't see them during the holidays, and they must've told him I was in the hospital. He probably wanted to come over and see what was going on for himself. He actually waited in the car while Joseph ran in the house to get something. I told him he didn't have to wait in the car, so he came to the front door and told me that the kids were great and that I was doing a great job."

"That's one thing he's said that is true…you have done a great job. No thanks to him."

"No kidding…he also asked me if I would give him a character reference because he and his wife were in the process of adopting a child. I said to myself, 'a character reference'? How could I possibly do that? He doesn't even take care of his own children!"

"Pretty cheeky to ask of you, don't you think? Enough about Dick…we're going to Canada skiing next month. Are you guys interested in coming up again?" Michele said.

"Actually, Sean and I were talking about that a few weeks ago. Yes, we'd like to go again. I don't think I'll be skiing this time," she said with a chuckle, "but I can relax in the condo and we can go to the spa together."

"That's okay; you'll ski next year. Besides, I don't have to ski all the time either, and the spa sounds good to me…we can just chill," Michele said.

A week before they were to leave for Canada, Carole hit a low point and was wondering if the long car trip was a good idea.

"If you want to stay home, you can come over my house and we'll go to the spa around here," Michele said.

"That's what Linda said to me last night. She was planning on coming over in March but is thinking she might come over a bit earlier. I'll talk to Sean and the kids about it and let you know."

Four days before they were to leave, Carole decided she would go up to Canada with her whole family and they would take their time travelling the 12-hour car journey.

A WINTER WONDERLAND

The Quebec Winter Carnival was under way, and the city was also celebrating their 400th anniversary of the founding of Québec City. Carole and her family took a detour and had a late lunch in the city before traveling up to the ski resort. There were crowds of people gathered at the site of a huge ice palace where live music was playing and people were dancing in the cold air, truly enjoying the entertainment and special lighting that was illuminating the palace behind the performers.

"Look at the big snowman!" little Cameron said.

Versions of the snowman seemed to be everywhere, and later they found out his name was Bonhomme, the King of the Carnival. Across the way in a park was a giant outdoor museum, with sculptures made from blocks of snow. The children quickly made their way over to the ice slides with their cousins, and they could hear screams of joy coming from the sledding rides at the far end of the park.

"Don't wait for me…I'll catch up," Carole said, as she saw the kids eager to run ahead. She held onto Sean's arm and enjoyed the festive surroundings; it was indeed a winter wonderland and she was pleased that she had decided to go to Canada after all.

However, it was brutally cold, and as she covered her nose with her scarf, she decided it was probably best if they started to head back to the car.

The ski chalet they were staying in was identical to the one they'd had the year before. Sean had a roaring fire going in the living room, as everyone else unpacked and got themselves organized for the week.

Kristy and Joseph had a good time with Bradley in ski school, as they recapped each day's lesson while eating snacks on the couch, and giggling about a student they nicknamed "Boston Boy." They also imitated their instructor scolding one of the other students in her French accent: "David, you must not go so fast...you must make more turns and stay with the group!" Carole loved watching the cousins enjoying each other's company.

Although Carole caught a little cold on the trip up and felt a bit under the weather for the first two days at the resort, by the third day she and Michele went to the spa and had a relaxing afternoon together.

"I'll have to make sure they go easy with my massage. I'm sure they will...I practically had to give them my whole medical history on this form," said Carole.

"Just ask them to stop if you are uncomfortable with anything. Do you want to get a bite to eat in the café after our massages?"

"Absolutely - let's enjoy the whole experience."

"Yes, and let's stay a little longer than we've planned, shall we? Only another three hours," Michele said with a giggle.

By the time they got back to the chalet, everyone was done skiing, Cameron was back from day care, and the house was buzzing with talk about the day's skiing, and preparations for dinner.

All twenty met at the local restaurant. Carole was feeling good and put on makeup for the first time in weeks.

"You're amazing, Carole," Deka said to his baby sister, as he sat across from her at the dinner table. "You look great, and you just plow through the challenges that are thrown at you."

"Thanks, I'm even going to try a glass of red wine for the first time in almost a year!"

Before Carole knew it, everyone was saying their good-byes in the parking area and getting ready to travel back home. On the drive down, Carole started to think about what else she had to look forward to. She had already had visitors come over from the UK during the first week in February. The Four Usuals (Jacqui, Daryl, Fay, and Carole) reunited for a shopping spree in New York City, and Carole got a new black Coach bag that she carried happily. Linda would be arriving on the 1st of March; Caroline, her childhood friend, was travelling over by herself at the beginning of April; and Julie, her husband, and daughter were coming over at the end of April. Carole was hoping she'd feel well during their visits. She had a treatment scheduled the day after she returned from Canada.

A Turning Point

Linda was flying into JFK Airport and had asked Carole not to take the hour long drive with Sean to pick her up. As she walked through the arrival doorway, the first person she saw was her sister, grinning from ear to ear.

"You are too much. I thought we agreed you wouldn't come out to the airport!" Linda said.

"No, you asked me not to come out, but that didn't mean I wasn't coming! How are you?" she asked, as she gave her a big hug.

"I'm good. More importantly, how are *you*?" Linda asked, as she looked at her frail sister.

"I'm okay…Now, let's get home quickly; the kids have been patiently waiting to see you."

Linda soon learned one of the reasons her sister looked poorly…she hadn't been eating.

"Carole, you've got to eat, even if it's just toast."

"I know, but I can't chew, and when I do get something down, it feels like it gets stuck in my throat…it kills my appetite and then sometimes I just can't keep it down."

"Are you craving anything?"

"I seem to like avocado salad these days…I can't stomach chicken anymore, and I used to love it."

Linda looked at her sister sitting on the chair with her oxygen tank, and it reminded her of when their father was ill. This was the first time in the eight years since Carole had been diagnosed with cancer that she looked as ill as she was.

Carole had a treatment scheduled for that Monday and Linda went with Carole and Sean to Sloan-Kettering. The doctor wanted to see Carole at 5:00 pm that day.

"Linda, would you mind looking after the kids when they come home from school?" Carole asked.

"Not a problem. I'll make sure their homework is done, and I'll feed them dinner," she said.

Carole sat in the doctor's waiting room as she and Sean had done hundreds of times before, but little did she know that she was about to have a conversation that every cancer patient fears the most.

"Hi, Carole, come on in," the doctor said.

For some reason Carole felt a sinking feeling in her stomach.

"I'm afraid we can't do anything else for you. The treatments are not doing what we thought they'd do, so we will be stopping them. We don't have any other alternatives," he said.

Carole sat there speechless, looking at the doctor and then at Sean, as she felt the tears run down her face.

"How much time do I have left?" she asked.

"That's hard to say…three to six months," the doctor replied.

As they left the office, Carole felt weak in the knees and again was trying to make sense of the whole situation.

"I don't want to talk to the kids about this until I'm ready," Carole said to Sean.

By the time they got home it was 7:00 pm, and Linda was starting to wonder what was taking so long. Dinner had been on the table for nearly an hour. As they entered the house, Linda took one look at Carole's red eyes and knew something was terribly wrong.

"Where are the children? I've got something to tell you," Carole asked Linda.

"They're upstairs."

They went into the family room and Carole shut the door. She took a deep breath and said, "The doctor told us there is nothing more they can do for me...the treatments aren't working," she said through her tears.

Linda walked over and hugged her sister. Sharing tears with her was more important than words at that point.

"I don't want to tell the children just yet," Carole told Linda.

Linda nodded in agreement.

Carole called Deka the next morning and explained to him what they had told her the day before.

"What does that mean...they've told you to get hospice in?" Deka asked.

"They've said they can't do any more for me," she cried.

"No, I'm not accepting that. As I told you before, going to your funeral is not on my calendar. So I know there has got to be something else out there. If that's what's in your head, you have got to get it out of there," he said through his tears.

"It's just so hard...every hurdle I get over, there seems to be another one waiting for me."

"It's going to be all right Carole...I just know it is," he said as they ended their conversation.

At breakfast Sean mentioned, "Do you remember when Lauren, from your support group, told you that one of her friends was given the same news and she went to a hospital in Philly?"

"Yes...I looked it up on the Internet and briefly read about the center. It's called the Cancer Treatment Centers of America," Carole said.

"Give them a call and let's see what it's all about," Sean said.

That afternoon Carole was on the phone with the Center, arranging an appointment. They gave her a date of Tuesday, March 11, and told her one of their oncology nurses would be calling her at home.

"The nurse will discuss your medical history and help address any questions or concerns you might have," the woman said. "Expect a call, and prior to your arrival at the Center we will mail you a personalized packet of information, okay?"

"Yes, I actually read that on your website," Carole said.

"Oh, great...then you know our medical records gatherers will need to obtain your medical records and other documents related to your previous cancer treatments prior to your first visit as well. It's a pretty simple process...all you have to do is let your healthcare provider know that we have authorization to collect this documentation on your behalf."

"I was also treated in Scotland," said Carole.

"Then you'll probably want to get on the phone and try to expedite that process. I'm not sure if they will accept the same medical release form that we'll be sending you in the packet. Or you can actually download it from our website if you don't want to wait for it to arrive by mail."

"I'll get onto the hospital in Scotland today," Carole said.

"The last thing I want to go over with you is the Medical History Form, which will need to be completed before your first visit as well. As I mentioned a few minutes ago, the medical record gatherers will request information from your previous hospitals and physicians. They will want to gather everything."

She was not exaggerating...they wanted *everything*: history and physical discharge summaries; x-ray films and reports, including CT scans; tumor marker reports; MRI and ultrasound films and reports; operative reports; complete chemotherapy records; radiation therapy records; nuclear medicine scans; original pathology/cytology records, slides and reports; current laboratory reports and progress notes.

"One thing is for sure...they are absolutely thorough," Carole said to Linda and Sean.

Two days later a representative from the center called Carole to confirm her appointment.

"I think I'm ready for the visit...I know I'll be there three to five days for my initial consultation and evaluation, and at the end of the testing we'll discuss my treatment plan. I'm to bring my insurance card, clothing, toiletries, and medication, right?" Carole said.

"That's right; you've done your homework," the woman answered.

Things seemed to be moving quite quickly, and Linda decided to extend her stay for another week to take care of the children while Carole and Sean travelled down to the hospital. Carole didn't like leaving the kids, but felt better that they were being cared for by Linda. They planned on staying at Michele and Deka's house the night before so the trip to Philadelphia would only be a little over an hour away.

"I don't know why I'm going," Carole said to Sean and Linda the morning they were to leave, "but I know one thing for sure...I don't want to die."

"Then that's why you are going. Let's give it a shot. As long as we have alternatives, we need to look into them, right?" Sean said. "And maybe, since we're already in Pennsylvania, on that Friday we can meet Michele and Deka at the National Centre of Padre Pio ... depending on how you feel, of course."

"Okay, let's see what they have to say at the hospital first," Carole said.

It was getting harder and harder for Carole to hold onto her hope, but she could always rely on Sean to help pull her back up.

They had an early dinner at Michele and Deka's and were up and out of the house at 7:30 the next morning in order to be in Philly by 9:00 am.

Carole quickly learned that the hospital's approach included several disciplines of care that would form her own care team. It wasn't just conventional cancer treatments; it also included nutrition therapy, naturopathic medicine, mind-body medicine, and spiritual support. The doctor explained to Carole and Sean that they specialized in treating many forms of cancer including complex and advanced cases. Throughout her three and a half days of testing, Carole met everyone who would be on her care team. She felt a connection with them that was different than a typical patient-doctor relationship and believed they'd be giving her the same advice if she were a sister of theirs. They developed an individualized plan together, tailored to Carole's unique diagnosis. She was starting to feel her hope being ignited yet again, but she still needed to ask the doctor the million-dollar question:

"What do you think my odds are of getting well?" Carole asked. She was quite pleased with herself that at least she didn't ask, "How much longer do you think I have to live?"

"Given the fact that you walked in here and we have choices to offer you, I'd say 80 percent" the doctor said.

"Wow, I didn't think you were going to give me such a high number," Carole said with a big smile. She also decided at that moment it would be the last time she'd ask that question. After all, how long she'd be on this earth was really up to God and herself...not some doctor.

"Well," the doctor said, "we're here to help you stay strong and maintain a good quality of life. So, when do you want to start your treatments?"

That visit gave Carole what she desperately needed...hope. They met Michele and Deka at the Padre Pio Centre, and that experience was just as hopeful. The four of them prayed in the chapel, visited the gift shop, and watched the video Michele had told them about. They waited for a gentleman to come to the gift shop with the relic, and the five of them prayed with Carole in a private little area. She held the glove next to her chest, lungs, and heart.

"I've got to get a miracle," Carole said.

"You will," Michele said. "You will, indeed."

That Sunday Michele, Deka, and the boys travelled to Great River, Long Island to see Carole and say good-bye to Linda before she travelled back to Scotland. Carole had befriended a priest named Monsignor Walsh and had invited him over to say a prayer with her family.

When she first met the priest, her first question to him was, "Why me?" and his reply was "Why not you?" They had long discussions about it, and he helped her make sense of it all.

"Boy, Carole, you seem to have a lot more energy than the last time we saw each other," he said to her.

"That's because my family is around me...I always feel better when I'm around my family," Carole said.

He led them in prayer and the ten of them, including the children, held hands in a circle and prayed with all their hearts for Carole's cancer to leave her body once and for all.

Carole had decided that she would start her treatments on Tuesday, March 25. On Easter Monday they travelled back over to Michele and Deka's house, stayed overnight and were up early again to go for her first session. It was the first time Bradley asked any questions about his Aunty's oxygen tank.

"It's okay, Bradley; I'm going to be fine," she said, and gave him a gentle hug.

She could see he was having a difficult time trying to understand how his aunt went from skiing, hiking, and running on the beach to an oxygen tank and losing a lot of weight. Carole was down to 110 pounds, and she was actually still trying to figure it out as well.

When they arrived at the hospital, the doctor went over what she'd be receiving. It would be four different types of chemo given to her all at the same time, with each dosage equally portioned. The doctor explained the risks associated with the combination of chemos and that the chances of it affecting her respiratory system were a thousand to one, which seemed like good odds.

WHERE THERE IS LIFE, THERE IS HOPE

Sean didn't realize what was happening, but could see from the sense of urgency on the part of the hospital staff that something serious was happening to one of the patients. A few minutes later he learned that Carole was the "one in a thousand," and the chemo had attacked her respiratory system. She was rushed to the ICU (Intensive Care Unit)…code blue. As soon as they were able to stabilize her, Sean was allowed to go into her room. She had a tube down her throat, and was coherent, but unable to speak.

She had a look on her face, which was saying, "what the heck happened?"

Sean explained to Carole what the doctors had told him: Since she had such an adverse reaction to the chemo, they'd have to take one day at a time to determine when she'd be able to go home.

Every day Sean spoke to Michele and Deka, giving them an update on Carole's condition, and they in turn would call Linda and Margaret and give them an update. Since it was supposed to have been an outpatient treatment, they had brought nothing with them to the hospital. Sean ran out to the nearest store and brought a few essentials until he was able to get home. One thing was for sure: He was not going to leave Carole alone for any length of time.

The tube in Carole's throat grew increasingly annoying and frustrating with each passing day because she was unable to communicate effectively. Sean tried everything…a white board, but Carole was having difficulty holding the pen. He wrote the alphabet across the top of the board and had Carole circle each letter, but that was taking too long for Carole's liking. He even tried reading her lips, but that wasn't working either, and Carole just rolled her eyes and shook her head.

"When are you getting out of there?" Michele asked Sean, as it had been over a week already.

"I don't know. She is swelling up with edema now."

"What's that?"

"Well, because of the adverse reaction Carole had to the chemo, she has what's called noncardiac pulmonary edema."

"You sound like a doctor. Can you give it to me in English, please?" Michele asked.

"Basically, the air sacs in Carole's lungs are filling up with fluid instead of air, which is stopping oxygen from being absorbed into her bloodstream. So each day she's getting more and more swollen. The doctors are trying to get it under control."

"Oh. Okay, do you want me or Deka to come on Friday to sleep over so you can get home?" Michele asked.

"Yes, I need to take care of a few things. I'll come back Saturday afternoon."

That Friday evening Michele stayed in the hospital with Carole. As she entered the room, Sean was massaging Carole's legs with lotion. Even though Sean had told Michele what to expect, she didn't think Carole would have been that swollen so quickly.

"Hi ya…how are you doing?" Michele asked putting a smile on her face and kissing Carole on the forehead.

She rolled her eyes and pointed at the tube going down her throat.

"That looks pretty uncomfortable," Michele said.

Carole opened her eyes very wide and said yes with a nod.

"Are you on a lot of pain medication?"

"Yes, she is," Sean said, "but I've been watching how much they are giving her, because she had so much in her the other day, her eyes were rolling to the back of her head."

Sean went over everything with Michele: what all the machines were doing for Carole, how often the nurses or doctors came in to check on her, and how to get help, if needed. There were only a half-dozen rooms in the ICU, and Sean seemed to know everyone already, and everyone knew Carole. After he had dinner, he said his good-byes to Carole and left for Long Island.

Michele tried to have a conversation with Carole, but Carole was getting frustrated that Michele wasn't able to understand her.

"Is it about you? Are you in pain?"

Carole shook her head: no.

"Is it Sean?"

Carole nodded her head: yes.

"He's gone home to get a few things. I'll be staying with you tonight, okay?"

Carole nodded.

"Would you like me to read to you?"

Carole shook her head: no.

"Okay…just rest and let me know if you need anything."

Carole lifted her swollen hand and examined it from front to back in disbelief.

"Don't worry," Michele said; "they will go back down again."

As it got later, Michele changed into sweatpants and made herself comfortable on the couch for a night's sleep. The nurses were in regularly to check on Carole's vital signs, and then at 2:05 in the morning Carole started to moan. Michele jumped up.

"Carole, are you okay?"

She was shaking her head with panic, trying to say "no, no" and was bringing her hand up to the tube in her throat.

"Carole, try not to touch that tube. I'll go get the nurse," Michele said.

Michele ran out and got the nurse and as they walked back into the room, Carole was pulling the tube out of her mouth.

"No, you can't do that," the nurse yelled, as she put the main lights on, and picked up the phone for assistance.

Before Michele knew it, an announcement was being made on the PA system, and she was being escorted into the waiting room a few doors down, as nurses and a doctor were running into Carole's room.

"This can't be happening," Michele said aloud to the pictures on the walls in the waiting area, as she paced back and forth.

Michele's grandfather had passed away at an early age when he was in the hospital because he had decided to rip out the tubes that were keeping him alive. All Michele kept on saying was, "Please, God…let her be all right. I can't be here alone, getting news I'm not able to handle. Please make this okay."

It felt like Michele was in that waiting area for a very long time, but finally the door opened and the doctor walked in. Michele put her hands up to her mouth in fear of what he might say to her. She was trying to read his face, but to no avail.

"I'm Dr. Foster. Are you Carole's relative?" he asked as he walked towards her with his hand extended.

To Michele it felt like he was walking and talking in slow motion.

"Yes, I'm her sister-in-law."

"She is a very lucky person. She is going to be okay, but she could have done a lot of damage by pulling out that tube."

"Whew, I was afraid you were going to tell me..." Michele stopped in mid-sentence.

"That could have happened. Like I said, she is a very lucky person," he said, as he held her hand.

"Thank you, Doctor. Can I go back in the room now?"

"Not yet. They are still cleaning her up and changing the sheets. The nurse will come and get you," he said and then left the waiting room.

When Michele was finally allowed back in the room, she saw that they had restrained Carole's hands, and she now had a tube inserted through her neck. The following morning, Carole didn't remember a thing. Michele explained to her what had happened and Carole kept on trying to ask her something.

"Is it about you? Are you in pain?" Michele asked.

No...she shook her head.

"Is it Sean?"

No, she said with her head again.

"The kids?"

"No," and this time pointed to Michele.

"Me?"

"Yes," she signed.

Carole mouthed, "Are you mad at me?"

"Am I mad at you? No...of course not, but if that sort of thing happens again, I'm surely going to have to color my hair weekly," she said trying to make light of it.

The days started to become weeks and before they knew it, Carole had been there for three weeks. By this time she was nearly 185 pounds of pure fluid. Her feet, legs, arms, fingers, and body were swollen beyond her normal identity. Sean was constantly trying to lessen the fluid build-up by elevating her legs with pillows and massaging them with lotion three times a day. He also managed to transform the room as much as he could from a cold hospital room to a room with warmth and some comforts of home. He had two of the portable hospital tables covered with family pictures, get-well cards, inspirational books, holy water, rosary beads, and religious prayer cards. When anyone walked into Carole's room, there was always soft music playing, which was usually Olivia Newton-John's healing CD, "Grace and Gratitude" or "Stronger Than Before." The music set the stage for what they were all looking for: inspiration, courage, and hope. It was as relaxed an environment as one could have with all the beeping machines Carole was hooked up to.

Every morning Sean said the Padre Pio Novena, the Hail Mary, and he'd do the rosaries with Carole, whether she was awake or not. He'd read *The Secret* to her, *The Power of Your Subconscious Mind*, and anything else that would give her hope. Throughout the day he would be on his laptop, updating family and friends on Carole's progress, or lack of it, and he continued to be Carole's rock, researching what the doctors would tell him so he'd feel comfortable with his level of knowledge on her prognosis.

"When do you think the children should come to see her?" Michele asked Sean.

"I thought she would have been home by now. Maybe we should see if we can get them here this weekend," he said.

"I think that's a good idea. I know we thought it would be too difficult for the children to see her in this condition, but after talking with Paula, who went through a similar situation with her own father, I'm of the mindset that it would benefit all of them. I'll ask my father if he'll go out and get them and bring them to Staten Island. Deka or I will meet them and bring them to our house before we travel down to Pennsylvania. We'll have to prepare the kids before they see her," Michele said.

That Friday afternoon, Deka drove down to the hospital, and Sean briefed him on everything before he left. About an hour after Sean left, the doctor came into the room and gave Deka an update on Carole, which wasn't very favorable. Deka was having a hard time seeing his baby sister in such a weak state, and the additional complications of a stomach infection made matters ten times worse.

"Michele, uh, the doctor just gave me an update," his quivering voice said, "and it's more bad news."

"Do you want me to leave work and come down there?"

"It's up to you. Sean left about an hour ago. I asked the doctor if he'd be around tomorrow afternoon to update Sean," he said.

Michele never heard her husband's voice sound so troubled, and she knew he needed her down there. It was raining cats and dogs outside, and as quickly as the windshield wipers were removing the rain, just as quickly were the tears running down Michele's cheeks as she held onto her steering wheel.

"*God, you cannot take her yet*...we need her here, her children need her, her husband needs her, and she has so much more to do...*please, God, don't take her from us*," she yelled at the top of her lungs in the empty car. She needed to find help from somewhere and got on the phone to the National Centre for Padre Pio.

"Please…is there any way someone could bring Padre Pio's glove down to a hospital to visit a patient?" she asked as she cried. Michele went into more detail of where Carole was and explained how they needed a miracle for her sister-in-law.

"What's her name?" the woman said.

"Carole, Carole McGarrigle."

"Oh, we received an intention to pray for her here at the center. It wouldn't be today, because it's Friday afternoon and the earliest would probably be the beginning of next week, but I can call you back once I get it confirmed."

"That would be great. What's your name?"

"Vera."

"Vera! The same little girl who visited Padre Pio in Italy and received a miracle?" she said with a very excited and hopeful voice.

"Yes, that's me."

"Oh my God, we need what you received. Please help us get that miracle."

"I'll pray for Carole and I'll call you back with a confirmation date and time on when we can get the glove down to the hospital."

"Thank you very much."

By the time Michele got to the hospital, she had talked to her parents, who were able to calm her down. Deka chatted with Julie, Carole's friend from the UK who was over visiting.

"Oh, you decided to come down," Deka said.

"Yes. How is she doing?"

"I've been reading *The Power of the Subconscious Mind* to her, hoping it's sinking in. You remember Julie - she used to work with Carole and then left to go work at Direct Line."

Michele had worked for Direct Line when they lived in England.

"Yes, of course. How are you?"

"I'm well, thank you. Now we just have to get Carole well."

"You said it...Deka, guess who I spoke to on the drive down? Vera, from the National Centre for Padre Pio!"

"Really, how did that happen?"

"I was so upset after I got off the phone with you, I called the center while I was driving, to ask if they could bring the glove down to Carole, and she answered the phone. I basically asked her if we could have the same sort of miracle she received. She is calling me back to tell me when they'd be able to get here."

"That's great."

"I know...isn't that a great sign, that I spoke to Vera!"

The following day Deka prepped Kristy and Joseph on the drive from Staten Island to New Jersey, and Michele did the same as she drove them down to Philly, explaining how their mother was going to look.

"Remember, she'll look different then the last time you saw her. She's very swollen, but the doctor's are working on getting the swelling down...and she also has a tube inserted in her neck to help her breathe, but it will be okay." Michele didn't mention the bag that hung on the side of the bed draining all the infected yellow fluid out of her body, nor the machines that surrounded her. She was starting to wonder if she was trying to comfort herself or the kids.

"Okay, Aunty Michele," they both said.

"All right, then, let's go up and see your Mum."

But nothing Michele said was able to prepare them for the shock they were about to see. They both stood at the end of her bed, just staring at her while she slept.

"Hi, Mummy," they eventually said with gentle voices.

Carole eyes opened wide with joy and mouthed "Hello" and gave them a big smile. Before too long they were sitting on her bed alongside their mother, updating her on anything and everything.

On the trip back to the house, Michele asked them if they were all right.

Joseph said, "Yep, that was my Mum…a little puffier than normal, but that was her."

"You're right, Joseph," Michele said in amazement at his ability to cope with the situation, "That's your Mum."

The kids were giggling and laughing on the trip back to New Jersey, saying hello to people in the cars that drove by, seeing if they'd say hello back.

Michele and Deka had been taking turns sleeping at the hospital on the weekends to give Sean a break. That particular weekend Deka stayed at the hospital on Saturday night as well, and Sean went back to stay at their house. During the middle of the night Michele had gotten up to take care of Cameron, who still was not sleeping through the night, and was hit with an idea…why don't we do a prayer chain, but not your typical prayer chain?

Sunday morning Michele shared her idea with Sean and suggested tying the prayer together with Padre Pio's glove being brought down to the hospital.

"What do you think about doing a prayer for Carole, but instead of a typical prayer chain, everyone will say the same prayer, at the same time, on the same day, for maximum prayer power!" Michele said.

"Sounds good to me," Sean said.

"I'll draft the email when we get down to the hospital today," Michele said.

After they had breakfast and went to church, they travelled back down to Philly and as soon as Michele got there she started writing the email.

It read…

From: Deka and Michele Rodger

Subject: WE NEED YOUR HELP – Time Sensitive

On Tuesday, April 8, at exactly 7:00 pm Eastern Time (USA) Deka's sister, Carole McGarrigle, will be blessed with Padre Pio's glove, which is a religious relic and has been known to help heal the sick and bring about miracles.

Here's where you come in. We'd like to have everyone say the same exact prayer at the exact same time, which means hundreds of us will be sending the same positive message out at the same time. The prayer is short and sweet:

Dear God,

Through the intersession of Padre Pio, Jesus, and the Blessed Mother, we ask that you bless Carole McGarrigle and cure her of her illness and sickness.
Amen.

Please say it with complete passion, conviction, and from your heart, and you will have played a part in creating a miracle. Also please send this onto everyone in your email address book and ask them to do the same. Lastly, please put in your subject line how you know Carole so people understand it's important to you.

The power of prayer and positive thinking will give a miracle to this 41-year-old wife and mother of two (10 and 13 years old). If you are with your family and have children, please include them, as they are powerful conduits to God.

*This **WILL** work and we will be in touch to let you know Carole's progress in her journey back to good health!*
*Thank you and **expect a miracle...***

Love,
Michele and Deka Rodger

P.S. Here is the link for the National Centre for Padio Pio <u>*www.padrepio.org*</u>

"That sounds good. I'll just tweak it a little and send it out from me to my whole email address book," Sean said.

"We'll need to get a copy over to Linda and everyone over in the UK as well," Michele said.

Michele got a confirmation call on Monday, telling her that a volunteer from the National Centre for Padre Pio would be there at 7:00 pm. Michele explained the importance of their being there on time, as they were trying to synchronize saying the prayer with hundreds of others while Carole held the glove. She was assured the person would be there.

People from all over the United States and the United Kingdom were ready to pray on Tuesday evening. Michele sent it out to her address book and told people at work throughout the day: Deb Stout, who was praying daily, also told her friends and family, Eric Radell did the same and asked his sister to have her prayer group pray, and Alan Cohen got on the phone and called his Rabbi to have him pray for her. Linda handed it out at work to all her friends, and Sean emailed it to everyone he knew at work plus his personal address book. They started to get word that their friends and family were sending it out to their friends and co-workers. Michael, Paula, and Howard drove to Philly from Long Island for the prayer, and Rose coordinated her prayer group to say the prayer as well. Twelve people around Carole's bed waited for the woman to arrive with the glove.

"Where is she? It's 6:50," Deka asked Michele.

"I don't know, but she told me she'd be here," she said.

With that, Michele's cell phone rang.

"Hello."

"I think I'm lost," the lady said on the phone. "Oh, is it a big brown building?"

"Yes, it is."

"Okay, I see it. I'll be up there in five minutes," she said.

At 6:57 she entered the room.

"Hi, I'm Carol, from the National Centre for Padre Pio," she said.

"Hi Carol. I'm Michele. Perfect timing...can we have the glove, please?"

Michele quickly explained what was about to happen, handed out copies of the prayer to everyone, and started the prayer off. It was a very special and spiritual moment. Padre Pio's glove was on Carole's chest and everyone in the room put one hand on Carole and prayed with their hearts:

Dear God,

Through the intersession of Padre Pio, Jesus and the Blessed Mother, we ask that you bless Carole McGarrigle and cure her of her illness and sickness.
Amen.

Sean had been telling Carole throughout the day what was happening that evening, and it all went off without a hitch. So many beautiful stories and good omens were shared with Michele, Sean, and Linda for days to come about the experience they had. Michele's friend George shared that he was out to dinner with his two children, wife, and in-laws, and at 7:00 pm sharp they stopped what they were doing, held hands, and said the prayer in the restaurant. Her college friend Anna was on her way home with her son from soccer practice, and pulled the car over to the side of the road to pray together exactly at 7:00 pm. Sean's relative in California who was a nurse was in the elevator with three priests right before the prayer was to be said, and they joined in. Carol, the volunteer from the National Centre for Padre Pio, was herself a cancer survivor. They calculated that nearly 1,000 people were all praying for Carole at the same time that evening.

The next day the doctor came in to examine Carole and said to Sean, "I can't explain it, but she is the strongest and healthiest sick person I've ever met."

When Sean told Michele what the doctor had said, she let out a big cheer: "YEESSSSS…that is awesome news. Tell the doctor we can explain it: It's called the power of prayer!"

Carole was looking better. Her edema was slowly going away, she was more coherent and able to sit up in bed, and was now able to suck on ice chips. Her friend Caroline arrived the following week from the UK, and she ended up staying with Sean in the hospital the week she was in town. Towards the end of her stay, she decided to stay for one more week, which would be Carole's fourth week in the hospital. Caroline had a quick break at Michele and Deka's house over the weekend and was back for the second week.

"The doctor told me this morning that the infection in Carole's stomach isn't draining as quickly as her first infection did, and they'll have to operate to clear it out," Sean said to Michele as she entered Carole's room.

"Is she strong enough for an operation?"

"They won't operate unless her numbers are better, but they want my consent and I'll need to ask Carole what she wants to do...if she wants the operation."

"Why are you asking Carole if she wants the operation? She's not in any state to make that decision," Michele said.

"I promised her that I'd always tell her what was happening. The doctor's biggest concern is kidney failure, but again, they won't do it unless her numbers are better," he said.

"I understand that, Sean, but how would this bit of information help her state of mind? It's not as if she'd be able to articulate her wishes or make suggestions ...she can't talk," she said.

"I've asked the nurse to slow down her meds so I can speak to her and she won't be so out of it."

Carole's medicines needed constant adjusting, depending on how she was reacting to them and if she was in pain, which meant sometimes she was a zombie and other times she understood everything.

With that, he walked over to Carole's bedside and started to talk softly to her about what was happening. Michele couldn't take it and walked out of the room.

Sean met Michele in the hall, and they walked down to get something to eat in the dining room. A nurse in the other unit stopped them and asked Sean how Carole was doing. Everyone on the entire floor knew Carole and was rooting for her.

"She's in the middle of a setback at the moment," Sean said, "and my brother-in-law doesn't agree that I should be telling Carole the truth about it."

"Oh," the nurse said; "it's important to be truthful with the patient."

"It's not only his brother-in-law who doesn't agree; I don't agree either," Michele said. "It's one thing to be truthful to the patient when she is lucid and fully understands what is happening to her, and can articulate her wishes, but when she is so drugged up that she can't possibly grasp what's going on, how can that benefit her? It's not as if she's sitting in a doctor's office, and Sean's being told something by the doctor and is not sharing it with her. In my opinion, why put that into her mind if she can't possibly do anything about it? In other words, what she doesn't know can't mentally hurt her. And when telling her hurts her mental health, which is really all she's able to control right now... well, we'll have to agree to disagree on this one," she added, as she wondered why he felt the need to say what he'd said to the nurse in the first place.

The nurse realized that perhaps she was getting in the middle of something she really didn't want to be part of and tried to become impartial. They said their good-byes and continued on their way down to the dining room.

"That was the Head Nurse of the floor," Sean said to Michele, making conversation.

"Oh, was it..." Michele said. She knew tensions were high with everyone, so she didn't bother asking him why he said what he'd said to the nurse. "Is Dominick working tonight?" she asked.

Dominick was one of their favorite nurses. He reminded Michele of a monk, in his brown scrubs, and she always felt Carole was in extra good hands when he was on duty.

"Yes, he's on tonight. Did I tell you I tried Reiki on Carole today, with Dana on the phone coaching me through it, and I felt the heat of the energy," Sean said.

"No, you didn't tell me, but I do remember Carole saying Dana came over to your house a few times to give her some sessions. What do you mean, you felt the heat?"

"It's supposed to help relax the body and promote healing. I looked it up on the Internet. In Japanese, Reiki translates to mean 'Universal Life Force Energy.' Dana told me I had to lay my hands on energy centers to boost Carole's Life Force Energy. It helps the body to naturally heal itself by balancing and realigning energy at the deepest level of the body. I actually felt the heat of the energy," he said.

"Wow. That's pretty deep, isn't it?" she said.

"Yeh...it also helps reduce stress and anxiety, but more importantly, it helps restore balance and equilibrium in the body and stimulates the immune system. Everything that Carole needs."

"You sound like a commercial for Reiki sessions...," Michele said with a giggle.

"I have a lot of time on my hands during the day, and I have to keep busy for my own sanity," he replied.

"You're a rock, Sean, and you're doing a great job, even though we might not agree all the time. I'm sure the Reiki will help Carole.

Mind you, she's looking a little yellow. Is there something wrong with her kidneys now?"

"Well, the doctors were saying that the kidneys are the cleaners in the body. They're supposed to clean the waste material from our blood, and Carole's kidneys aren't functioning properly at the moment, but they seem to think they can get that under control," Sean said.

"We so need a miracle," Michele said.

"We get little ones every day," Sean said.

"You are absolutely right."

The day before Caroline was to leave to go back home, Linda and Carole's mum arrived. Linda stayed in the hospital with Sean, and her mum went to their house on Long Island to take care of Kristy and Joseph. The kids had begun complaining that they didn't like being home with Sean's mother alone.

Carole remained on an emotional rollercoaster for the two and a half weeks Linda was in town. She had good days and bad days, and Linda quickly learned when Carole was feeling good. She'd watch Oprah at 4:00 pm, and everyone knew not to talk until the commercials.

A few days later the doctor consulted with Sean on Carole's operation.

"We don't have a choice…her numbers aren't where they need to be for an operation. She will have a hard time recovering from this infection," the doctor said to Sean while Michele and Dominick, the nurse, were in the room.

"Well, it's in God's hands…where it's always been," Michele said and saw Dominick nod his head in agreement, as if to say, "You got that right, girlfriend!"

"Look at it this way," Michele said to Sean once the doctor had left the room. "You didn't have to make the decision...it was made for you, which I think is a blessing in disguise."

"Yes, I suppose so," he said. Deep down Sean was relieved. For days he had been wrestling with what to decide if he was told her numbers were good enough to undergo an operation, and now he was able to release that from his mind.

That weekend was a special one, as they were celebrating Joseph's eleventh birthday. They brought a cake and presents up to Carole's room, and she enjoyed being part of the celebration and singing "Happy Birthday" to her son. Michael and Paula got to the hospital late Saturday afternoon - they were doing the night shift that weekend. Sean prepped them, as he did with anyone who stayed overnight.

By the time Linda was due to return to Scotland, Carole had been in the ICU for six and a half weeks. Christine, their other sister, was due to fly in on Thursday, and Linda would be flying out the following day.

"You know, I'm not very good at good-byes, Carole, so I'll just say, I'll see you in a few months, okay?" Linda said.

Carole nodded her head and could feel tears welling up in her eyes.

"Keep strong...I love you," Linda said, fighting back her tears.

"I love you too," Carole mouthed.

Margaret did not go home with Linda and continued to take care of the children. Every weekend it was the same routine: Howard drove 40 minutes east to pick up the kids and Margaret in Great River and drove them for one and a half hours, to the Bradley Avenue exit, off the Staten Island Expressway. Michele or Deka would meet Howard at the Starbucks parking lot and drive the children to New Jersey, which took another 45 minutes, and after lunch, they drove for 1 hour 15 minutes to Philly to see Carole. Kristy didn't look forward to that drive every week, but wanted to see her Mum. Joseph just went with the flow and loved seeing his cousins every weekend. Bradley and Cameron's favorite part was having them sleep over every weekend…it was like an ongoing slumber party to them. When Michele heard them playing in the basement, it was as if they didn't have a care in the world, and she so wished that were the case.

Carole's system was slowly closing down and, if her blood pressure didn't start improving, her whole body would eventually shut down. During the time Christine stayed with Sean in the hospital, Carole's vital signs improved a bit, and she seemed eager to sit up in her bed. Christine left on May 16, but before she went, they celebrated Carole's birthday. Carole would turn 42 on May 20. Deka drove down that day to be with his sister and then drove his mum to the airport the following day for her to return home. It had been a month since she had been home, and she felt confident Carole was going to receive her miracle.

Carole had now been in Intensive Care for nine and a half weeks, and all the additional support that had come for extended periods had gone home, which meant Sean was now at the hospital alone during the week. Michele and Deka were on call to drive down at a moment's notice. The days seemed longer for Sean, and the light at the end of the tunnel was getting dimmer by the day. Carole's kidneys were failing, and the doctor said that her unusually low blood pressure and longer pauses in her breathing rhythm normally would last for three days before the body started to shut down. Sean did not leave Carole's bedside. Deka took Kristy and Joseph to see their mother on Saturday and, as always, they kissed their mother good night and said, see you in the morning. That night Sean prayed and kept telling her, "Come on Carole - you have to fight."

THE DREADED PHONE CALL

Sunday, June 1, was a lovely, sunny morning. The children were already downstairs playing in the family room, and Michele was cooking breakfast before they ran out to church and then to the hospital. The phone rang at 9:00 am and Michele answered.

"Hello," she said, as she walked into the pool room to get away from the noise the children were making. Deka followed her and closed the French doors.

"She's gone…," Sean said through his tears.

"*What?*" said Michele in disbelief.

"She's gone…," he repeated.

"When?" she sobbed.

"Ten minutes ago."

Michele looked at Deka. He knew what she was about to say, and he grabbed his head and pulled it down to his bent knees.

"**NNNNOOOOO,**" he bellowed.

"Oh, my God, Sean…one of us will come down to be with you, and Deka will call Linda and Margaret now. Sean, I can't tell those kids…I just can't," she cried.

"Okay, I'll tell them when I get to your house," he said.

"All right, one of us will be down as soon as possible,"

Michele and Deka went downstairs to call his sister and mother and, from where she was standing, Michele could hear Linda scream as Deka gave her the news. As sick as Carole had been, nobody entertained the thought that she'd be taken from them...it just was not supposed to be in the cards.

Two hours later Deka met Sean in Carole's room. No words were necessary. They just hugged and wept together.

"I stood by her side and prayed with her all night, and I kept asking her to fight because I could tell by reading the machines that her system was starting to slowly shut down, so I was whispering in her ear 'Come on, Carole...you have to fight'," Sean told Deka. "I told her I had to sit down and when I did, I just collapsed on the couch and woke up to alarms going off...she actually passed at 3:00 in the morning, but there was no reason to call you that early. She was a fighter...," he said through his tears.

"Yes, she was...she just couldn't fight anymore. She had too much going against her. She's at peace now," Deka said choking on his words.

"Yes, she is," Sean said.

They sat for some time, trying to take it all in, shaking their heads in disbelief, and hoping they would wake up from their nightmare.

"What needs to be done now?" Deka finally asked.

"I've already started to make some phone calls. I'd like to get Carole back to Long Island today."

"You'll need to rethink that plan. We'll need to get back to the house, because the kids need to be told. Michele emailed us some info she found on the Internet on how to tell children. It's basically saying not to tell them that she 'died' or that she is 'dead'," Deka said.

"Right, okay…we'll do that now and get Carole back to Long Island tomorrow."

Michele took the kids to the park for a picnic to avoid any phone calls prior to the children getting the news from Sean. She just wanted them to be happy for as long as possible before their lives would change forever. Kristy asked a few times when they were going to the hospital.

"Uncle Deka is going to the hospital first, and once we get a call from him, we'll know what the plan will be for the day," Michele said.

She watched them play and was getting sick to her stomach, knowing what was to come. As soon as Michele got the call from Deka that they were on their way back to the house, she told the children they'd be leaving the park in half an hour, and Uncle Deka and Sean would be at the house.

They all arrived back at the house at the same time. Michele gave Sean a hug and started to cry. He met Kristy and Joseph in the foyer, and before anyone knew it, he said to them:

"Your Mum…your Mum is dead," he said as he began to sob.

"**What!** *NO, NO*," Kristy wept, covering her mouth with her hands.

Joseph was in shock, and Sean hugged both of them as the three of them cried.

"Sean, thank you for taking such good care of my Mum…she would not have been with us for so long as she was if it weren't for you," Kristy said minutes later.

Sean kissed the top of her head and hugged her.

"Why don't we go sit down in the family room?" Michele said.

Sean walked into the other room, and Joseph looked up at Michele with his big blue eyes and said, "Aunty Michele...Sean just said, 'Your Mum is *dead*.' "

"Yes, I know, but what he really meant to say is that your Mum passed away," she said and gave him a big hug.

They followed Sean into the family room, and Michele hugged them both on the couch. Sean explained to the children what would be happening over the next few days and the preparation that would be required. He thought it would be a good idea to keep their minds busy by getting them involved with the planning. For the next few hours they went through Michele and Deka's photo albums, selecting the best pictures of their mum to create a photo collage.

"Can we stay with you, Sean?" Kristy finally asked.

"I will do whatever you want...there will always be a place for you and Joseph with me," Sean said.

After dinner, Sean, Michele, and Deka sat in the back yard, under the stars.

"What are you going to do about the children?" Michele asked.

Sean looked up at the hundreds of stars in the sky, shook his head, and put his hands behind his head, "I don't know...I just don't know."

"You can't lose them...you have raised them for the last five years. They are your family."

Sean shrugged his shoulders, not knowing what to say.

THE DAYS THAT FOLLOWED

"I'm going to ask my sister to help me pick out the casket. Carole wanted to be cremated so we'll need to arrange that as well…and I'll have Kristy and my Mum pick out something for her to wear," Sean said to Michele and Deka.

Michele couldn't believe her ears: "He is having his sister help him!" she thought. "The person who wouldn't even go over to the house to see how Carole was feeling when she was still at home, the person who never visited her in the hospital the whole time she was there, should not be part of such an important decision that only a true loved one should be part of. Not to mention his mother, who clearly had had issues with Carole!"

"He's got to be kidding!" she said to Deka once they got upstairs. "Carole has got to be saying, 'Are you crazy? I don't want *them* making those decisions on my behalf.' I don't understand why Sean wouldn't have asked us to get involved. We're Carole's immediate family and have always been there for her."

That night everyone had slept very restlessly; Michele could not get Sean's plans out of her head.

"I have to say something to him," Michele said to Deka the following morning.

"Okay, then…let's talk in the sun room, away from the kids."

"Sean…can we have a word?" Michele asked as she walked into the room. She didn't want to upset him, but certainly didn't want Sean's sister or mother to be the only people involved in helping with the arrangements.

"Sean…I'm really sorry, but I couldn't help but think about this all night, and I don't think your sister should be part of picking out Carole's casket…I mean….she didn't even like Carole and, in turn, Carole didn't like her. And I'd like to pick something out for Carole with Kristy," she said, as she started to cry.

"They had their differences, but they worked them out. Look, I only want what's best for Carole," he said.

"We do, as well. I'd like to go with you to pick out the casket," Deka said.

"That's fine…like I said, I only have Carole's best interest at heart," Sean said.

"We know that, Sean…we all do," Deka said.

A few minutes later Sean said, "Can I ask my sister to come for support for me?"

"Of course you can - we just want to be part of organizing it as well," Michele said, thinking to herself that this was an odd question to ask.

There was a lot of preparing to be done. Sean and Deka ended up going alone to pick out the casket and make arrangements at the funeral parlor, as Sean's sister couldn't make it the day they eventually went. Sean and Deka did all the major planning together, and they were there for each other through this trying time. Although Michele and Kristy did pick out an outfit for Carole, another one was needed because they weren't able to find a dress with long sleeves and a high neck. Sean and Deka went to the shop that the funeral parlor director recommended, and they found the perfect dress, in Carole's favorite color. This was by far one of the hardest things they had to do.

"What was the name of the prayer you thought would be good for Carole's mass card…I can't find the one you gave me," Deka asked Michele, as he called her from the funeral parlor.

"I don't know the name of it, but it starts with 'Do not stand at my grave and weep…'."

"Okay, the man knows that saying, and we're going to put Padre Pio on the front."

"Oh, that will be nice. I'll meet you back at the house, I have to go and get some clothes for Joseph, and I'll take Kristy to the mall tonight."

Even though it was clear as day that Carole had passed, it was all so surreal…like a nightmare that they couldn't wake themselves up from. Until the moment they had been told she'd passed, her family still believed that somehow, some way, she'd get the miracle they were all praying for, and she'd eventually walk out of the hospital, but the reality was God had other plans for her.

Sean and the kids put together eight photo boards of Carole, which were displayed on easels all around the room at the funeral parlor. Between the photo boards were dozens of floral arrangements that were arriving at a steady pace. Things that were dear to Carole were displayed in the parlor. Her climbing gear was there, as well as her gardening clothes. Deka did a digital photo display of pictures that they played at the funeral parlor as well, and Michele got all the kids' clothing ready for the next three days. Linda and her mum flew back over from the UK and were at Carole's house on June 3 just in time for the first day of the wake.

Hundreds of people came to pay their final respects. Kristy and Joseph's friends, teachers, and principals were there. Sean's work colleagues and bosses were there and, of course, Carole's family, friends, coworkers, and neighbors. Having being in the States for only five years, she had managed to touch hundreds of lives.

The children wrote letters to their mum, and on the last day put them in the coffin. Bradley and Cameron seemed quite comfortable running up to their Aunty Carole to see if she was all right, and then going back to whatever they had been doing. Like most wakes, the crowds of people helped distract the loved ones from going too deep into their sorrow, and Sean, Kristy, and Joseph seemed to be doing remarkably well.

"It seems like Deka and Linda volunteered you to say a prayer at the church," Sean said to Michele.

"That's fine. I just hope I get through it," Michele said.

"You'll be fine...I'll be saying one too," he added.

Sean had arranged for Monsignor Walsh to say her mass, and Carole would have a full police escort from the funeral parlor to the church.

The police car sped past the funeral precession and stopped the traffic up ahead, to allow the cars to continue without stopping. Four police cars rotated the procession through the neighborhoods until they reached the church, but not before they drove Carole past her house for one last time and left a red rose on her doorstep.

"Carole would have liked this sendoff," Linda said.

"Yes, it's quite the proper sendoff, isn't it?" their mother added.

They were greeted at the church with the pipe-and-drum band of the Suffolk County Police, who had volunteered their services. They stood proudly in their kilts in a circular formation, playing "Amazing Grace" outside the church.

"Wow, that's pretty touching," Deka said, as a tear ran down his cheek. He certainly was not the only one shedding a tear, as it hit everyone to their core.

"I asked them to play for Carole. They sound good, don't they? That's the band I'm in when I do parades and competitions," Sean said.

"Yes…they sound excellent," Deka said.

The last day was a difficult one, but by the time they got to the restaurant to have their last meal in honor of Carole, they were all pleased that she had a perfect sendoff - anyone who witnessed it from afar would have thought it was a dignitary who had passed.

The following day, Sean, Michele, and Deka spoke about Kristy and Joseph, and where they would live.

"We'll move out here and help you raise them," Deka said.

"Yes…you won't have to do it alone," Michele said.

"Well, there is a really nice area on the water about ten minutes from here. Do you want to take a ride over?" Sean asked.

"Yes, let's go have a look…just to get an idea," Deka said.

"Did I tell you that Dick stopped the kid's money from going into Carole's account two days after she passed? He sent me an email saying that a dead lady can't sign checks," Sean said.

"Please tell me you are kidding," Michele said.

"I wish I was…" Sean said.

"He is a pathetic asshole and a sad excuse of a human being," Deka said.

"Unbelievable…no wonder why Carole didn't want the kids to be with him," Michele said.

A Proper Scottish Sendoff

Prior to leaving the States to attend her mother's memorial service in Scotland, Kristy made it very clear to her father that she didn't want to live in England and had asked him how he could take care of them when he hadn't been able to take care of them in the past.

"Are you nervous at seeing your father?" Michele asked her one day when they were walking on the beach.

"No...why would I be?" she replied, as if it were a silly question.

"I don't know...maybe he'll be upset with you that you've been so honest about your feelings."

"I'll be fine, Aunty Michele," she said.

Sean organized a memorial service, to be held at Houtoun House Hotel, where he and Carole had had their wedding celebration. All Carole's friends and family who weren't able to travel over to the States were now able to pay their respects...in true Scottish style.

The children travelled over to Scotland with Sean, and Kristy prepared something to say about her mother. Deka attended, but Michele and the boys stayed home. Mick and Sue travelled up, as did Jacqui, Fay, and Daryl…three of the Four Usuals, along with nearly 65 other friends and family.

Dick had been telling the children that he was going to attend. At the last minute he didn't, although his brother and parents attended.

There were eight speeches, wine, and great stories about Carole being shared throughout the room. Deka started it off: "Where does one start?" he said to Carole's friends and family. "As her big brother, there was our childhood; she lived with me as an adult in London we shared birthdays, Christmas's; we went on holidays together and New Year's celebrations…there were many. When Carole moved to the States, we were able to spend much more time together, although not always during the best of times. Nevertheless, I'm very blessed to have had the last five years with her, and I know that now. So what memory does her big brother leave you with? You all knew Carole, and you knew that she was a very kind, loving person who was fun to be around. I don't need to tell you that and, if Carole thought you were a bit off with her, she had a very pleasant way of letting you know, which in itself was an art. I'd like to share a little story with you…Cameron, my 2-year-old, has the same flaming red hair as Carole. Although I'm not saying that when I look at him, he reminds me of Carole, because as his father I'm changing his diaper on a regular basis, but he can sit down with his cars and he will line them up perfectly beside each other, or directly behind one another, and he will spend a lot of time analyzing each car, making sure it's absolutely perfect and in place. Now who does that remind you of? When we told Cameron last weekend that his cousins were coming over for a visit, he asked if his Aunty Carole was coming. Michele explained that she was up in heaven, but would always be with us. He in turn asked, 'Why did she leave me?' This is a two-year-old! This was a typical characteristic of Carole, that by just being herself, she had an astounding effect on people, so today that's the memory I share with you: Carole's innate ability to touch people in a way that we will never forget...and that's why most of you are here today. Thank you."

Christine read Carole's favorite poem, *Footprints*. Kristy said a few words about her mum and, before Sean finished off the speeches, he invited Julie up, followed by Jacqui, Fay, and Daryl, who recited a poem that Daryl had written about their special friendship. Jacqui cleared her voice and started them off...

THE FOUR USUALS
"This is Carole Rodger"
Announced Julia from Personnel
"She'll be joining you from today –
So I hope you'll look after her well!"

"A fourth person in our office
How would this work out?"
"Please don't corrupt her," thought Julia
And sashayed off with a pout

Carole Rodger stood there looking lovely
So poised and well groomed and all that
From top to toe everything matching
If she could she'd have worn a hat!

Pretty she was as a picture
With a mane of luscious, red hair
She spoke in a soft lilting Scottish
And we all fell in love with her there

So we christened ourselves the Four Usuals
Four so different, yet one of a kind
Jak, Raz & Faz, and Wee Cazzie
From that day on our lives were entwined.

We developed our own way of talking
There were "Usual" phrases galore
Our days were spent making mischief
And our plans for the evening our focus

Reliving the night's antics next morning
There'd be howls of laughter all round
Dave and Rave would drop in for coffee
Soon our office was dubbed "The Playground"

Caz was summoned one morning by Julia
Pouting a lipstick particularly red
"You are destined for greater things, Carole"
"You're partner material" she said

So Caz cleared her desk and belongings
Picked up her bag, scarf and gloves
She turned as she walked through the Playground
And said "See you for lunch – OK, luvs!"

So we tearfully bade her goodbye
And drank Cointreau the rest of the day
We knew our friendship ran deeper
Than Julia moving her away

We learned everything about one another
All our thoughts and our lives lay bare
Through the good times and hangovers
For each other we were always there

Then one by one we took off on life's journeys
To whatever our futures might hold
There were weddings and children and good times
Relocations and exploring the World

Our reunions were magical times
We created one hell of a din
Reminiscing and laughing 'til crying
Our jokes just never wore thin

Our time spent together was precious
Always something new to amuse
A weekend of restaurants and shopping
Caz nearly always bought shoes

Then trials and dark times came knocking
And nothing could prepare us for the day
When our courageous, beautiful and treasured
Wee Sweet Cazzie was taken away

We can't say, Caz, how much we miss you
Our hearts will never completely mend
So many wonderful memories of you
Our funny, compassionate, true friend

But we know you haven't gone far, Caz
You're here now with your Raz, Faz, and Jak
And we're all so very proud of you
And we love you to the Moon and back

So now when we have our reunions
Though in body, Caz, you're here no more
Your spirit will always be with us
And we'll still book a table for Four"

As they all recited the last verse of the poem in unison.

Carole was finally back home amongst her own kin. The following day, her ashes were scattered on the Cuillin Ridge, on the Isle of Skye – where she had always felt at peace. She was indeed home at last.

Kristy and Joseph spent a week with their father before they were to return to the States with Sean.

"When are you bringing the kids back here before they travel back home?" Linda asked Dick.

"I'm not…they are not going back to the States. They want to stay here," Dick said.

Linda couldn't believe what he was telling her.

"That's funny, because only last week they wanted to be in America," Linda told him. "Can I speak to the children?"

"No...nobody is speaking to the children until I get them home and settled," Dick said. "They aren't with me," he said, and hung up the phone.

Linda tried to reach Sean, but he was up in the mountains. She then called Dick's parents to get his brother's phone number, so she'd be able to speak to the children. They told her they didn't have his number. "You don't have your son's phone number?" she said to herself.

It was Labor Day weekend in the States, and Linda called Michele and Deka to give them the news.

"Dick is now saying they want to stay with him in England," Linda said.

"What! That can't be true! All along, they've said they wanted to come back to the States. Have you talked to the children? Did you hear it from them?" Michele asked.

"No...Dick won't let me talk to them, and I've been trying to get in touch with Sean, but he's not answering his cell. He must still be up in the mountains."

"Oh, my God. How could Dick do this to them? Haven't they gone through enough? Let them live where they want to live!" Michele said.

"I'll call you as soon as I get in touch with Sean."

"Okay, they have to get back here. School starts on Wednesday. This is like something out of a movie," Michele said in disbelief.

When Linda was finally able to reach Sean, he didn't seem too surprised by the news. He tried to contact the children via Dick and was able to speak to Kristy.

"There is too much pressure on me," Kristy said.

"Who is putting pressure on you? I'm not putting any pressure on you," Sean said.

"No, from this side," she said, and the phone was taken away from her. He could hear her crying in the background.

Sean quickly got in touch with a solicitor, who put him in contact with another lawyer down in London.

"I'll be driving down to London to get counsel from this solicitor and get the paperwork started to get a judge involved," he told Linda.

"I'll go with you, if you want," she said.

As they drove down to London, they got a text message from Dick, telling them to meet him in the car park of the Cumbria Police station, where they'd be able to see the children and speak to them. ·

"If I feel like the children are being held against their will, we will continue to drive down to London and get the process started to get them back," he told Linda.

Dick was there with his wife, his brother, and the children.

Sean and Linda met Dick and his brother midway between the two cars.

"I'd like the children to speak to Linda," Sean said.

"No, not on her own...my wife will be with the children as well," Dick said.

Every time Linda asked them a question, his wife answered for the children.

Sean said, "I want a word with them by myself," and walked away with them.

"Is this what you want?" Sean asked Kristy.

"It's what we want right now," she said.

Dick was pacing and saying, "We need to get them away from Sean...now, now, we have **got** to get them away from him," Linda heard him say to his brother."Give them a chance to say their good-byes," his brother said, looking very disturbed by the whole ordeal.

Linda walked over and hugged Kristy goodbye and said to her, "Are you sure about this?"

"Well, ya…for right now."

"Kristy, you don't have a choice. You can't change your mind next week,"

Kristy looked surprised by what her aunt was saying, and with that Dick called for her. She hugged her Aunty Lindy and walked away towards her father.

A YEAR LATER JUNE 1, 2009 - LIVERPOOL, ENGLAND

Kristy and Joseph's father gave them a choice to go to school or stay home by themselves. They decided to stay home on the first anniversary of their mother's passing. Dick went to work, and his wife and their adopted son were out of the house for the day. Joseph ran outside into the garden and cut a white rose, and they walked down to the beach, a place they knew their mother had loved. The tide was going out, and the sand was wet, except for a little spot that was big enough for them to set up their small memorial area.

"Let's put the rose in the sand over here," said Joseph.

They knelt down and made a perfect area for their mother. Kristy drew a heart in the sand and wrote, "We Love You," and Joseph placed the rose inside the heart.

"I think Mum would like this," Joseph said.

Kristy agreed with a nod of her head and took her Mum's mass card out of her pocket and started to read it aloud.

"Do not stand at my grave and weep:
I am not there, I do not sleep.
I am a thousand winds that blow:

I am the diamond glints on snow.
I am the sunlight on ripened grain:
I am the gentle autumn's rain.
When you awaken in the morning's hush,
I am the swift uplifting rush of quiet birds in circled flight.
I am the soft star that shines at night.
Do not stand at my grave and cry. I am not there: I did not die," said Carole.

The children sat in silence for a few minutes in deep thought.

"Do you want to take a walk on the beach?" Joseph asked.

They rolled up their pants and walked along the beach, holding hands, comforting each other. As they did, they felt a warm, loving, familiar touch that only their mother could give them. They looked at their hands and smiled at each other, knowing their mother would always be with them -- she did not die.

The End

MESSAGE FROM THE AUTHOR

What is the moral of the story? There are many, but the one I will leave you with is this: Be inspired to live life to its fullest. Know you can achieve goals, which you thought were impossible. Whatever the goals are, stick with them until they are achieved. It might be climbing mountains; flying planes; getting an academic degree; searching for true love until you find your soul mate; having a family; learning to ski; or simply enjoying the company of family and friends. Or it might be having a dream to write a book to immortalize a special person in your life and knowing from the day you started writing it that it would one day be so successful that it would significantly contribute towards finding an alternative treatment for cancer.

ACKNOWLEDGEMENTS

To my son, Cameron, who at the age of three, asked me if Aunty Carole was still sleeping in the "Treasure Chest." I reassured him that she was no longer there, but was up in heaven, hanging out with God. He always knew his Aunty was *A Scottish Gem,* thus giving me the title for this book.

My son, Bradley, who shared the writing literacy knowledge he gained in third grade to help contribute to the detail of the book.

My sister-in-law, Linda, as I would have never been able to remember all the memories and details of Carole's life without our weekly chats, input, and counsel.

My husband, Deka, for being the first reader of the book, for being my biggest supporter, and for giving me guidance on how to market the book.

My parents, Rose and Howard, and brother, Michael, for listening to my dreams and plans for the book. They always encouraged me to forge ahead.

To my sister-in-law, Paula, for being one of my early readers, and for giving me guidance and support through the initial editing process.

To Anna Orologio, my college friend, for being one of the five original people asked to read the book. She was the first non-family member to read it and gave me great feedback and encouragement.

To Sara Ungerleider, who has been gifted in recognizing grammatical errors without effort and giving another viewpoint that was of great value.

My colleagues at work, Eric Radell, Brittany Paxson, Linda Emma, John Cop, Ruth Wilson (and the list goes on) for listening, encouraging, and cheering me on every step of the way.

To all the survivors out there, I applaud you and wish you continued good health.

To all those people who are looking for hope: Hang in there - an alternative method is on its way.

To all those who have passed - we will never forget you and we will find an alternative that works in honor of you.

Lastly, to you, all the people who have purchased this book. You have taken action, you have contributed towards finding an alternative to treating cancer, and you have become part of this unique journey of hope.

ABOUT THE AUTHOR

   Michele M. Rodger has worked both in corporate America and in the United Kingdom, as a human resources professional for the past 19 years. She earned her bachelor's and master's degrees from Adelphi University's School of Social Work and always had an overwhelming desire to help people. However, it wasn't until her sister-in-law's encounter with cancer that her own life was changed in a profound way. Michele vowed to support alternative treatments to cancer until people diagnosed with stage 4 cancers would not need to die from the disease. That would be the ultimate happy ending to this story. This is her first book.

   Michele and her husband, Deka, live in Readington Township, New Jersey, with their two sons, Bradley (9) and Cameron (4).